ORIENTALISM AND IDENTITY
IN LATIN AMERICA

Orientalism and Identity in Latin America

Fashioning Self and Other from the (Post)Colonial Margin

Edited by
ERIK CAMAYD-FREIXAS

THE UNIVERSITY OF
ARIZONA PRESS

TUCSON

THE UNIVERSITY OF
ARIZONA PRESS

© 2013 The Arizona Board of Regents
All rights reserved

www.uapress.arizona.edu

Library of Congress Cataloging-in-Publication Data
Orientalism and identity in Latin America : fashioning self and other from the
(post)colonial margin / edited by Erik Camayd-Freixas.
    p. cm.
  Includes bibliographical references (p.   ) and index.
  ISBN 978-0-8165-2953-7 (cloth : alk. paper)   1. Spanish American fiction—
20th century—History and criticism.   2. Orientalism in literature.
3. Orientalism—Latin America.   I. Camayd-Freixas, Erik.
  PQ7082.N7O66 2013
  860.9'98—dc23
                                                                      2012025837
CIP

*Publication of this book is made possible in part by the proceeds of a permanent
endowment created with the assistance of a Challenge Grant from the National
Endowment for the Humanities, a federal agency.*

18 17 16 15 14 13   6 5 4 3 2 1

To my Cuban Lebanese grandparents,
Emilio (Najib) Camayd and Argelia Zogbe

Contents

Acknowledgments

I would like to thank José E. González of the University of Nebraska at Lincoln, Ivan A. Schulman of the University of Illinois at Urbana, and Debra Lee-DiStefano of Southeast Missouri State University for their generous discussions, advice, and assistance. A special note of gratitude is due to my graduate assistants, Lucas Katz, Svetlana Tyutina, and Sara González, for their valuable help in the editing process and the translation of some of the chapters. I am indebted to Maida Watson and Steve Heine, director of the Asian Studies Program, both at Florida International University, for their encouragement and recommendations, as well as their leadership in organizing conferences and lecture series on Orientalism in Latin America, with the participation of various contributors to this volume. I am especially grateful to Patti Hartmann, senior editor at the University of Arizona Press, for her expert editorial advice. The support and inspiration of my family were a constant among the many variables of life and work. This project was made possible in part by support from the Asian Globalization and Latin America Title VI grant, the FIU Foundation, and the Faculty Senate, the Asian Studies Program, and the Department of Modern Languages at Florida International University.

ORIENTALISM AND IDENTITY
IN LATIN AMERICA

The Orientalist Controversy and the Origins of Amerindian Culture

Erik Camayd-Freixas

Defining a New World identity has proven to be a challenging cultural enterprise, one that has risen to a multidisciplinary debate. The question itself is coeval with the rise of recorded culture in the Americas. All from migratory origins, Native American peoples developed foundational myths of origins to lay claim to their native land. In turn, colonial writers theorized that Amerindians had migrated from the East in a not-so-distant past.[1] This "orientalization" of Native Americans, which depicted them as foreigners in their own land so as to justify colonization, is a direct antecedent of modern Orientalist discourses about Latin America.

Native America presented a cultural tapestry of hundreds of distinct linguistic groups, none having succeeded in establishing cultural hegemony (beyond the regional dominions of Aztec and Incan imperialism) at the point in their history when their development was interrupted by the European arrival. There is mounting evidence of pre-Columbian discoveries by various transatlantic and transpacific seafaring peoples who left an uncertain trace on the native cultures with which they came in contact.[2] But only the Europeans succeeded in establishing a hegemony that would incorporate the "New World" into Western culture, as a colonized domain.

Yet at the time of the discovery, the Europeans were themselves in the process of establishing their own myth of cultural homogeneity as the "West," based on exclusion of the "Orient." Crucial to European identity construction was the Westernization of Christianity through differentiation from its Semitic roots. This was a process that began with Greek as the language of the New Testament, was expanded westward by the Roman

Empire, and developed into doctrine by early European theologians, until it culminated in the Crusades.[3] Still fresh in European collective memory, the mentality of the Crusades provided Columbus with an ulterior, messianic motive for finding an overseas trade route to the East: to finance a private army with which to liberate Jerusalem.[4] His sponsors, Spain's Catholic monarchs, had just expelled the Jews and barely completed their Reconquest of the Moors in 1492, after 721 years of Islamic occupation, which left its mark in the language, culture, infrastructure, and political institutions of the Iberian Peninsula and colonial Spanish America.

In line with the Crusades–Reconquest–Conquest military and ideological model, forced Christianization and socioeconomic machines such as the plantation economy soon came to mold the new colonial societies.[5] With Amerindian populations decimated by harsh treatment and disease, the need to fuel such machines led to the African Diaspora, counteracted after Independence by new European immigrations fostered by the policies of social "whitening" of the nineteenth and early twentieth centuries. As Black slavery declined, this economic fuel was supplemented by imported contract labor, some of it supplied by impoverished European immigrants but much of it by "coolies" from China who came by the hundreds of thousands (and in lesser numbers from India and Malaysia) to various points of the Americas after the late 1840s. They brought a renewed presence of the Orient bolstered by further Middle and Far Eastern immigrations in the twentieth century, up until their current absorption into a new colonialist myth of Western homogeneity: our newfound awareness of "globalization."

The common denominator among these various non-Western cultures is the perspective from which they were evaluated, which could be no other than that of hegemonic culture: Eurocentrism, the self-proclaimed universality of Western man, the standard against which "others" would be measured. And to the extent they were not the same, racially or religiously in particular, they would be considered inferior. Thus Eurocentric identity was constructed not only through differentiation and exclusion but also by the biased attribution, projection, and transference of negative traits onto its "others"—an exercise Edward Said collectively termed *orientalization*.[6] Furthermore, the different out-groups of the West were bundled together as one, indiscriminately orientalized. The "primitive" Africans, the "degenerated" Asians, and the Amerindians, those "primitive Orientals," were imbricated stereotypes conceived by colonialist discourses as an exotic continuum of otherness.

Our earlier collection of essays, *Primitivism and Identity in Latin America*, revealed a close relationship between the terms primitivism and

Orientalism, since the West's "primitive others" were also orientalized.[7] Eventually the pejorative concept of primitivism, evolved by the West, was adopted in Latin America as a new way of looking at itself, with both positive and negative results, ranging from exaltation of the past to self-prejudice and pessimism about the future. The present collection, *Orientalism and Identity in Latin America*, explores the diverging appearance that Orientalism assumes in the periphery, not from the standpoint of hegemony but from the layered perspective of the colonized.

The essays in this collection explore both historical contacts and literary influences in the formation of Latin American constructs of the Orient and the self, from colonial times to the present. Following a chronological, north-to-south organization customary in Latin American studies, these essays analyze the "other" great encounter, not with the Europeans but with Arabic, Chinese, and Japanese cultures, as they marked Latin American societies from Mexico, Central America, and the Caribbean, to Peru, Argentina, and Brazil. Given the impossibility of exhaustive coverage, we offer instead a sampler of a much wider array of multidimensional points of encounter. Nevertheless the perspectives, experiences, and theories discussed in these examples offer a comprehensive frame of reference for understanding other manifestations of Orientalism in Latin America and elsewhere in the developing world.

We have avoided dividing the book into parts, given our aim to establish a comparative dialogue not only among the different cultures, points of insertion, and periods that have shaped Latin American Orientalism but also between historical experience and imaginary constructions of identity and otherness. As such, these essays juxtapose historical, biographical, and literary depictions of Middle Eastern and Asian migrations, of both people and cultural elements, as they have been received, perceived, refashioned, and integrated into Latin American discourses of identity and difference. Underlying this dialogue is the hypothesis that the discourse of Orientalism and the process of orientalization apply equally to Near Eastern and Far Eastern subjects, as well as to immigrants regardless of provenance, and indeed to any individual or group who might be construed as Other by a particular dominant culture.

Given that Orientalism as defined by Said is fundamentally a discourse of domination developed by colonial powers, its application in Latin American studies presents various problems from the standpoints of critical and postcolonial theories. For this reason, our volume opens with a seminal theoretical essay by Brett Levinson, who examines some fundamental contradictions in the Latinamericanist critique of Eurocentrism and Orientalism. Levinson deconstructs the discourse of Anglo-American academics who purport to redeem the "silenced" Third World voices. He shows that such discourse ultimately reinforces the Western hegemonic concept of "truth"; perpetuates Saidian Orientalism's obsolete First World/Third World "othering" structure, which hinges on a now defunct Second World and has been superseded and decentered by globalization; and is fundamentally extraneous to Latin America and to the very voices it seeks to redeem.

Heeding Levinson's penetrating critique, this volume brings together multiethnic academic perspectives from across Latin America, North America, and beyond. A first cluster of essays focuses on Arabic influences in the colonial and independence periods. Hernán Taboada analyzes ideological continuities from the Iberian Reconquest to the Conquest of America, tracing the assimilation of Amerinds and Muslims to the formation of Eurocentric identity in the Renaissance. Christina Civantos defines D. F. Sarmiento's ambivalent conflation of gaucho and Arab in Argentine identity as a Creole Orientalism that differs from its European counterpart. In a second cluster of essays, Blake Seana Locklin examines the role of Orientalism in Mexican nationalism as reflected in two fascinating figures of popular culture: the Chinese-born mystic Catarina de San Juan as precursor of the nationalist China Poblana costume. Julia Camacho documents the anti-Chinese movement in 1930s Mexico as it impacted the fate of one Chinese Mexican family. A third cluster of essays is devoted to Orientalist poetics in Latin America. Ivan Schulman illuminates the cult of the Orient in nineteenth-century *modernismo*. Zoila Clark revisits the peripheral Orientalism of Guatemalan *modernista* in Enrique Gómez Carrillo's Japanese travelogues. Erik Camayd-Freixas traces the influence of Eastern thought and haiku on Mexican avant-garde poetics as a substitute for the indigenous heritage severed by the Conquest. A fourth cluster of essays centers on the Chinese diaspora in the Caribbean and Central America. Rogelio Rodríguez Coronel writes on the Chinese presence in Cuban literature and culture. Kathleen López chronicles the government-sponsored "revitalization" of Havana's Chinatown. Margarita Vásquez surveys the literature on the Chinese experience in Panama and the hybrid culture that results. A final cluster focuses on contemporary Asian migrations in South America and the changing question of identity. Debra Lee-DiStefano studies literary accounts of marginality of Chinese Peruvians in the context of neglectful historical exclusion from the "trinity" of Amerindian, European, and Black, held as the composite ethnicity of Latin American identity. Cristina Rocha delves into the transculturation of Zen in Brazil as it accommodates to the ideals of traditional Japanese immigrants, their creolized descendants, and the neo-Orientalism in vogue among

Brazilian intellectuals. Closing the volume's theme of transnationality, Karen Yamashita recounts her autobiographical journey in search of her roots, a communal voice, and a collective memory among the Japanese peasants in Brazil who inspired her remarkable series of novels. These various multidimensional viewpoints offer perspectives across national, cultural, linguistic, generational, and even gender identities. Intellectualized theory, collective history, and interethnic imagination are intersected and humanized by diverse individual voices and compelling personal stories.

The Orientalist Controversy

When Said defined Orientalism as a colonial hegemonic discourse corresponding to an intricate structure of cultural domination, which it served to justify and legitimize, he stated that one of his main objectives was to warn the readers of the so-called Third World about "the dangers and temptations" for formerly colonized peoples "of employing this structure upon themselves and others" (25). In a Latin American context, however, Said's formulation of French and British Orientalism as a discourse of otherness requires substantial qualification, this being a key point of departure for understanding the essays in this book.

First, the profound Arabic and Hebraic cultural influences in the Iberian Middle Ages led to the late fifteenth-century formation of Spain and Portugal as nominally European but truly hybrid nations in denial. Moreover the colonial hegemony they established in Latin America led to a hybrid Creole culture. Thus, as these essays demonstrate, it is not unusual for Latin American subjects to perceive the Orient not as Europe's Other but rather as a reflection of the Other within, variously and conflictually affirmed or denied. Second, there is the fact that Latin American Orientalism arises not in the centers of colonial power but in the periphery, where it presents itself at times as an alternative to both indigenous and Western constructs of cultural history and identity. Third, Latin American Orientalism may even take the form of a foundational discourse, based on the remote Asian origins of Amerindian populations.

Given these differences, many Latinamericanists, and other Third World readers, may not fully identify with the hegemonic Orientalism so appropriately condemned by Said. For example, in *Orientalism in the Hispanic Literary Tradition*, Julia Kushigian actually reacts to Said, arguing for a Hispanic "spirit of veneration and respect for the Orient."[8] This benign version of Orientalism evokes the multicultural richness of the Toledo School of

Translators (ca. 1126–1284), where Arabic, Hebrew, and Hispanic scholars collaborated to disseminate the works of the Islamic Golden Age (ca. 750–1258) and reintroduce classical Greek science and philosophy, lost to the European Dark Ages. It constitutes a utopian ideal that Kushigian attempts to project across the colonial period to modern Latin America.

Spanish medieval Orientalism, however, was really the product of a tense coexistence between Christians and Moors, along a shifting and porous frontier where periods of war and peace alternated during centuries of Reconquest.[9] This historical reality gave rise in the ninth century to the cult of Santiago Matamoros (Saint James the Moor Slayer), patron of the Orders of Chivalry, the Crusades, the Reconquest, and the Conquest of America. The conflict with the Moors accounts for the first great work of Spanish literature, the epic *Cantar de Mio Cid* (ca. 1140), as well as the later "Moorish romances" like *El Abencerraje* (1565) and *Guerras civiles de Granada* (1595). On a positive note one finds Christianized adaptations of Sufi mysticism in the poetry of San Juan de la Cruz and the prose of Santa Teresa and Baltasar Gracián. Thus Kushigian is forced to recognize a degree of "ambivalence toward Islam" manifested by a certain intellectual curiosity together with the eagerness to destroy it.

This ambivalence, however, becomes radicalized in the New World. In *La sombra del Islam en la conquista de América* (The Shadow of Islam in the Conquest of America; see Selected Bibliography in this volume) Hernán Taboada details how fifteenth-century Italian travelogues about the Turks influenced the chronicles of the Indies, leading to constant comparisons between the "barbarism" of Amerinds and Muslims. Taboada, following Said, sees this as another example of the negative orientalization of the Amerindians, a transfer of supposed Islamic attributes onto a new enemy, resulting in the fashioning of a homogeneous Other with respect to the construction of a Eurocentric self.

Whether such orientalizing trends prevail through the late colonial period is a matter that awaits further study. But in the nineteenth century, after Independence (see Civantos in this volume), we have a notorious example in Sarmiento's essay of national interpretation, *Facundo: Civilization and Barbarism* (1845), where his ambivalent comparison of gauchos and Bedouins foreshadows his later project for the Europeanization of Argentina as president of the republic and author of *Conflicto y armonía de las razas en América* (1882). Such Latin American social "whitening" policies, which extended well into the twentieth century, bear the influence of Comte's positivism and Taine's determinism, compounded later by the evolutionism of Darwin and Spencer, to produce a host of pseudoscientific theories about the congenital psychic traits of human races and their inter-breeding, according to the proportion of "bloods" in a given people or representative individual.

On the basis of such racist scientism, the prejudice of European Orientalism, and the sudden influx of Chinese coolies (the new surrogate Indians), there arises the grouping of Native Americans, mestizos, and Asians within a single psychoracial concept. Consequently, during the naturalist-positivist period in Latin America (1880s–1940s), regionalist novels and sociological essays echoed European racial discourse, exhibiting what could be called an "auto-Orientalism," a self-prejudice that explains economic underdevelopment as a consequence not of four centuries of colonial exploitation but of a presumed "social pathology" ascribed to racial inferiority and degeneration from interbreeding.[10] Accordingly the Indians, and proportionately the mestizos, had inherited the "Asian abulia," the "treacherous" and "retrograde" character of the Chinese or, as the Argentine sociologist Carlos Octavio Bunge puts it, their "vengefulness" and "ancestral indolence," their "passivity" and "Oriental fatalism":

> We soon recognize that the organization of the two great pre-Columbian empires, the Aztec and the Incan, shows remarkable similarities to that of the ancient Asian empires. What is the foremost psychological trait of the latter peoples, in contrast with the Europeans? Without a doubt it is the passivity of the large masses of men, the resignation to their fate. . . . Indeed, Oriental fatalism constitutes the characteristic trait of Mexicans and Peruvians, and this trait explains, in part, their easy conquest and domination.[11]

Still in the 1930s, following the Bolivian Alcides Arguedas's sociological essay *Pueblo enfermo* (1909) and invoking nineteenth-century phrenology as well as Spengler's cultural organicism about the decadence of civilizations, the Peruvian César Augusto Velarde is capable of writing infamous yet widely acclaimed pages on "the infiltration of Asian blood into our veins":

> It is no longer that of the Mongol, full of warlike vigor, which conquered China, India, as well as central and southern Asia. It is rather a stock physically depleted by defects of nutrition and opium abuse, as well as morally and intellectually degenerated by the tiredness of a millenary civilization in a terrible crisis of death. . . . And the men issuing from such a breakdown are to contribute their blood for the benefit of the future "cosmic race"! . . . That brachycephalic race of rachitic contexture

and slanted eyes, traits that can only disappear after the fifth or seventh generation. . . . Now we must correct daunting defects of blood that run deeper than those which originally burdened us.[12]

The "social therapeutics" that Velarde hails as "axiomatic" according to many "men of science" says it all: "to regenerate or suppress the autochthonous Indian race" (62), together with "a vigorous injection of Saxon blood" (217). Perhaps the saddest note about Velarde's book *Patología indolatina* is that it was received with admiration and praise across the Hispanic world, not only by popular opinion but also by writers, jurists, academics, and even ministers of education, not to mention its raving press reviews throughout South America. Said's warning had indeed arrived too late: colonized America had already applied onto herself the Orientalist structure of cultural domination (see Camacho, Vásquez, and Rodríguez Coronel in this volume).

A "veneration" of the Orient in the Latin American literary tradition would only begin to surface with *modernismo* (1880s–1940s), although by virtue of French influence (mainly Pierre Loti, the Goncourt brothers, and later Judith Gautier) on the poets Rubén Darío (Nicaragua, 1867–1916), Julián del Casal (Cuba, 1863–93), Julio Herrera y Reissig (Uruguay, 1875–1910), Enrique Gómez Carrillo (Guatemala, 1873–1927), Efrén Rebolledo (Mexico, 1877–1929), Guillermo Valencia (Colombia, 1873–1943), and others (see Schulman and Clark in this volume). Beyond the lure of the exotic and the search for artistic refinement in an idealized Orient (tendencies common to French Parnassians, Symbolists, and Impressionists), Spanish American Orientalist *modernismo* includes an identity-building dimension, where that which Said calls the writer's "strategic location" departs from hegemonic paradigms to reconfigure the Orient in parallel with Latin America's own peripheral, uneven, and conflictive modernity. Surprisingly, humanistic *modernismo* was contemporaneous with its antithesis, the positivistic scientism discussed earlier, such that the same period sees the culmination of both, the respectful and the racist versions of Hispanic Orientalism (no longer ambivalent, as it was in early Spain, but radically bipolar). In the long run, humanism prevailed: *modernismo* paved the way for a deeper inquiry into the importance of the Orient for Latin American identity and cultural expression, an inquiry that led through avant-garde poetics to Eastern thought and through the process of creolization to social acceptance (see Rodríguez Coronel, Camayd-Freixas, Lee-DiStefano, Rocha, and Yamashita in this volume).

This newer tendency of Latin American Orientalism centers more on Asian influences, both ancient and modern, than on a fading Arabic

Iberian heritage. Kushigian, Taboada, and other researchers included in Silvia Nagy-Zekmi's collection of essays, *Moros en la costa: Orientalismo en Latinoamérica* (2008), recognize that a foundational Arabic Iberian heritage distinguishes Hispanic Orientalism from Said's paradigmatic formulation. Another collection, Ignacio López-Calvo's *Alternative Orientalisms in Latin America and Beyond* (2007), includes essays on Asian influences in modern Latin American literature. Yet the (no less foundational) Asian Amerindian connection has never been fully factored into the Orientalist debate. The overlooked question of the Asian origins of Native American populations sets Latin American Orientalism apart, not only from the Iberian tradition and Said's hegemonic critique but also from expressions of Orientalism in other postcolonial societies. It is uniquely a New World concern.

The Origins of Amerindian Culture

The Orientalist concept of the migratory origins of Amerindians is ever-present in colonial writings since the Discovery. According to Peter Martyr (1511), Columbus identified Hispaniola with the biblical Ophir, whence King Solomon's fleet returned loaded with gold after a three-year journey; the Greek Bible refers to it as Sophir, the Coptic name for India, while some located it in the Malay peninsula, and later authors placed it in Peru.[13] Eventually it blended with the various legends of El Dorado. Fray Diego Durán (1570) documented Aztec attempts to locate their ancestral land of Aztlán but acquiesced to the prevailing view that Amerinds proceeded from the Lost Tribes of Israel. Sahagún (1577) affirmed that they descended from Adam and inferred from Nahuatl chronicles that Mexican ancestors migrated from the north in search of the earthly paradise. Joseph de Acosta (1590) reasoned from the Bible that they came from Adam and the ancient Orient, across lands "somewhere joined and continuous." Father Acosta placed American migration thousands of years earlier and argued that Amerindians had long forgotten their origin and created new myths with no relation to the first settlers; hence they had to be indoctrinated anew and reintegrated into the biblical tradition. It was an argument that ultimately justified evangelization and colonization.

Fray Gregorio García in *Origen de los indios del nuevo mundo e Indias occidentales* (1607) held that the "indios" descended from Noah (a thesis advanced in 1571 by Benedicto Arias Montano, the Spanish Orientalist and editor of the Polyglot Bible). According to García, Plato's Atlantis and the distant lands mentioned by Aristotle, Seneca, and others alluded to the

American continent. He figured that Noah's Israelite descendants sailed through the legendary Strait of Anian from Tartary or China, bringing also Phoenician and Egyptian influences, a theory he rested on physical similarities (facial features, pigmentation, lack of hair) and cultural affinities (idolatry, the calendar, the use of knots as a system of registry).[14] His influence on Mexican colonial literature is notable in Sor Juana Inés de la Cruz (*Neptuno alegórico*, 1680) and Carlos de Sigüenza y Góngora (*Theatro de virtudes políticas*, 1680). The latter asserted that Amerindians issued from Nephtuhim, son of Noah, founder of Carthage, deified as Neptune by the Greeks, who led a maritime exodus toward Atlantis, which his descendants continued on to America.[15] However, while Friar García, a Spanish anti-Semite, orientalized the Amerindians as "cowardly" heathens for their "Israelite ancestry," Sigüenza, a precursor of Mexican nationalism, extolled indigenous political virtues, becoming one of the first to adopt a distinctively Latin American brand of Orientalism.

Ideological interpretations continued well into the twentieth century. In 1871 the Argentine historian Vicente Fidel López suggested, after some lexical comparison, that the sacred language of the Incas (mentioned by the mestizo historian Garcilaso Inca de la Vega in 1609) was none other than Sanskrit, while the rest of Peruvians spoke Quechua. It was an outlandish idea that, nevertheless, the archaeologist Chaman Lil revived in 1949. According to López, every page of Inca poetry bears the marks of the *Ramayana* and the *Mahabharata*.[16] As late as 1887, another nationalist, pioneering archaeologist, Alfredo Chavero, in *México a través de los siglos* (Mexico through the Centuries) discarded as absurd the passage of man through the Bering Strait, accepted Atlantis, and concluded from linguistic analysis that the Chinese actually left America to populate Asia. In 1916 the anthropologist Manuel Gamio in "No hay prehistoria mexicana" (There Is No Mexican Prehistory) found it necessary to react to the radical monogenism of the Argentine paleontologist Florentino Ameghino, who placed the cradle of *Homo sapiens* in the Argentine pampas. Gamio set out to refute the cultural chauvinism of those who insisted on speaking of an autochthonous human being in America, pointing out instead that American man issued from Asia and is therefore more recent (and less "developed" historically) than European man.

Ideologically the idea of Asian origins, especially if posited as a recent migration ("no American prehistory"), constitutes a religious and cultural affront to Amerindian nations. Without exception, all native religions of the Americas profess that American man was created from American soil (a thesis shared, in fact, by many nineteenth-century polygenists) and that their culture is original, giving rise to their territorial rights and their designation as "native" Americans or "first peoples." On the other hand, while the orientalization of the Amerindian was a useful discourse to the Europeans for the purposes of conquest, evangelization, and colonization, it was later useful as well to the white Creole elites, the Founding Fathers of the new republics, as a means of asserting their own national identities based on difference and cultural independence from their former European colonizers. In the twentieth century a further twist of orientalization served to legitimize new myths about the universality of "Mestizo America" as propounded by José Vasconcelos's answer to Darwin, his influential essay *La raza cósmica* (1925), which hailed the evolution of a Mestizo Latin American race as a heightened synthesis of all races.[17] In a word, the orientalization of the Amerindian has variously served the ideological interests of Europeans, Creoles, and Mestizos, at the expense of Amerindians themselves.

In this context, North American anthropology sought a less tendentious perspective. Vitus Bering's discovery in 1728 of a fifty-five-mile strait separating Siberia from Alaska cast doubt upon the migration theory. But in 1856 Samuel Haven revived Acosta's 1590 assumption ("lands somewhere joined and continuous") with his hypothesis that during the Pleistocene (60,000–11,000 years ago) glacial accumulation and lower sea levels exposed the Beringia land bridge. Evolutionism favored the theory of a single migration or common Asian ancestor. Its main proponent was the Smithsonian anthropologist Aleš Hdrlička (1937) who, based on cranial traits, attempted to define an American "general type" of Central Asian Neanderthal ancestry. Morris Swadesh (1952) also posited the existence of a common ancestral language irradiating from Eurasia, but further linguistic and blood group studies suggested three distinct migrations. Yet these methods offered no decisive evidence.[18]

Only recently have mitochondrial DNA tests established genetic similarities suggesting a common ancestry for today's Amerindian, Siberian, and Asian populations, although American peculiarities also prevail. There is evidence that only four mtDNA lineages characterize 95 percent of all current Amerindian populations, while each lineage encompasses a range of ethnic groups and geographical distribution.[19] This suggests that a few founding groups migrated from Asia to the New World. Current scientific consensus is that the land bridge was available for various periods between 60,000 and 13,000 years ago, enabling different migrations at different times.

Once Asian migration is accepted, the question is no longer that of biological origins but that of the rise of pre-Columbian culture in the Americas. This is a decades-old debate between two opposing hypotheses:

cultural isolationism and diffusionism, with various intermediate positions. Modern viewpoints on this topic belong to three general categories.[20] First there is the theory of independent invention, which maintains that Asian settlers (late Quaternary and early Neolithic) brought such a rudimentary culture that one must view the high cultures of the Americas as fundamentally autochthonous. It assumes land migration and, once the Beringia land bridge vanished, total or relative isolation and therefore independent development of Amerindian culture. Similarities between ancient Asian and Native American cultures are considered the result of similar biological, psychic, and environmental conditions rather than historical contacts and cultural diffusion.

The second theory posits an integral cultural cycle, or *Kulturkreise*, a term coined by Leon Frobenius to refer to a core culture, in contrast with particular elements developed later. According to *Kulturkreise*, whole cultures, fully formed in their fundamental aspects, migrated from particular regions of Asia to different points of the Americas. Transpacific similarities would represent the remnants that, after a long period of separation, have survived the process of transculturation.

Third, an intermediate position, the theory of transpacific contacts holds that despite a relatively independent initial development, Amerindian cultures continued to receive Asiatic influences from sporadic pre-Columbian sea contacts, first by primitive fishermen and then by Asian seafaring cultures. Among its chief proponents, Robert Heine-Geldern (1885–1968) and Gordon Ekholm (1909–87) pointed to numerous Asian similarities in the symbolic arts, sciences, rituals, political organization, and social practices of the high cultures of Mexico and Peru, including the caste system.[21]

The probable settlement of the South Pacific has served as a model to explain that of the Americas, according to the theory of the "three main waves" of migration and the resulting gradient of cultural complexity. This model assumes that a first and most primitive migration composed of nomadic Paleolithic hunters without agriculture may have attained low-density distribution throughout the South Pacific and the Americas. Much later a second wave of migrants of more complex agricultural tradition may have reached the intermediate regions, conquering the earlier culture and displacing it toward more remote regions. Centuries later a third wave, composed of cultures of greater political organization and population density, would have finally conquered and displaced the previous ones from the regions closer to the continental center of irradiation, but without reaching the more distant regions, where the primitive settlers continued to develop in relative isolation.

In the Americas the most primitive regions belonging to the first wave are also the most remote and isolated, to the east of the Andes: Amazonia, the Pampas, and Patagonia. The second wave is represented mostly by the cultures of North America, and the third and last by the more complex Eskimo cultures of Alaska and the Arctic. The cultural gradient fits perfectly, except for a huge anomaly: the high cultures of Mesoamerica and the Andes, located at a great distance from Beringia but with access to the Pacific coastline. Whether they migrated from the north to settle in more temperate zones, resulted from maritime colonization or transpacific contacts, or developed independently remains an unresolved matter. All three theories are plausible and not mutually exclusive, such that Amerindian developments could be explained by a combination of scenarios.

However, at the landmark 35th Conference of Americanists (in Mexico City in 1964), the Mexican philosopher and archaeologist Alfonso Caso (1896–1970) debunked diffusionist theories, showing slides of almost identical vases from different cultures and periods in Palestine and Monte Albán, México, among which any claim of contact would be ludicrous.[22] This impacted Caso's pupil, the Nobel Laureate poet and essayist Octavio Paz, who promptly offered a conciliatory solution, "independent germinations of a single seed": "American man is of Asiatic origin. Without a doubt the first migrants brought with them the rudiments of a culture. In seed form among those rudiments, there was a worldview—something infinitely persistent that, by virtue of being passive and unconscious, can more successfully withstand the changes in techniques, philosophies, and social institutions."[23] Paz's metaphor reconciled the theories of independent invention and *Kulturkreise*, while affording little credence to transpacific contacts, which he saw as an obstacle to his poetic project.

Paz sought to ground his poetry as genuinely Mexican despite his Orientalism. Positing a common "seed" was crucial to his poetic legitimacy. Transpacific contacts, on the other hand, explained the sudden rise of the high "matrix" cultures—Olmec in Mesoamerica and Chavín in the Andes—as the product of foreign influence by Asian civilizations. "Geneticists," Paz argued instead, "believe that evolution is not gradual but produced by mutations that are more or less abrupt" (143). The high American matrix cultures, which represent a leap in the gradient of civilization, would then be explained by a sudden flowering owed to fecund inventions and independent advances. Paz charged that diffusionists paid too much attention to superficial similarities in style, design, or technique, while he, as a poet and essayist, looked for the fundamental conception or deep structure of cultural epiphenomena. Discrete elements, Paz argued, following his teacher Alfonso Caso, "are found in many other parts of the world; hence similarity does not imply direct contact" (144).

> Mexican pyramids, like the ziggurats of Asia Minor, the stupas and the pagodas, are independent developments or versions of a primitive belief: the tendency to see the world as a stepped mountain. The true similarity lies not in the architectural forms and structures but in the worldview. It is not influence but rather, as in the case of the cosmological beliefs of Chinese and Amerindians, a matter of diverse developments of a single, very ancient idea, which probably had its origins in Asia. (145)

Paz adopts a genetic model of culture based on a structuralist conception of myth: a primeval "seed" or common ancestor whose cultural DNA transmits the blueprint of a foundational "worldview."

The inevitable question is what constitutes that "seed" or archetype that lies at the bottom of the hypothesized Asian Amerindian worldview. Ironically evidence for such an archetype may be found only in the superficial similarities that Paz dismisses. Moreover, severed by the European conquest, the codes for interpreting pre-Columbian cultures have been lost forever. Any interpretation must look for clues in what surviving Amerindian culture lacks, that is, in what the Conquest destroyed. Another of Paz's mentors, the Dominican critic Pedro Henríquez Ureña, defined this missing evidence with characteristic clarity:

> The Conquest decapitated Amerindian culture, destroying its higher forms (not even the art of reading and writing Aztec glyphs survived), while only familiar and popular forms were preserved. Given that only a minute portion of the numerous and broadly scattered native population was able to be fully integrated into a European type of civilization, nothing filled for the Amerindians the void left by those higher forms of their autochthonous culture.[24]

Having lost the art of pictographic writing, on which oral tradition rested, what little survived of the Amerindian worldview was refashioned and Christianized by colonial missionaries. Thus the European destruction of the "higher forms of culture" ("decapitation," not any supposed racial deficiency) explains the diminished state of surviving Native American populations.

Interestingly, Henríquez Ureña's brilliant observation sheds light on Paz's messianic cultural project. The reconstruction of those "higher forms" would mean a restoration of high Amerindian culture and a symbolic redemption of today's marginalized "Indians." This was Paz's unavowed poetic agenda: to posit an Asian Amerindian seed; to reach it via poetry, supplying the missing worldview by means of an archaeology of knowledge, a regression *ad ovo* along the continuity of Eastern thought (which no colonization severed), in order to arrive at the shared archetype on which to ground the symbolic reconstruction of a bridge of continuity linking original Amerindian culture with modern Latin American poetics, as though the Conquest had never taken place. This would in fact be a poetics of counterconquest, a countercolonial Orientalism.

The "higher forms" that Henríquez Ureña referred to are the system of thought (what Paz calls "worldview") and the system of writing (which, being ideographic, is scarcely distinguishable from the system of thought itself). That is, thought and writing formed a unity or, better still, a duality. Along these lines, Miguel León-Portilla, based on Ángel María Garibay's studies of Nahuatl philology, interpreted the Aztec worldview as fundamentally dualistic, based on the concept of a dual god, Ometéoltl/Omecihual, "Master and Mistress of Duality."[25] Paz, following his own concept of the "fluid unity" of Amerindian culture, extends this dualistic worldview to all Native American peoples:

> Religious dualism . . . is apparently a permanent trait of American cultures. . . . Levi-Strauss also emphasizes this dualistic or binary conception, not without analogy to the yin and yang of the Chinese, among the tribes of Amazonia. Thus, by means of the invariable structure of myth, it would be a matter of reconstructing the historical and unrepeatable gestures of events—, to read on the rigid mask of myth the variable and instantaneous features of history. This is a task that, for now, is beyond the capabilities of historians and anthropologists. (138)

In other words, for Paz, it is a task for the Poet.

It is not clear, however, to what extent dualism resides in autochthonous Amerindian thought rather than in the eye of the modern beholder, influenced by Americanist Orientalism's desire for a common origin to circumpacific cultures. Curiously, in asserting the dualism of the Aztecs, León-Portilla avoids any reference to the Orient. The French structural anthropologist Claude Lévi-Strauss, on the other hand, did not consider *duality* and *binarism* to be synonymous. Like his structuralist precursor, the Russian linguist Roman Jakobson, Lévi-Strauss held that binarism is not a cultural trait but a tendency of the entire human species. Still, for Paz, this mythical-metaphorical evidence was enough for grounding a poetics: "Beyond truth or error—the discussion remains open—the Asiatic theory makes us see with different eyes the works of the ancient Americans. It is a bridge" (154).

Paz's poetic quest—to return to Asia in order to arrive at America through the time bridge of dualistic thought and ideographic writing—may be considered a culmination of Hispanic Orientalism. Yet we might ask what would be the real dividends for today's testimonial Amerindian peoples of such an intellectual project aimed at the Orientalist reconstruction of their autochthonous cultures: perhaps a new cultural colonization? It is difficult to see any *indigenista* redemption in a pursuit that Native American nations reject, precisely because it denies their originality and devalues their accomplishments. The poetic restoration of a possible dualistic system of thought and writing will not return to the Amerindians the higher forms of their autochthonous culture; after centuries of colonization, their destruction is irreparable. It might be more realistic to see in Paz's neo-Orientalism another self-serving project of affirmation of Creole universality as a sort of "cosmic culture"—a mere update of Vasconcelos's *Raza cósmica*. In view of such contradictions, it is scarcely possible to claim without great reservation that we have finally achieved an Orientalism free from manipulations. As Paz pointed out, "the discussion remains open."

Nevertheless, beyond a merely symbolic achievement, if the transpacific project could lead to the affirmation of the fundamental unity and rights of Native American peoples, long denied by modern nation-states (with their closed borders established by European newcomers), or if it served at least to open an inclusive transnational dialogue that incorporates the more recent immigrations, then Hispanic Orientalism would take a legitimate first step toward its own redemption as a humanistic discourse. The essays collected in this volume are in various ways an invitation to that meaningful dialogue.

Notes

1. Lee Eldridge Huddleston, *Origins of the American Indians: European Concepts, 1492–1729* (Austin: University of Texas Press, 1970); Eduardo Matos Moctezuma, *Ideas acerca del origen del hombre americano (1570–1916)* (Mexico City: SEP, 1987).

2. Nigel Davies, *Voyagers to the New World* (New York: William Morrow, 1979); Paul Tolstoy, "Asia and the Americas Trans-Pacific Contacts: What, Where and When?," *Review of Archaeology* 20.1 (1999): 19–30.

3. Samuel Silva Gotay, *El pensamiento cristiano revolucionario en América Latina y el Caribe: Implicaciones de la teología de la liberación para la sociología de la religión* (San Juan, P.R.: Ediciones Huracán, 1989).

4. Tzevetan Todorov, *The Conquest of America: The Question of the Other* (Oklahoma City: University of Oklahoma Press, 1984).

5. Antonio Benítez Rojo, *The Repeating Island: The Caribbean and the Postmodern Perspective* (Durham, N.C.: Duke University Press, 1996).

6. Edward Said, *Orientalism: Western Conceptions of the Orient* (New York: Pantheon, 1978).

7. Erik Camayd-Freixas and José E. González, eds., *Primitivism and Identity in Latin America: Essays on Art, Literature, and Culture* (Tucson: University of Arizona Press, 2000).

8. Julia A. Kushigian, *Orientalism in the Hispanic Literary Tradition: In Dialogue with Borges, Paz, and Sarduy* (Albuquerque: University of New Mexico Press, 1991), 3–4.

9. Américo Castro, *La realidad histórica de España* (Mexico City: Porrúa, 1964).

10. Martin S. Stabb, *In Quest of Identity: Patterns in the Latin American Essay of Ideas (1890–1960)* (Chapel Hill: University of North Carolina Press, 1967), 12–33.

11. Carlos Octavio Bunge, *Nuestra América: Ensayo de psicología social* (1903), 6th ed. (Buenos Aires: N.p., 1918), 123. Unless otherwise noted, all translations are mine.

12. César Augusto Velarde, *Patología indolatina (sociología latinoamericana)*, 2nd ed. (Madrid: Ediciones Góngora, 1933), 60–62. See also Alcides Arguedas, *Pueblo enfermo: Contribución a la psicología de los pueblos Hispano-Americanos*, 1909, reprints from the University of Michigan Library; Michael Aronna, *Pueblos Enfermos: The Discourse of Illness in the Turn-of-the-century Spanish and Latin American Essay* (Chapel Hill: University of North Carolina Press, 1999).

13. Paul Rivet, *Los orígenes del hombre americano* (1943; Mexico City: FCE, 1960), 11–17. See also Huddleston; Matos Moctezuma.

14. Gregorio García, *Origen de los indios del nuevo mundo e Indias occidentales* (1607; Madrid: Consejo Superior de Investigaciones Científicas, 2005).

15. Carlos de Sigüenza y Góngora, *Obras históricas* (Mexico City: Porrúa, 1983).

16. Vicente Fidel López, *Les races aryennes du Perou: Leur langue, leur réligion, leur histoire* (Paris: Librairie A. Franck, 1871).

17. José Vasconcelos, *The Cosmic Race / La raza cósmica* (1925), trans. Didier T. Jaén (Baltimore: Johns Hopkins University Press, 1997).

18. Joseph de Acosta, *Historia natural y moral de las Indias* (Seville: Juan de León, 1590); Samuel Haven, *Archaeology of the United States* (Washington, D.C.: Smithsonian, 1856); Aleš Hrdlička, *The Question of Ancient Man in America* (Washington, D.C.: Smithsonian, 1937); Edward Sapir, "The Similarity of Chinese and Indian Languages," *Science* (New York) 52.1607 (1925): 1–12; Morris Swadesh, "Linguistic Overview," *Prehistoric Man in the New World*, ed. Jesse D. Jennings and Edward Norbeck (Chicago: University of Chicago Press, 1964), 527–56; R. C. Williams, "GM Allotypes in Native Americans: Evidence for Three Distinct Migrations across the Bering Land Bridge," *American Journal of Physical Anthropology* 66.1 (1985): 1–19; Joseph Greenberg, Christy G. Turner II, and Stephen L. Zegura, "The Settlement of the Americas: A Comparison of the Linguistic, Dental, and Genetic Evidence," *Current Anthropology* 27.5 (1986): 477–97.

19. T. G. Schurr et al., "Amerindian Mitochondrial DNAs Have Rare Asian Mutations at High Frequencies, Suggesting They Derived from Four Primary Maternal Lineages," *American Journal of Human Genetics* 46.3 (1990): 613–23; Ugo Perego,

et al., "The Initial Peopling of the Americas: A Growing Number of Founding Mitochondrial Genomes from Beringia," *Genome Research* 20.9 (2010): 1174–79. See also "Historia genética de los indígenas de América" (Internet article).

20. Terence Grieder, *Origins of Pre-Columbian Art* (Austin: University of Texas Press, 1982), 12–19; Paul Shao, *The Origin of Ancient American Cultures* (Ames: Iowa State University Press, 1983).

21. Robert Heine-Geldern and Gordon F. Ekholm, "Significant Parallels in the Symbolic Arts of Southern Asia and Middle America," *Selected Papers of the 29th International Congress of Americanists* (Chicago: University of Chicago Press, 1951), 299–309; Robert Heine-Geldern, "Representation of the Asiatic Tiger in the Art of the Chavín Culture: A Proof of Early Contacts Between China and Peru," *Actas del 33 Congreso Internacional de Americanistas*, 33:1 (San Jose, Costa Rica, 1959), 321–26; Robert Heine-Geldern, "Traces of Indian and Southeast Asiatic Hindu-Buddhist Influence in Mesoamerica," Gordon F. Ekholm, "The Possible Chinese Origin of Teotihuacán Cylindrical Tripod Pottery and Certain Related Traits," and Paul Kirschhoff, "The Diffusion of a Great Religious System from India to Mexico," all in *Proceedings of the 35th International Congress of Americanists*, 35:1–3 (Mexico City, 1962–64).

22. Davies, 115–17.

23. Octavio Paz, "Asia y América," *Puertas al campo* (Barcelona: Seix Barral, 1966), 141–42.

24. Pedro Henríquez Ureña, "La América española y su originalidad" (1937), *La utopía de América* (Caracas: Ayacucho, 1978), 25.

25. Miguel León-Portilla, *Aztec Thought and Culture: A Study of the Ancient Nahuatl Mind* (Norman: University of Oklahoma Press, 1963).

CHAPTER ONE

The Death of the Critique of Eurocentrism

Latinamericanism as a Global Praxis/Poiesis

Brett Levinson

Latinamericanism

The term *Latinamericanism*, deployed by critics as a possible new name for the discipline of Latin American studies, has been viewed in three different ways.[1] Some have viewed it negatively, as Latin America's version of Orientalism, that is, a First World or U.S. discourse that appropriates and misrepresents the actual Latin American situation. Others have understood Latinamericanism as a critique of Orientalism, a means to call into question precisely this First World appropriation of Latin America. Still others have posited Latinamericanism as a theoretical reconsideration of Latin American cultural and literary studies. In this reconfiguration Latin America is not posited as a given (present or lost) geographical area or culture but as a "scene" within the movement of globalization, as belonging to domains such as the market, the diaspora, late capitalism, the new world order, and transnationality.

Latinamericanism, in this third case, addresses a *post*–Latin America, which emerges after the disappearance of a particular Same/Other structure, a (cold war) First World / Third World mapping, hinged on a now defunct Second World. The *post* materializes, therefore, after the dissolution of both Orientalism and the critique of Orientalism, discourses that rest on this First World / Third World dichotomy.[2] This does not indicate the actual dissipation of Latin America or the Third World, or that because the former Third World has now entered global processes such as the liberal market, the world is getting better and the struggle is almost over. The *post*, in fact, points to neither the resolution nor the eradication of world destitution. It merely marks the decline of Latin America and the Third World as sovereign categories, as classifications capable of grounding the Latinamericanist or postcolonial project. Passing on is the figure of Latin America (and therefore the figure of Orientalism). Latin America, as the former foundation of a certain discourse and praxis, is falling into globalization.

My purpose is to explain why the radicalization of Latin American and postcolonial studies depends upon this third Latinamericanism, why their discourses would do well to abandon Orientalism and its critique and move toward a different Latinamericanism. Only this third Latinamericanism addresses what needs to be addressed: the sloping and passing on of Latin America, the Third World, and postcolonial studies.

Orientalism is a term that Edward Said excavates and retools in his books *Orientalism* and *Culture and Imperialism.* He labels Orientalist any Western discourse that, by constructing and imagining the non-Western world in prejudicial or violent modes, generates and affirms Western hegemony. Orientalism deals with the way a particular First World, Western subject, in its representations of peoples and sites of the Third World, establishes itself as the universal subject. The critique of Orientalism, which I shall call *de-orientalism* (not to be confused with Occidentalism or the reversal of Orientalism), tries to dismantle this Orientalist discourse. It unveils the misconceptions and biases that Orientalism itself both deploys and conceals. De-orientalism also attempts to restore the wronged or violated discourses. For if Orientalism abjects other worlds, it only makes sense that the critique of Orientalism would attempt to recover that excluded domain, to recuperate a subjectivity of difference. One cannot be at all sure, however, that this critical response to Orientalism actually avoids participating in the very discourse that it contests, especially when one considers the project in terms of its overall teleology.

Before pursuing this last point, a word on this study's use of the term *Other* is necessary. Said's critique of Orientalism does not intend to define the Third World Other. Rather Said demonstrates how certain cultures and races have been Othered. Orientalism is not about the devaluation of the Other, as many seem to believe; it is about Othering as devaluation. Indeed non-Western sites are abjected the moment they are Othered. Said's Third World Other is not an ontological but an existential category. It emerges when, in a particular historical, cultural, or political situation, a Western discourse objectifies the foreign or the unfamiliar. In this structure, any person, group, class, or site can potentially occupy the place of the Other or that of the Same.

Therefore much Latin American scholarship that seems faithful to Said's project actually betrays it (although it must be noted that Said too at times betrays his own undertaking). This scholarship assumes Latin America to be a priori Other, reveals how this Otherness has been violated, and then tries to recover that alterity.[3] It presupposes an authentic Other who preexists an inauthentic Othering, whereas Said's critique succeeds insofar as it does not make such presuppositions. This (perhaps inevitable) slippage in Latin American and postcolonial studies between the ontological and the cultural, the essential and the existential—between a reading that posits Third World inhabitants as Other (an ontological statement) and one that studies the way that, at a specific historical moment, particular discourses and peoples have fabricated this Otherness (a cultural statement)—is of course of enormous interest. However, critics striving to expose the radical aspects of Said's work should not forget that the Saidian Other is not a given but a construct: a product of the West, racism, metaphysics, and global capital. Thus when I implement the word *Other* in this study, I am referring to those figures who have been named and posited as Other by Western discourses, not to peoples or sites supposed to be *really* (ontologically) Other. At the same time, my analysis is attentive to de-orientalism's (and Said's) tendency to slide from the cultural to the ontological, for this is precisely my point: Latin American de-orientalism repeats Orientalism rather than critiquing it, because it ontologizes alterity and cultural difference.

The Uses of Truth

The previous reference to teleology may seem unnecessary. In fact one could maintain that the value of de-orientalism lies in its conscientious and innovative counterreading of Eurocentric texts and rhetoric, regardless of its goals. Yet de-orientalism's most common claims are not hermeneutical, formal, or rhetorical but political. De-orientalism is not about the Western misrepresentations of the Other per se but about the fact that these misrepresentations are part of hegemonic social and ideological practices. Similarly when this critique recalls the voices of the excluded, it does so with the expressed intent of uncovering the alternative or resistant political possibilities that these hidden voices often symbolize or reflect.

The nature of these politics will become apparent shortly. For now, I emphasize the perspective that overarching this political dimension is the issue of truth, a concern with the falseness of Western misrepresentations.

It is precisely this concern that blocks de-orientalism's attempt to address the problem of alterity. De-orientalism ultimately replaces the Other with truth, sacrificing Otherness in the process. Latin American de-orientalism wants to rescue Otherness from its false, Western representations when, in fact, the present and future status of Latin American studies hinges on another task entirely, a deconstructive task: that of detaching the Other from truth.[4]

Before demonstrating how Latin Americanist de-orientalism loses alterity, we would do well to review the traditional understanding of truth in Western thought since Plato. For Plato the real world, the world of the *eidos*, is ideal, beyond the physical universe, and therefore never directly visible or accessible. The task of the truth seeker is nonetheless to locate this actual realm. He or she accomplishes this by studying the finite images, linguistic depictions, earthly reproductions, or mimetic reflections of the *eidos* that are available to the human eye. That is, he or she learns to look critically at the mimetic, lower world of the senses, to understand that these reproductions are mere representations, and to intuit the authentic Idea beyond such fraudulent images.

Plato's epistemological and educational platform hinges on a single, metaphysical *difference*: between the realm of the *eidos* and the realm of mimesis. It is only through this opposition between the higher world of ideas and the familiar, fallen world of representation that the truth can be sensed, understood, and operationalized. The "true" world, then, occupies a kind of unobtainable Other site, but not a site of Otherness, for what is really at stake within Plato's paradigm is fallen man's and fallen language's attempt to retrieve and recall the off-stage *eidos*. What is on the line in the *eidos*/mimesis difference is the redemption of authenticity via inauthenticity, of the factual via the erroneous: representation's reappropriation and restitution of its mislaid, unreachable essence.

Eidos, then, is not truth. Truth is a process and a structure. The process is any that seeks to recuperate a lost essence or *eidos*. The structure is any that posits a false or illusory field and an Other that lies beyond that field. The Other might be called the body, materiality, the subaltern, the oppressed, silence, Being, and so forth, but this renaming makes little difference since truth is grounded on a logic and a structure, not on any enunciation. Metaphysical truth survives its rearticulations for it is by definition Other than articulation itself.

At first glance de-orientalism appears to have nothing to do with this structure of truth. It appears to function, rather, as a powerful critique of ideology, a critique of the manner in which a particular, contingent fiction of a dominant group or class (for example, Orientalism) passes for universal, necessary reality. Yet it is more accurate to associate de-orientalism with demythification. De-orientalism attempts to demonstrate that the "truths" about the Other, which have been repeated over centuries and have come to be accepted, are nothing but myths used to construct and support the illusion of Western superiority, as well as of the naturalness (the necessity) of that superiority. De-orientalism demythifies the myths, the false paradigms that, according to Said, are "still prevalent, unchecked, uncritically accepted, recurringly replicated in the education of generation after generation."[5]

This last citation suggests that, in general, Western institutions teach that hegemonic representations of the Other are true, making the critique of those representations counterhegemonic and anti-imperialist. Indeed de-orientalism, like ideology itself, requires not only a dismantling of certain misrepresentations but also a prevalent (and blind) belief, among its audience, in the truth of those (mis)representations. For example, the fact that Cortés's depictions of the Mexica Aztec peoples can be shown to be Eurocentric and prejudicial is not sufficient. For a de-orientalist or de-mythifying operation to work, those Western depictions must be accepted by the audience in question: "uncritically accepted, recurringly replicated in the education of generation after generation" (Said 20). Thus a modern scientific discourse based upon the idea that the world is flat can be shown to be false, but it cannot be demythified since no modern scientist believes the statement is true. Likewise it would be redundant to proclaim as untrue a Western myth that the reader of such a proclamation believed to be untrue in the first place. Yet one must ask if this is not precisely what is happening in much of Latin American studies today. The person most likely to read or teach the Latin Americanist critique of Eurocentric discourses is also likely to know beforehand that such discourses are coercive, misleading, and orientalist.

This does not mean that orientalist and imperialist attitudes have in any way diminished. Western myths about the Other are constantly being created and recreated. Indeed one might well maintain that the majority of Westerners believe in these representations and that they are thus in need of a good dose of de-orientalism. People who in 1992 joyously celebrated the five-hundredth anniversary of the so-called discovery of America, for instance, would have done well to read a de-orientalist text such as Mary Louise Pratt's *Imperial Eyes*. However, this supposition amounts to suggesting that the ideal audience for Latin American de-orientalism is the person, however intelligent, who has read very little about Latin America, colonialism, or imperialist discourses, or who has read them in a completely ingenuous manner: the subject-supposed-not-to-know.[6]

In fact only the latter can potentially *learn* the main point that the Latin American de-orientalist wants to teach: Western discourses about Latin America are not unbiased depictions but ones put forth to silence (oppress) the Other and establish and reestablish the Same. This subject is also supposed not to know that de-orientalism is only one of various critiques of Eurocentrism. (Heidegger's critique of technicity, which questions not Western categories but categorization itself, is another.) Scholars even minimally trained in Latin American cultural theory or in postcolonial studies are already aware of this. For decades, analyses of Latin America, especially of the colonial period, have emphasized that Western discourses, however innocent they may appear, are in complicity with colonial repression, ideology, and tyranny. In fact not only is Said's claim that the Orientalist myths are "replicated in the education of generation after generation" not applicable to Latin American studies (which is not to deny that his point is valid for other fields), but the exact opposite is the case: the critique of those myths, de-orientalism, is one of the most effective and most prevalent pedagogical tools deployed in Latin American studies today.

De-orientalism, then, can disclose a great deal to the contemporary Latin American scholar: it rereads certain Eurocentric texts and reads others for the first time; it exposes in often brilliant fashion the exact rhetorical devices of imperialism; it tracks down excluded voices. But it cannot accomplish its main political task, which is to demythify dominant, First World discourse. This is because for the contemporary Latin Americanist those discourses are "under suspicion" before they are even read. This is not to suggest that enlightened Latin American or postcolonial critics do not often end up producing new myths about the Other. De-orientalism and demythification may themselves be two of those myths. It is merely to insist that in today's scholarship on Latin American culture Western representations of Latin America are rarely viewed as a priori true (and therefore they are rarely demythifiable).

If pedagogically the de-orientalist text subverts certain Western truths that the reasonably trained scholar of Latin American culture does not necessarily accept as true in the first place, epistemologically this same text demonstrates that certain Western representations are false when in the West *representation, mimesis, is by definition false*. Likewise the claim that Western representations of the Other are spurious is absolutely true, for such a claim merely repeats the discourse of truth itself, the discourse that trains us to see reproduction or mimesis not as real but as imitation, as false. We would thus do well to exercise caution in our celebrations of the splendid rhetorical critiques of Eurocentrism and colonialism put forth in studies such as *Imperial Eyes* and Stephen Greenblatt's *Marvelous Possessions: The Wonder of the New World*—not because these texts are too good to be true but because they may well be too true to be good.

In Latin American studies de-orientalism is too true to be good because the operation is antiquated, no longer any good. Good for what? one might ask. The question has already been answered: for the politics of heterogeneity that de-orientalism purports to be. Part of the problem, related to the (pedagogical) subversion of so-called Western truths, has been exposed. Yet the subversion of Western representations is only one part of the politics of de-orientalism; the other part, as already stated, concerns the representations of the Others themselves. *Imperial Eyes*, for example, not only critiques Western discourses but also alludes to the articulations of the Other that these same discourses have silenced (see, for instance, Pratt's discussion of Inca history on 135–36). Pratt's goal is not to speak for the Other but rather to uncover the presence of Other voices that have already spoken but were then stifled by the West. In effect, Pratt wants to affirm that the Other is not an object of knowledge but a producer of knowledge, a subject.

Pratt's political undertaking in *Imperial Eyes*, like Said's in *Culture and Imperialism*, might be understood as one of liberal democracy at a transhistorical, transnational level. Pratt wants the voices of all players on the stage of world history to be heard, not only the dominant voices. She wants the representations by the Other, the agency of the Other to be recognized. However, such a reading is not quite accurate since for Pratt it is not sufficient that the Other speak and be heard; it is necessary that the Other speak differently, as Other. Thus when Pratt notes that Humboldt deployed and then suppressed an entire Latin American intellectual tradition in his examinations of New World botany, zoology, and mineralogy (136), she is not merely pointing out that in the early nineteenth century there existed skilled, though unacknowledged, Latin American scholars. She is also implying that these scholars produced discourses that were distinctive, not simply European duplicates or spin-offs. Said, in *Culture and Imperialism*, repeatedly makes the same point (see especially 258–59): Orientalism suppresses not only other voices, other peoples, but other forms of knowledge, other narratives, other worldviews.

It is here that the de-orientalist conflation of Otherness and truth, and the subsequent erasure of Otherness, begins to come into view. Consider Said's reading of Frantz Fanon in *Culture and Imperialism*. After examining

Fanon's anticolonialist discourse, Said points out that Fanon was unable to follow up his critique with a viable alternative, noting also that this inability is "symptomatic of the difficulty millions of people are facing today" (236). Rather than move beyond *Orientalism, Culture and Imperialism* can only restate the arguments of the earlier text, this time by placing the de-orientalist critique in the mouth of the Third World intellectual. Yet in Fanon's texts, Said does not find the ignored "enormous contributions to knowledge" (258) but another discourse that reveals how and why these contributions have been ignored. Said (via Fanon) articulately shows that the imperialist suppresses the colonial subject, yet he cannot dredge up this subject's repressed perspectives or even provide evidence that such perspectives exist.

The above discussion was put forth with the sole intention of setting up the following questions: How can Said and the Latin American de-orientalists be so sure that when the Other has spoken, he or she has spoken differently, that his or her "enormous contribution to knowledge" (now perhaps silenced) is a *different* contribution, if they themselves never locate those other discourses? How can they be certain that a non-Western locus of enunciation automatically leads to a distinct perspective or vision?

It is not a question of whether or not Other sites of enunciation exist. Obviously they do. The question is whether those subaltern loci can be transferred to the domain of knowledge or discourse, whether the Other's singularity, location, dislocation, and perspective is somehow preserved as it is relocated onto a given epistemological or discursive field. One must ask how de-orientalist critics are capable of presenting conclusions about the being of subaltern discourses when the crux of their argument is that those discourses have never been allowed to come forth or have immediately been assimilated into Western discourses.

Before answering, a brief detour through the de-orientalist discussion of silence is in order. As the above suggests, de-orientalism always runs the risk of interpreting the silence of non-Western peoples as both the ground and the muted voice of difference. Such a discourse strongly suggests that the difference of the Other's voice is dependent not upon what the Other says but upon the fact that this voice was once silenced, oppressed. This, at best, is a dangerous proposition. It sets up the silence and oppression of the Other as the indispensable *essence* not only of the imperialist's discourse but of that discourse's opposite number: the voices of heterogeneity. The formulation makes a former silence (the wound of oppression) the precondition and ground of any articulation of alterity. It thereby holds that what is politically necessary (the silence of the subjugated) for the oppressor's definition of the Other is just as politically necessary for the Other's self-definition.

But it is important to add that this Other silence is a de-orientalist metaphor, not a fact. The Other is not literally silent except in death. The Other is a speaking being. Marginal or subaltern communities have a voice. The problem is that these voices have not been sufficiently heeded by a particular public sphere: scholarship, historiography, the media, literature, and so forth. In fact not even the most brutal colonizers' descriptions claim to impose silence upon the living Other. These portrayals have suggested that the Other's tongue is babble, irrational, forked, barbaric, underdeveloped, uncultured, animal-like, nonsensical, childlike, innocent, immature, naïve, meek, even poetic, charming, godlike, and Christ-like. But of all the adjectives that the orientalist has used to depict the Other's voice, *silent* does not figure among them.

To be sure, Orientalists often imply that the Other is silent by nature and that therefore its speech is counter to nature, unnatural, dangerous. But the Orientalist can never actually impose this silence upon a living being, neither through political action nor through discursive argument. Indeed, for the colonizer, the living Other is always making too many noises: speaking, breathing, weeping, singing. And de-orientalism knows this: that the Others have always broken through silence, even if their voices, sighs, and screams (of joy and pain) have rarely been heard. De-orientalism is well aware that the metaphor of the "formerly silent native" (*Culture and Imperialism* 212) is just a metaphor and not literally true. Why, then, must the de-orientalist deploy this metaphor of silence? What is de-orientalism trying to sneak onto the postcolonial scene when it posits the Other's unrecognized speech and noise as nonspeech and nonnoise?

Simple logic dictates that the de-orientalist metaphor of silence reflects a desire for precisely the Other's silence. In fact only this silence can guarantee the nonideological, emancipatory, and alternative character of the Other's speech. But it also assures the same character for the de-orientalist discourse itself. After all, the only guarantee of speech is that it will disrupt silence. (First, of course, the silence has to be supposed.) Therefore when de-orientalism speaks out against this silence, which it itself imposes through metaphor, it a priori emancipates both itself and the Other from suppression and oppression, from the enforced silence. De-orientalism most definitely opens the way for the Other's insurgent speech, but it is just as true that the Other's silence opens the way for de-orientalism's claims. This is why de-orientalism desires the Other's silence before it desires the Other's speech, why it grounds that speech on an imaginary or metaphorical silence, on a fantasy or a blatant misreading. It wants the Other to speak. But first it wants the Other to be silent so that de-orientalism itself can speak more securely, so that its critique is assured to be radical, known to be Other, guaranteed to upset the imposition of silence.

In short, the colonizer and the decolonizer are unaware of their common desire for the Other's silence (or death). Matters are of course complicated. The colonizer wants the Other's death and silence but also his labor, his life. No doubt the Orientalist's imposition of babble upon the Other's speech is geared to communicate this double desire: for an irrational, thus animal-like, and exploitable life. But insofar as the colonizer truly desires the Other's silence, he or she accomplishes it through murder, violence, and annihilation. De-orientalism, on the other hand, executes its desire for this silence by simulating violence through rhetoric, through a poetics. It silences the Other through a turn of phrase. It kills the Other's voice in order to bring back that voice, to redeem it through "poetry," through trope.

This simulated murder is desired not because it opens the way for the Other's redemption or restitution but because it allows for the redemption of the discourse of redemption itself—the discourse of the West since the institutionalization of Platonism, that is, since the birth of Christianity. Saved is not the Other but salvation and thus truth as the Other of language, as salvation from the fallen word. De-orientalism is less a politics than a poetics of the Other, an act of *prosopopeia*, a rhetorical tool seeking to redeem the deceased (redemption itself), to overcome not the dominant discourse of Eurocentrism but a greater master: death. De-orientalism stages the Other's metaphorical death or silence in order to save itself—a postcolonial discourse that perhaps should have dissolved along with the Second World in 1989 and the end of the First and Third Worlds as sovereign categories.

In such a manner de-orientalism betrays its desire for the return of truth as master. This return is made necessary by deconstruction's assault on truth, its claim on the death of truth. Deconstruction, once viewed as a radical critique of the West, has emerged for postcolonial studies as one of those Western, Eurocentric, dominant discourses. Yet this is not because deconstruction is Eurocentric but because it blocks de-orientalism's desire for the Other as truth.[7]

The trope of the formerly silent Other thus unconceals what the de-orientalist wants to hide, namely, that de-orientalism's desire is not for an Other or alternative discourse, a non-Western articulation, but for the Other of language: truth; and that this language, Western or otherwise, cannot be overcome: the Other of language that one reaches by overcoming language is not ready to hand. The de-orientalist, struggling to get past a deceitful language (that of Orientalism), needs another deceitful language, the trope of *prosopopeia*, in order to do so. It is not the West's rhetorical language or false representations that bother the de-orientalist critic. If this were the case, he or she would seek the Other through a more literal language and not through silence. Nor is such a critic truly bothered by the Orientalist's reduction of the Other's language to babble, to the irrational. If this were the case, he or she would strive to recover the Other's voice by demonstrating the logos or reason behind that voice.[8] The pain that never goes away is language as such, which is why de-orientalism grounds its theory of the Other on the Other of language: silence.

Here one perceives the real reason for the de-orientalist's demands for the study of other cultural productions, the Other of literature. Literature in fact represents language in the de-orientalist imaginary and is thus the symbol of the dominant discourse, the master, the Western hegemony that de-orientalism must overcome.[9] And yet de-orientalism cannot win this battle, cannot defeat language, since the linguisticality of language keeps resurfacing. Indeed de-orientalism tries to get past language to the real through the thickest form of language, the language that presents the most obstacles, that most presents itself as language: the trope, the trope of silence. De-orientalism wants to straighten out the forked tongue of the Other, a forking imposed by Eurocentrism, so as to lead that language directly back to its source, return it to the good and the true. But in doing so, it runs smack into language, into its own rhetoric, the moment it turns away from Orientalism and back toward that silent Other.

This all explains how the de-orientalist, when faced with the erased documents, the repression or silence of the Other, can nonetheless put forth theses about the Other's perspective as truth. The de-orientalist comprehends the Other's visions by catching them in the rearview mirror of the Eurocentric Same that he or she critiques. He or she then draws a metaphysical line between the false mirror itself (the Same, discourse, Orientalism) and the intuited (rather than manifest) lost Other that the mirror reflects: truth, or silence as truth. In brief, the de-orientalist Other, supposedly a construct, is Other precisely because it transcends construction. It is not the Other at all, then, but the *eidos*. The structure of de-orientalism is that of truth because, as in Platonism, it separates an off-stage "Other-than-representation" domain from a visible, on-stage, field of representation.

The fact that de-orientalism stands today as one of the most truthful and accurate means by which to analyze imperialism is therefore not surprising. But nor is it surprising that the critique, when it tackles the

unavoidable second project, the analysis of the Other of imperialism, necessarily falls back into the paradigms it seeks to undo. Indeed due to his or
her investment in truth, the de-orientalist does not dismantle but restages
Orientalism by turning the question of Otherness into a reflection of or
upon the Same. De-orientalism is too true to be good because it ignores
the collusion of Western metaphysics and Western politics. It refuses to
acknowledge that the political discourse that critiques the West (de-
orientalism) is identical to the epistemological discourse (of truth) that
grounds the West, since both discourses are founded on the same critique
of representation.

Redemption: From Truth to Subjectivity

In essence, the dilemma refers to a Latin Americanist cultural poetics of
the postboom and of the future, a Latin American project that addresses
the limits of both Orientalism and de-orientalism. Yet one must begin to
ask whether Latin American studies is today up to the task of forging a
cultural politics of alterity or whether it remains a discourse whose principal concern is the redemption of a decadent Western modernity (or postmo-
dernity). Any answer to this question must consider at least two matters.

The first concerns language. Within Western epistemology language
has traditionally been treated as a fallen language, as deception, error, distortion, even iniquity. De-orientalism, of course, does not claim to critique
language per se but a particular language, that of imperialism. However, it
often sets up its critique by first opposing actual territories, histories, and
peoples to the linguistic depictions of those histories. It then places a
higher value on the real (or on experience) than on language. And insofar
as it makes this gesture, de-orientalism is caught in a metaphysical structure in which Other experiences are to Western discourses what truth is to
deception. In its desire to overcome Western representations, de-orientalism
cannot help but slide, via this recovery of a prediscursive reality, into the
very foundations of the Western modernity (Orientalism being one of those
foundations) that it wants to undermine.

Second, de-orientalism, whether openly or covertly, holds onto a notion
of the subject, be it non-Western or marginal. This aspect of the de-
orientalist project must be placed in its context. The so-called poststruc-
turalist antihumanist discourses that announced the death of the subject
did so, at least in part, because they believed that the subject could construct itself and the world only by appropriating, silencing, and excluding

difference. As long as the subject is preserved, these discourses suggested, no thinking of alterity is possible. And since the violent Western *subject* grounds not only modern epistemology and the politics of the West (colonialism) but also modern "humanist" values (particular values passing for universal values), the critique of the subject also calls into question those values. This gives us a hint as to why proponents of the death of the subject are often accused of being nihilists. They are indicted for eradicating certain values that come part and parcel with the subject.

De-orientalism is implicated in these debates in an odd way. To be sure, the marginal or excluded subject that the de-orientalist wants to recover cannot a priori be reduced to this universal subject. Yet when de-orientalism posits the marginal subject as the emancipatory, virtuous, victimized (thus innocent) subject in relation to a violent Western "I," it also redeems the notion of the subject.[10] It reconstructs, often despite its own intentions, modernity's crumbling ground. Over against both the imperialists who deploy the subject for totalizing ends and the supposed nihilists who dismiss this subject as brutal, de-orientalism retools, reappropriates, and replaces this "I." It reconstitutes it as once more necessary, liberating, enabling. What this discourse saves is not difference or the Other but the Same: the West. Latin American de-orientalism picks up from a deathbed Western modernity's foundational concept, the subject, and then metamorphoses, adapts, and remarkets it for postmodern and postcolonial concerns such as "Otherness." And since this "I," as various thinkers have demonstrated, is a modern representative of Plato's *eidos* (or of the Christian God), the retrieval of the Other as Other Subject can never be separated from the retrieval, once more, of truth.[11]

At stake, however, are not merely some abstract notions of subjectivity and truth. At stake is real freedom, as can be shown by analyzing the marginal subject according to Jean Baudrillard's theory of the duopoly. Baudrillard suggests that ideology no longer functions through a monopoly logic. It no longer imposes a single dominant discourse, state apparatus, company, and so forth, upon the many.[12] It functions, rather, via the logic of the duopoly. It does not offer one choice but at least two and often many choices. Indeed ideology erects choice upon choice. It does not coerce the subject into taking what is given but invites him or her to select from a wide range of options. But of course, these options are merely products of the market, commodities whose difference, like that between two laundry detergents, is wholly imaginary. Such options therefore simulate freedom. The subject autonomously opts for his or her own exploitation by choosing between the market value of different commodities, by misconstruing this price difference as difference itself, and by viewing the decision to buy into the market as real choice, as true freedom.

In Latin American studies one has perhaps witnessed the construction of precisely this sort of market strategy. Having promoted the notion of the marginal subject, many Latin American critics no longer feel forced, as they once did, to choose a particular subject—the Western, dominant subject—but feel free to invent and select from an array of subject positions. And yet whatever this choice, the choice is subjectivity (just as, in Baudrillard's paradigm, whatever product one chooses, one chooses the market). Choice and freedom are simulated as the critic opts for the Sameness that he or she was previously forced to accept, as the monopoly is replaced by the duopoly, and as homogeneity and Eurocentrism are supplanted by a controlled pluralism. The critic splits the subject into many subjects and then chooses this subject or that subject, the subject or the subject (which, according to Baudrillard, is a choice of the type Pepsi–Coke). He or she does not choose difference; he or she imagines a difference in order to choose or make a claim on the Same.

Yet this freedom to pick from a pool of subjects is not one liberty among others, since the modern subject has always itself been a name for that liberty: for freedom as self-determination and for self-determination as selfhood. Thus the following reading must be entertained. As Latin Americanists continue to set up a "market of subjects," and then from out of this market to select (and invite Others to select) the Other subject or the Other as subject, they simulate their own emancipation in the name of the oppressed. The Latin Americanist's or the academic's freedom to create a market of discourses and to make market choices, his or her subjectivity and self-determination, easily passes in today's Latin American scholarship for the political and cultural liberation (and truth) of the Other. The de-orientalist always runs the risk of not freeing but of capitalizing on the Other, of using the Other as a means to enter the (academic, intellectual, discursive) marketplace. He or she is always in peril of falling toward selfishness, of profiting from the Other, of emancipating his or her own intellectual subjectivity, of advancing his or her academic position through the appropriation of the Other. De-orientalism, in sum, is dangerously close to becoming a clone of Orientalism. It is almost a discourse in which the Same (the academic) takes the Other (the oppressed) in order to both produce and increase its own space. This has not yet happened; it may never happen. But it is close to happening.

What is at stake? It is not a question of absolutely discarding de-orientalism, returning to Orientalism, or disposing of them both. It is a question of being wary of the impending convergence of the two paradigms as they contend within the market. The task is to articulate their difference, which could happen only through a third discourse, a discourse at the limit that binds and separates the one from the other, at the finitude of postcolonial studies itself. Between Same and Other today lies not the Second World but the limit, which also marks the limit of the current discourse of postcolonial studies, the end of the enterprise.

The challenge for Latin Americanism is not to take for granted these differences *between* Orientalism and de-orientalism, Same and Other, bias and correction, dominance and liberation, conservatism and revolution. Difference is not given, inherited, or recuperated. No Other and no speech are ever *necessarily* or *essentially* different from the Same. No loss is necessarily the loss of the Other. Nothing in the archive of Latin Americanism is certain to be Other when it is discovered. Difference is a *praxis*, an engagement with alterity, that is also a *poiesis*, a making. The question is whether that making is in-the-making for Latinamericanism, whether the third Latinamericanism will emerge.

Notes

Author's Note: An earlier version of this essay appeared in *Revista de Estudios Hispánicos* 31.2 (1997): 169–202.

1. I am here following up on Enrico Mario Santí's seminal article "Latinamericanism and Restitution," *Latin American Literary Review* 20 (1992): 88–96, which traces the roots of Latinamericanism to Orientalism. Santí's work on restitution, put forth both in this article and in "Sor Juana, Octavio Paz, and the Poetics of Restitution," *Indiana Journal of Hispanic Literatures* 1 (1993): 101–39, has especially influenced my own study. Alberto Moreiras's brilliant follow-up to Santí's studies, "Restitution and Appropriation in Latinamericanism," *Journal of Interdisciplinary Literary Studies* 7 (1995): 1–43, has been equally important for my reading. It is in fact Moreiras who points to the three possibilities for "Latinamericanism" that I am describing.

2. See the last third of Moreiras's "Restitution and Appropriation" for a discussion of this "other" Latinamericanism.

3. This gesture can be found, for example, throughout Mary Louise Pratt's *Imperial Eyes: Travel Writing and Transculturation* (London: Routledge, 1992).

4. This, of course, was above all the task of Michel Foucault.

5. Edward Said, *Culture and Imperialism* (New York: Knopf, 1993), 20.

6. I introduce this term as an inversion of Jacques Lacan's subject-supposed-to-know. The Lacanian notion is perhaps best presented in *The Four Fundamental Concepts of Psychoanalysis*, ed. Jacques-Alain Miller, trans. Alan Sheridan (New York: Norton, 1977), 203–60.

7. De-orientalism's resistance to deconstruction is palpable. Further evidence of this is discussed in George Yúdice, "*Testimonio* and Postmodernism," *Latin American*

Perspectives 18 (Summer 1991): 15–31. Yet deconstruction's assault on truth is not a dismissal of truth (for deconstruction, truth cannot be dismissed; one is never outside of the discourse of truth) but a deconstruction of truth as ground.

8. One hears the call for a literal language all the time, of course. But it is grounded on a desire for the Other's "silence" as "ground." Silence is the detour that grounds the call for a literal language. The same goes for any discourse on "reason." Latin Americanists often try to straighten out the Latin American tongue, to make the discourse of Latin America's alterity more reasonable and less poetic or "irrational." But again, this invariably takes place through the detour of silence. See Yúdice, Pratt, and Said for evidence of this, in addition to John Beverley, *Against Literature* (Minneapolis: University of Minnesota Press, 1993); Doris Sommer, "Rigoberta's Secrets," *Latin American Perspectives* 18 (1991): 32–50; Georg Gugelberger and Michael Kearney, "Voices for the Voiceless: Testimonial Literature in Latin America," *Latin American Perspectives* 18 (1991): 3–14.

9. This is Beverley's position in *Against Literature*. Yet neither he nor many others would confess that this is their stance. They would say that literature represents hegemonic culture and thus must be overcome. Yet it is the canon and the book that represent hegemonic culture. Since Plato, literature is irreducible to the book. Getting rid of the book and the canon may be a revolutionary gesture, but getting rid of literature through the book and the canon only reveals that the problem is much deeper than the book. The true culprit for Beverley and de-orientalism is the hidden enemy that often hides in the book but is never itself the book: literature as the symbol of language itself, in the academy and in Latin Americanism. But literature is not more or less linguistic than any other cultural form; it is just imagined to be.

10. See Enrique Dussel, "Eurocentrism and Modernity," *Boundary* 2 20 (1993): 65–76, for a discussion of innocence.

11. For a fine summary of the ways that subjectivity and truth are linked, see the introduction and the first two chapters of Marc C. Taylor's *Altarity* (Chicago: University of Chicago Press, 1987).

12. Jean Baudrillard, *Symbolic Exchange and Death* (London: Sage, 1993), 58.

CHAPTER TWO

The Mentality of the Reconquest and the Early Conquistadors

Hernán G. H. Taboada

The continuity between the war against the Moors and the war against the Indians was so evident that the Conquistadors called the temples of the New World mosques.

JACQUES LAFAYE, *Quetzalcóatl and Guadalupe*

This quotation suggests an ideological continuity between the Reconquista and the Iberian conquest of America.[1] At the roots of such a widespread idea we find a set of assumptions, as well as a heated debate about the (feudal or capitalist, medieval or Renaissance) character of colonial Iberian America. Given the importance of this debate, it would be useful to examine this continuity more in depth, even though we are often faced with testimonial evidence of a rather superficial nature. These testimonies indeed reveal to some extent the mental heritage of the Middle Ages or, conversely, influences and developments of a "modern" type, in keeping with the historical debate. To go beyond such general assumptions requires an analysis of several subtopics: the discourse that equated conquistadors with the heroes of the Reconquest, institutional similarities, and the identification of Amerindians with Muslims. These are the questions whose initial discussion is the focus this inquiry.

Indians as Muslims

Typical of the writings of the Conquest is recourse to Islamic geographies and societies as a means of explaining America. African warmth and Arabian spices, camels, Moorish houses, burnouses, African spears, jewels, dances, Arabic language, tattooing, nomadic life, marabous, impalement, circumcision, heritage laws, fire signals—these are some of the terms and images used to explain alleged American peculiarities. In order to make the city of Tlaxcala understandable, it is compared to Granada; Tenochtitlan, the Aztec capital, to Istanbul; the court of Moctezuma to that of the Moors of Granada, with "very Moorish" rooms and riches that "the Moor never saw," while Moctezuma suffered the same fate as the last king of Granada, Boabdil of the Nasrid, the last Muslim dynasty of Spain. Writing far from America, Bernáldez repeats that the beautiful Indian houses were of Moorish style. We can also see that, besides explicit comparison, direct assimilation is used as well: Indians become "Arabs," their temples "mosques," their priests "fuqaha" and their chieftains, "sheiks."[2]

In many cases, we are facing a terminological migration: when Columbus speaks about a "Turkish bow" he designates a generic weapon; when he speaks about *almadías* (canoes), *alfaneques* (Moorish tents), and *almaizares*, he uses words already incorporated into Spanish, although of Arabic origin. This origin, however, generally was unknown to the speakers and does not necessarily imply a deliberate Islamic reference. Juan Gil has noted that Bernal Díaz believes that the word *adive* is of Nahuatl (Aztec) origin, though it derives from the Arabic term for "wolf."[3] The confusion is understandable at a time when terms of such pedigree began to diminish, while American words began to enter the various languages of Spain. Columbus began by naming Taino canoes *almadías* but later uses the autochthonous *canoa*; he also moves from the illustrious term *kings* to the more contextually appropriate *caciques*.

But sometimes assimilations occurred consciously, out of the need to explain the new; Islam and Christianity (or Judaism) provided a common ground that made communication possible (albeit questionable), whereas the symbols of Amerindian cultures were alien to Europeans. Other familiar frameworks were used, for example, Spain, classical antiquity, and indeed anything that could evoke an association: local Amazons worship Apollo, as had the Moors of the *Chanson de Roland*.[4] When Suárez de Peralta speaks about the "satraps" of the Aztecs, and Gutiérrez de Santa Clara informs us that the Nahuatl term *Aculhuaques* is the same as saying *caesars* or *pharaohs*, they were not thinking about mysterious connections between Farsis, the Nile, and the Anahuac valley of Mexico.[5] They were instead trying to be understood by their readers; indeed sometimes examples were used *a contrario*—Indians do *not* do as Moors or Jews—and sometimes the chroniclers were simply trying to display erudition.

In more numerous cases, especially for those writing far from America, a blurring of identities is noticeable. It is well known that American novelties were associated with Orientalist exoticisms: words such as *turkey*, *granturco*, and *arabósitos* were used for American products. Collections of curiosities in European museums showed mixed objects from Mesoamerica and Japan; iconography made no clear distinction (camels appear in triumphal arches, engravings, and even travelogues as typically American, while Mexica buildings exhibit Moorish features); and in theater too names were often confused.

In this context, when Lizárraga, among many others, informs us that the Mapuche of Chile believe in Muhammad's paradise, and fray Diego de Landa supposes the same about the Maya,[6] we do not know if they are proposing to us an analogy or an identity. Yet when similarities are noted by such an acute observer as Father Joseph de Acosta, we can safely assume that he goes beyond the anecdotal: "The manner of slaughtering cattle, big or small, that the Indians used, in keeping with their ancient ceremony, is the same as the Moors have, and call *alquible*. . . . They gorged themselves and feasted, in the Moorish manner."[7] Some ceremonies and rites of the Indians are similar to those of the Jews, "others to those of the Moors" (265), others to the Christians; their buildings are "badly distributed and used, just like mosques or like the buildings of barbarians" (298). Acosta is considered among the first to attempt a systematic structural comparison among cultures, and thus the elements he points to must be understood in the context of that methodological intent.

Only in a few instances does it seem that Europeans actually believed that the Amerindians had some relationship with the Moors.[8] Fray Toribio Motolinía says "a number of Spaniards considered some rites and ceremonies of these natives to be of Moorish origin."[9] This suspicion eventually vanished, as did the myths about Cynocephali and Amazons, as opposed to the more persistent myths that associated Indians with Jews. But it is telling that a Peruvian priest deemed it necessary to correct Acosta by stressing that the Moors never came to these lands, nor could they have taught the Peruvians their religious ceremonies or the teachings of their Koran.

The Ideological Comparison

Imprecision, rhetoric, and ignorance seem to be plausible causes for many of these examples of association, but there are others in which the comparison is motivated by the emotional reactions of sixteenth-century Spaniards. Peter Martyr, an Italian unfamiliar with these reactions, depends on Cortés for his account of the Conquest of Mexico, yet he does not reproduce Cortés's references to mosques.[10] The conquistadors, on the other hand, depicted the Indians as Muslims, in large measure out of emotional response: they sought legitimacy for themselves, a legitimacy grounded in the master narrative of a unified monarchy, the product of eight centuries of warfare against Islam.

Therefore a commonplace in their writings is the claim to deeds tantamount to those of Pelayo's chieftains during the Reconquest of Spain from the Moors, and thus deserving of similar rewards.[11] The first heraldry of the New World employed the motif of the "Indian's head" instead of the "Moor's head" exhibited on the coat of arms in the Middle Ages.[12] We are also told that the checkerboard plan of Spanish American cities reproduced the strategy of superimposing the rational Western grid onto the supposed anarchy of the Islamic plan.[13] This assumption, of course, derives from a marked Orientalist bias about Islamic cities. Somewhat more convincing, however, is the observation about Reconquest toponyms in America: "We called it Pueblo Morisco . . . because in this town forty-some of Narváez's soldiers died, as did many of ours. . . . They robbed . . . and Cortés ordered Sandoval not to leave this town without its good punishment."[14] In his second letter, Cortés refers to the city of Nautecal, where an Indian rebellion began, as Almería, leading us to think that he hinted at the Spanish Almería, where the Morisco rebellion of 1501 began. Names like Castilblanco and Segura de la Frontera would have been moved to America because of their military importance during the Reconquest.[15]

When colonial society was consolidated, a few ethnic terms that derived from Mediterranean confessional categories were reproduced in America: the very common one of *morisco*; that of the christened Indians called "janissaries" for no apparent reason; the *ladinos* and *tornadizos*, which were used in Spain before being applied in America, the former for those who had learned Spanish and the latter for those who had "turned" from Judaism or Gentility to Christianity. The name of the Brazilian *mamelucos* probably derives from a Guarani word, but its phonetic adaptation related them to the Mameluks of Egypt. Arab etymologies are also given for other human groups: impossible in the case of *gaucho*; plausible in that of *cholo*, which probably originated in the context of the coexistence of Moors and Christians; more surely in regard to *albarazado, cambujo*, and *jarocho*.[16]

Although the matter would require a more extensive study, it is even possible to correlate such linguistic usage with some attempts of applying to the Indians certain policies already used with the Moors. This was done in systematic fashion in the case of evangelization, where pastoral guidelines and manuals frequently referred to the Moorish experience, although it could certainly be said that such insistent priestly reference to Moorish evangelization is just a logical use of past experience. More erratic in their application and obscure in their purpose were certain prohibitions imposed upon the Indians, such as those banning them from riding horses or using firearms. Even if these can be said to be consistent with public safety and political control, it is difficult to find a clear explanation, except as a Moorish remnant, when it comes to the prohibition banning Indians from selling meat.

Elsewhere I have argued that the frequent references to the European fight against Islam were rarely the result of direct personal experience but rather of family traditions and the new myths propagated by the growing production of the printing press. In this regard, Lafaye's epigraph is inaccurate. Alongside the motifs of the peninsular Reconquest, there appear the more recent, and therefore more vivid, motifs of the fight in Mediterranean waters. We can suspect, for instance, that the Greek Pedro de Candia had seen action in the Aegean, whence originated his first explanations of the Andean world. In other cases, the similes came from previous contacts with the Ottoman Empire and the Barbary Coast. Well-known tales of the Muslim enemy were transferred to the résumé of the conquistadors. Traditional Oriental fables were interwoven in the accounts of Ponce de León's search for the Fountain of Youth. A motif once in Ibn Battuta is found in Diego de Ocaña's 1599 account of his travels through South America. When we learn that Cortés "burned his ships" (he actually sank them), it was so only in a rhetorical manner, born in the classical world but also applied to Tariq ibn-Ziyad when he moved from Africa to conquer Spain in 711, across the rock that now bears his name, Mount of Tariq or jibal al Tariq (Gibraltar). There are also plain inaccuracies: Cervantes de Salazar explains that he calls the Mayan temples "mosques" because of their similarity to "the houses of Mecca that the Moors had"—a typical confusion.

In short, a mixture of oral traditions and bookish news was being recycled among those conquistadors who aspired to establish their feudal dominions in the New World, opposing the centralizing efforts of the Crown. It is perhaps pertinent to note that the most evoked heroes of the Reconquest—Pelayo, the Cid, and Bernardo del Carpio—showed a mixture of loyalty and rebellion toward the Crown, like the conquistadors themselves, who nevertheless might not have consciously made such a connection.

In any case, their Orientalist discourse proved ephemeral, as were the pretensions of the conquistadors. Cortés in the end seems to have grown tired of speaking of "mosques," while his successors preferred the word "temple" and ceased to point at *sheiks* and *fuqaha*. The toponyms of the Reconquest did not last, and the names for the social and ethnic castes lost their first Islamic connotations. In 1696 Madrid officials were stunned by the presence of "Moriscos" in the Indies, only to be candidly informed that this was the name given to a human group without connection to the descendants of Ishmael. So even though official zeal prohibited, to no avail, the use of the term *morisco* in the Indies, this simple misnomer, much like the word *turkey*, no longer evoked any conscious relation to the Orient. By the eighteenth century, when caste paintings (*cuadros de castas*) became popular, there was nothing in their pictorial motifs to recall Islam. The old ballads and stories of the Spanish-Moorish frontier (*romances fronterizos*) brought to America were lost or significantly changed subject and protagonists, such that even the heroic names of Pelayo and the Cid fell into relative oblivion, as Alexander von Humboldt attested at the beginning of the nineteenth century.

The Uses of Narrative

But before their decline, the prestigious names had established their influence, becoming assimilated into new discourses bearing a different intention. Thus we see that Indian figures also received Spanish heroic qualities: Tlacaélel, like the Cid, won battles after his death, as Dorantes de Carranza affirms, while Gonzalo Fernández de Oviedo finds no better proof of the gallantry of Amerindian warriors than calling them "a Hector, or a Bernardo del Carpio, or a Cid Ruy Díaz."[17] Perhaps this is simply a rhetorical device, but we must remember that Alonso de Ercilla's great epic of the conquest of Chile, *La Araucana*, shows the noble Araucanians with a patina of heroism not found in their Spaniard enemies. America is thus the last refuge of chivalric values that modernity was eliminating in the Old World.[18]

Conversely the assimilation of old discourses into the new arena reached a point of reversal. A sort of counterdiscourse "orientalizing" the conquistadors is seen in Las Casas and his followers. Bartolomé de las

Casas was an expert in such rhetorical reversion; he referred to the conquistadors as "tyrants," an epithet that the conquistadors themselves had
previously used against the Inca rulers (meaning that they were illegitimate
rulers). In the same vein, he found an effective device in his insistent assimilation of conquistadors and Moors.[19] Las Casas's use of the term *wolves*
(of Evangelical reference) to describe the conquistadors (while Indians are
"tender sheep") is also found in medieval chronicles with reference to the
Moors who attacked the Christian population.[20] The concept of destruction was traditionally linked to the "destruction of Spain" by Arab conquerors and is the subject of many religious commentaries. Hence the word
significantly appears in the title of Las Casas's famous treatise, *The Destruction of the Indies*, as well as in the pages of various other authors. Las Casas
also argued that the wars against the Indians were worse than those waged
by Turks and Moors against the Christian people and that forced conversion was the mark of Saracens and not a Christian practice.[21] In time, Las
Casas found more and more comparisons between conquistadors and Muslims, and so did his followers. Acosta, for instance, finding systematic similarities, goes as far as identifying two peoples as descendants of the Scythians:
the Spaniards and the Turks.[22]

In time, the friars too abandoned the old rhetorical references to Islam.
Much as in the rhetoric of colonial writers and in the popular imaginary,
there was an initial continuity of Orientalist motifs from the Reconquest
in the legal writings and legislation pertaining to the Indians, but at the
same time such continuity exhibits ever more radical changes in content
and is eventually replaced by phantom forms, mere shadows of the old Islamic referent, which linger in the Indies. Thus Creole rhetoric did not
persist in the references to Islam. The Indians, however, seized the comparison and did not let go. While identifying themselves as Christians,
they Islamized their adversaries. Thus Tarascans warring with Chichimecs
represented them as barbarians in castles where they had captured the
Holy Cross.[23] When confronting Ladinos and Creoles, they used the imported terms; Muñoz Camargo tells us in his *History of Tlaxcala* that the
Indians called the Spaniards that mistreated them Jews and Moors. One of
the several explanations of the odd assimilation between Cortés and the
Moorish king in the play *The Conquest of Jerusalem* (1539) is that the Indians, or the friars who wrote for them, intended to malign the principal character among conquistadors. Centuries later an indigenous play about Saint
Paul shows him as a Moor before his conversion. Perhaps it was because
the Moor was the archetypal infidel, but also we cannot help recalling that
peninsular pride insisted that Spain had been evangelized by Saint Paul

(see Romans 15:24). More systematically, the indigenous Peruvian chronicler Guaman Poma de Ayala uses comparisons with Moors and Jews. In the Moros y Cristianos dances of the Zinantecs, the Christians are the indigenous, facing the Moors-Ladinos. Santiago Matamoros ended his American career by aiding the Indians against the royalist Spaniards in the wars of Independence in Mexico and Peru.

The omnipresent Moor of the Middle Ages and Golden Age vanished in late seventeenth-century Spain, from both the physical and the imaginary world, because of his actual expulsion from Spain in 1609 and because the ideological uses of him fell into oblivion. He disappeared more completely from America, and it is noteworthy that he returned at the end of the colonial period, transmogrified into the Oriental, not because of a new real presence but because of the new dimensions he had acquired in European discourse beyond the Pyrenees, and above all for ideological reasons.[24]

Notes

Author's Note: This chapter was translated by Gregory Hutcheson and Erik Camayd-Freixas.

1. I use the term *Reconquista* hesitantly throughout this study, given its long-standing usage in historical literature, and yet fully aware that from its very etymology it is a tendentious term, which translates into a very partial conception of Spanish medieval history.

2. For the historical context, see my book *La sombra del Islam en la conquista de América* (Mexico City: FCE/UNAM, 2004).

3. See Consuelo Varela and Juan Gil, eds., "Introducción" and "Glosario," *Cristóbal Colón: Textos y documentos completos. Nuevas cartas* (Madrid: Alianza Editorial, 1997).

4. Glen F. Dille, "El descubrimiento y la conquista de América en la comedia del Siglo de Oro," *Hispania* 71.3 (1988): 492–502.

5. Juan Suárez de Peralta, *Tratado del descubrimiento de las Yndias y su conquista* (Madrid: Alianza Editorial, 1990), 89.

6. Fray Diego de Landa, *Relación de las cosas de Yucatán* (Mexico City: Porrúa, 1973), 44.

7. José de Acosta, *Historia natural y moral de las Indias* (1590), ed. Edmundo O'Gorman (Mexico City: FCE, 1962), 246–47.

8. See chapters 5 and 6 of *La sombra del Islam*.

9. Fray Toribio de Benavente o Motolinía, *Memoriales o libros de las cosas de la Nueva España*, ed. Edmundo O'Gorman (Mexico City: UNAM, 1971), 14.

10. Jean-Pierre Tardieu, "Las Casas et le 'chemin de Mahomet,'" *Bulletin Hispanique* 2 (2003): 303–19.

11. See examples in *La sombra del Islam*. Spain's founding hero, Pelayo, was the first king of Asturias, crowned in 718, and founder of the Spanish dynasty and its Visigothic myth. He defeated the Moors at the Battle of Covadonga, the first Christian victory that marks the beginning of the Reconquest.

12. See Bernal Díaz del Castillo's description of Cortés's coat of arms in his *Historia verdadera de la conquista de la Nueva España* (Mexico City: Porrúa, 1955), 156, 327.

13. Erwin Walter Palm, "Los orígenes del urbanismo imperial en América," *Contribuciones a la historia municipal de América* (Mexico City: IPGH, 1951), 239–63.

14. Díaz del Castillo, 296.

15. Luis Weckmann, *La herencia medieval de México* (Mexico City: FCE, 1994), 114.

16. About *ladinos* and *tornadizos*, see *Tesoro de la lengua castellana o española* by Sebastián de Covarrubias (1610), and the article by G. Cirot, "'Ladino' et 'aljamiado,'" *Bulletin Hispanique* 38 (1936): 538–40. The word *genízaros*, after its primitive meaning, became also "en Italia al que es nacido de español y de italiana, o al revés" (Covarrubias), and in America it enters the vocabulary of the castes. About *cholo*, see Elena Pezzi, *Los moriscos que no se fueron* (Almería: Cajal, 1991), 62–63, which assigns its etymology to the Arabic *shaul* (agile, quick, able, and one who serves promptly, domestic servant); about the *mamelucos*, see Maxime Haubert, *La vie quotidienne au Paraguay sous les jésuites* (Paris: Hachette, 1967), 302; about *albarazado, cambujo,* and *jarocho,* see Manuel Alvar, "Las castas coloniales," *Actas del I Congreso Internacional sobre el Español de América,* ed. Humberto López Morales and María Vaquero (1982; San Juan: Academia Puertorriqueña de la Lengua Española, 1987), 17–32.

17. Gonzalo Fernández de Oviedo, *Historia general y natural de las Indias* (ca. 1548; Madrid: Biblioteca de Autores Españoles, 1959), book 25, ch. 19 (3:53), ch. 22 (3:60).

18. Michael Rössner, "¿América como refugio de los ideales caballerescos? Apuntes sobre la *Numancia* de Cervantes, la *Araucana* de Ercilla y algunos textos americanos en torno a 1600," *Actas del XII Congreso Internacional de Hispanistas, III Estudios áureos II,* ed. Jules Wickler (Birmingham, U.K.: University of Birmingham Press, 1998), 194–203.

19. Expressions about the Muslims abound in the works of Las Casas. See Juha Pekka Helminen, "Las Casas, los judíos, los moros y los negros," *Cuadernos Hispanoamericanos* 512 (1993): 23–28.

20. André Saint-Lu, "Des brebis et des loups (à propos d'une image lascasienne)," *Las Casas indigéniste: Études sur la vie et l'oeuvre du défenseur des Indiens* (Paris: L'Harmattan, 1982), 35–44, n22.

21. Tardieu, 303–19.

22. Monique Mustapha, "L'après lascasisme au Pérou chez les pères de la Compagnie de Jésus: Acosta," *Ibero-Amerikanisches Archiv* 11 (1985): 267–81.

23. Manuel Gutiérrez Estévez, "Mayas, españoles, moros y judíos en baile de máscaras: Morfología y retórica de la alteridad," *De palabra y obra en el Nuevo Mundo, 3. La formación del otro,* ed. Gary H. Gosen et al. (Mexico City: Siglo XXI, 1993), 323–76.

24. See my article "La sombra del Oriente en la independencia americana," *Moros en la costa: Orientalismo en Latinoamérica,* ed. Silvia Nagy-Zekmi (Frankfurt: Vervuert, 2008).

CHAPTER THREE

Orientalism Criollo Style

Sarmiento's "Orient" and the Formation of an Argentine Identity

Christina Civantos

As nineteenth-century Argentine intellectuals grappled with the question of national identity, they brought images of "the Orient" and the figure of the Arab into their formulations. Domingo F. Sarmiento, a prominent statesman and author, in his *Facundo: Civilization and Barbarism* (1845) makes frequent comparisons between gauchos and Arabs and references to deserts and cities of the Orient. Later, in *Viajes por Europa, África y América 1845–1847*, Sarmiento writes about his travels in the Arab world and again relates Arabs to gauchos as he tries to establish a "civilized" yet *criollo* identity.[1] A reading of these two works reveals how "the Orient"—as imagined and experienced by a founder of Argentina and its literature— has played an important but unacknowledged role in Argentine identity and how conceptions of Orientalism can be reconfigured in a Latin American context.

The cultural backdrop that informs Sarmiento's Orientalism includes the particular moment of nation formation through which he lived and, linked to this, his relationship to Iberia, both as *España* and as *al-Andalus*. In Sarmiento's time, the newly independent administrative units of the Spanish Empire were struggling to decide on political systems and national borders. Although the Viceroyalty of the Río de la Plata, which included most of today's Bolivia, Paraguay, Uruguay, and Argentina, declared independence from Spain in 1810, it remained "Provinces of the Río de la Plata" through the mid-1800s. In 1853 a constitution confederated the interior provinces of what would become Argentina, while the province of Buenos Aires continued to fight for dominance over the interior. It was not until after 1860 that all the provinces united in a federation stable enough to create the nation of Argentina. Thus Benedict Anderson's definition of the nation as "an imagined political community—and imagined as inherently limited and sovereign" can be applied in its most literal sense to the Argentina that Sarmiento writes about in *Facundo*.[2] To further emphasize the importance of the imaginary in Sarmiento's textual and political project, it is worth noting that when he writes *Facundo* not only does he conjure up the Orient without ever having visited it, but he evokes the Argentine pampas without ever having seen the pampas proper. He knows both only through books. In fact he visited North Africa before his first travels to the pampas as an army officer.[3]

The struggle for power in the River Plate region primarily consisted of the conflict between Unitarians, who wanted power to be centralized in Buenos Aires, and Federalists, who wanted the provinces to be autonomous. In 1829, in the midst of these clashes, Juan Manuel de Rosas was elected governor of the Province of Buenos Aires. When the authoritarian leader left office, the stability he had created—or enforced—crumbled, and he was reelected in 1834. As governor, Rosas took on such powers as to become a veritable dictator of the province, until he was ousted in 1852. Nominally a Federalist, he actually increased Buenos Aires's control over the interior provinces with the support of various other provincial leaders, or *caudillos* (such as Juan Facundo Quiroga), and their gaucho militias.

Sarmiento himself is difficult to categorize as strictly Federalist or Unitarian. Born into a struggling rural family of Federalists, he was an autodidact who became aware of the discrepancies between his concept of Federalism and Federalism as it was practiced by the local *caudillos*. Moreover his political opinions were similar enough to some Unitarian ideas for him to link himself to the Buenos Aires literary salon known as the Generation of 1837, a group of young writers and intellectuals who shared the desire to rid the Argentine provinces of Rosas and the *caudillo* system in general. They sought to delineate what problems hindered unification and how the provinces could develop into a modern nation. In the process they produced, in Nicolas Shumway's words, "some of Argentina's most durable guiding fictions."[4] Foremost among these nation-building fictions propagated by the Generation of 1837 is the binary opposition between *civilization* and *barbarism*, central to the construction of an Argentine national identity. These discursive categories, emerging from the European Enlightenment, are first used in the River Plate provinces by early Romantics in the 1830s and finally popularized by Sarmiento's *Facundo*.[5]

As part of the Generation of 1837, Sarmiento had a conflictive relationship with all things Spanish. Anti-Spanish sentiment stemming from independence reached particular intensity among these young liberals, who blamed Argentina's political turmoil on its having been colonized by a "backward" country, which they saw as distinct from and inferior to Europe. In their view, both the indigenous inhabitants and the Spanish legacy produced Argentina's barbarism. During the same period Spain was involved in one of various stages of questioning its own relationship to Europe versus North Africa, and the relationship of each of these to civilization versus primitiveness. Spanish and Latin American thinkers questioned the legacy of centuries of Arab and Jewish presence in the Iberian Peninsula: Was it this contact that brought about Spain's decline, or did the process of the Reconquista that expelled Arabs and Jews bring Spain down? Although Sarmiento tended toward the strain of thought that blamed the expulsion for Spain's downturn,[6] his different positions toward Arabs ran the gamut of the stances found in Spain. With his characteristic ambivalence as well as his Romantic leanings and readings in French Orientalism, he saw Arabs not only as the erstwhile civilizing force in Spain but also at times as barbarians and at other times as romanticized figures. It is possible, as some have suggested, that Sarmiento's more sympathetic views of Arabs came from his awareness of his mother's Arab ancestry.[7] This can be taken only so far, however, when we consider that Sarmiento's more immediate Spanish heritage was not enough to alter his views of Spaniards. I propose instead that he uses the multivalent figure of the Arab as a way of translating Argentina's difference—its cultural identity in formation— for himself as well as for Europeans.

The way Sarmiento employs the concept of barbarism and relates to it elucidates the function of the Arab in his texts. While he often invokes the barbaric in order to define himself by opposition, he also expresses identification with elements of barbarism as he delineates his hybrid, Spanish American *criollo* position. Moreover his imitation of and identification with the barbarian is linked to his practice of Orientalism. He participates in Orientalism not only when writing about his travels in the Arab world but also when writing about Argentina.

The Arab Gaucho in *Facundo*

The Latin American classic *Facundo* contains some of the earliest Argentine images of the Arab and the Orient. *Facundo* is largely a historical and political essay that Sarmiento fashions as the biography of Juan Facundo Quiroga, the leader of La Rioja Province during the Rosas dictatorship. It is Sarmiento's attempt at understanding the turmoil in the "Argentine Republic," an upheaval so puzzling that he calls it "the Argentine Sphinx."[8] As he looks out over the provinces in the throes of disunity he identifies civilization and barbarism as struggling forces. The traditional reading of *Facundo*, and of Sarmiento's literary and political career as a whole, focuses on the positioning of the civilized above the barbaric, as sharply separate categories. However, as late twentieth-century scholars have shown, *Facundo* (as well as the Algerian travelogue, as I demonstrate below) is in fact marked by deep ambivalence. In *Facundo*, for instance, Sarmiento points to the struggle between civilization and barbarism as that which gives Argentina its particular poetic essence. The ambiguous use of these terms— their constantly shifting values—reflects Sarmiento's efforts to combine them both into a distinctly Argentine identity.

As Sarmiento describes the landscape and human types of the interior, all those who inhabit the pampas are outside the European urban ambit and thereby marked as barbarians. There are three groups: the indigenous peoples, the usually *mestizo* cattle herders and ranch hands known as gauchos, and the *criollo* farmers and ranch owners. But Sarmiento focuses on the gauchos in a broad sense to include Facundo Quiroga and his soldiers, although these men were from western provinces rather than the plains the gauchos called home. Thus in Sarmiento's text the term becomes "roughly synonymous with country-dwelling nomads whom he viewed as natural supporters of *caudillismo*."[9]

Sarmiento praises the gaucho barbarians' intelligence and poetic sensibility. Yet his descriptions are a form of classification, an attempt to define and control what is threatening in the barbarian. He describes their special form of knowledge using gaucho types, which he lists and characterizes: the tracker, the guide, the bad gaucho, and the singer. Each one has his own "science," skill, or art (44–53). Julio Ramos notes that when Sarmiento cites their special knowledge, oral narratives, and distinctive vocabulary, he seeks to maintain the voice of the Other, understood as poetry, in opposition to "modern, rationalized knowledge."[10] However, Sarmiento comments on how disorganized, inconsistent, and inexact their knowledge and poetry are, and his collection of types, as well as the always italicized gaucho words, have the function of ordering and domesticating barbarism. As a result, the gaucho's special knowledge remains in a subordinate position.

Sarmiento examines "uncivilized" rural society as a doctor would a sick patient. He prescribes the cure for barbarism and at the same time determines what the cultured city (Buenos Aires) needs in order to be a Latin American rather than Spanish or European city. Thus, while the civilized needs the barbarian's special forms of knowledge, the barbarian needs much more; without the Europeanized urban center, it is impossible for the interior to develop.

What is particularly striking about *Facundo* is that in imagining both the status of Buenos Aires vis-à-vis the barbarous interior and the character of the barbarian, Sarmiento repeatedly makes references to "the Arab" and "the Orient," a stylized or stereotyped version of West Asia and North Africa. Furthermore his images of the Orient and the Arab are as ambivalent as his attitudes toward Argentine barbarism, both being deeply intertwined. Thus he participates in the ideology of essentializing the Oriental Other, but in doing so from his particular cultural context and in his distinct ways, he leads us to a more complex conceptualization of the essentialist construction of West Asia and North Africa.

Sarmiento deploys images that range from evocations of biblical antiquity to deterministic geographical descriptions and equations of the Argentine gaucho with Arab and Asian nomads and tribal leaders, at times in a negative and at times in a positive light. He invokes the figure of the biblical patriarch to expound upon the connection between a people's dress, their level of civilization, and their system of ideas. He then states that Facundo and the dictator Rosas reject suits—the clothing of high civilization—and any changes in fashion. Thus if one fixes thought and enslaves it, styles of dress will be invariable. As an example, he mentions Asia, where man lives under governments like Rosas's and has worn the same tunics since the time of Abraham (120–21). Wrapped around this theory of fashion are his thoughts on the significance of the color red, the official color of the Rosas regime that was harshly imposed on the people. For Sarmiento this is another matter "that reveals the spirit of the Arab, Tartar herding power that is going to destroy the cities" (118–21). This leads to ruminations on the color red as the universal color of barbarism.

Conversely he claims that Buenos Aires, as the only Argentine port city, "would already be the American Babylon, if the spirit of the pampas had not blown over it" (25). This usage of the Orient reflects positively on Babylon but laments the stifling of Buenos Aires at the hands of Argentine barbarians. The comparison is woven into descriptive passages that reflect a deterministic conception of geography. In describing the pampas Sarmiento observes, "This expanse of plains imprints upon the life of the interior a certain Asiatic tinge, that is not unpronounced" (27). He then states that many a time he has been inspired to salute a moonlit landscape with a quote from Volney's *The Ruins of Palmyra* (1791).[11] This reference to Volney displays Sarmiento's familiarity with European Orientalism and its role in his writings. Volney was a French Romantic whom Said describes as one of the "orthodox Orientalist authorities."[12] Jaime Concha notes that Sarmiento had a broad exposure to nineteenth-century European Orientalism "as an assiduous reader of *Revue de Deux Mondes*."[13] Slimane Zeghidour indicates that at the time of writing *Facundo*, Sarmiento was reading Sallust's *De la historia de las guerras de Yugurta* (*Bellum Jugurthinum*) and Alix's *Précis de l'histoire de l'Empire Ottoman*.[14] Sir Walter Scott's descriptions and ideas about gaucho barbarism and its connection to the "Oriental qualities" of Spaniards also influenced him.[15] Such European writings on the Orient and Argentina itself are the material that Sarmiento uses to present places he has yet to see. Yet in replicating Orientalist discourses, he also expresses identification with the objects of his Orientalist descriptions.

After quoting Volney, Sarmiento invokes the Fertile Crescent to claim a "something," an "analogy," a "kinship" between the solitude and "spirit" of the pampas and those of the Asian plains flanked by the Tigris and the Euphrates, "between the solitary troop of wagons that crosses our solitudes to arrive, after months of travel, in Buenos Aires, and the caravan of camels heading to Baghdad or Smyrna" (27). Similarly, a few pages later he describes his great Argentine city as a "narrow oasis of civilization" besieged by savagery (31). Thus in order to establish the civilization of Buenos Aires and the barbarism that threatens it, he turns alternately to symbols of a cultured Orient, the cities of the ancient Near East, and to a symbol of the savage, merciless Orient: the desert.

Sarmiento continues to employ geographic determinism, shifting his focus to the desert and combining topography with images of the people of Argentina as Arabs. He notes that the landscape of the Argentine interior looks so Asian that without thought we imagine "the tents of the Mongol, the Cossack, or the Arab" (32). He later compares La Rioja to Jerusalem and expresses "concern" that the Argentine city and province is geographically too similar to Palestine, "a strange combination of mountains and plains, fertility and aridity" (87). Here the Middle East arises as an anxiety of similarity, but one that is to be fostered and even reveled in, despite its sometimes troubling nature. In this passage he immediately shifts to the people: "What most brings these Oriental reminiscences to my imagination is the truly patriarchal appearance of the farmers of La Rioja." He expresses surprise at seeing people who speak Spanish yet wear full beards and have an "appearance that is sad, taciturn, grave, and sly—an Arab who rides a donkey and sometimes wears goat skins" (87–88). Sarmiento has absorbed so fully his readings in European Orientalist texts that he himself has vague "memories" of the Orient in spite of not having been there. He takes as fact the images of his readings—the oddness of the landscape and the primitiveness and craftiness of its people—and relates it to vast areas of the region he is trying to build into a nation.

In particular Sarmiento directly links the aggressive survival tactics of the indigenous people, the roaming, unfixed lifestyle of the gauchos, and even the seasonal lifestyle of the interior's *criollo* subsistence farmers to the nomadic and the tribal, more specifically to savage, desert-dwelling nomadic Orientals. For instance, he describes an Argentine caravan traveling through the pampas: its leader must fend off marauding savages—the indigenous people of the region—and Sarmiento refers to them as "American Bedouins" (28). His preoccupation with people not rooted to a particular place or bound in social units stems from his view that such groups do not contribute to the construction of a nation; instead they challenge the power of national authorities and the very existence of the nation as a unified community. Paradoxically he uses the gaucho as the figure that represents the national character or temperament that in turn can delineate a unified national community.

Sarmiento artfully juxtaposes gauchos, *caudillos*, and Arabs under the rubric of barbarism. However, part of the ambivalence in *Facundo* stems from his contradictory depictions of the gaucho as an orientalized yet distinctive national type. Sarmiento struggles between building a nation favoring either *criollo* or European values, but potentially difficult to distinguish from Europe culturally.

He also attributes positive qualities to the gauchos, again in connection with "the Orient." He credits the gauchos for being skilled, devoted horsemen and having a great appreciation for music, noting, "Here the life of the Arab, the Tartar appears again" (51, 55). When he refers specifically to Facundo Quiroga, he perceives in Facundo's public life "a great man, a man of genius, despite himself—without his knowing it—a Caesar, a Tamerlane, a Muhammad. He was born that way, and he is not to blame; he will descend social strata to rule, to dominate, to fight the power of the city" (83). Thus the terrible Facundo Quiroga emerges as an innocent, natural man who was simply born to rule.

However, the characterizations continue to contradict each other. In a later passage Facundo, like Attila in Rome and Tamerlane in the Asian plains, is a "barbaric genius" who leaves civilization in ruins (94). Then the tone of the characterization shifts, and in a completely negative portrayal

Sarmiento describes Facundo as worse than Muhammad Ali, Ottoman governor of Egypt. While Ali can "desire European civilization" and inculcate it in those he oppresses, Facundo rejects and destroys any element of civilization (96).

The depictions take yet another turn when Sarmiento describes Facundo's terrifying sideways glance as similar to that of the "Ali Pasha," a title of Muhammad Ali, in a painting by Monvoisin (76).[16] Sarmiento recounts anecdotes about Facundo and notes that the countless stories and popular sayings about him in people's collective memory "have a stamp of originality that gave him a certain Oriental air, a certain tinge of Solomonic wisdom in the conception of common folk" (85). In a similar vein, in the midst of an anecdote about Facundo's visits to the province of Tucumán, Sarmiento asks his reader, "Do you think, by chance, that this description is plagiarized from *One Thousand and One Nights* or other Oriental fairy tales?" (175). For this *criollo* intellectual, Facundo and his American environment constitute an unbelievable, fantastic, and yet fascinating reality.

Several critics have considered the function of Sarmiento's Orientalism in *Facundo*. Ana María Barrenechea explains his Orientalist images as support for his thesis of geographic determinism and a source of "local color and distance that charges them with poetic value in the Romantic period" as well as "historical or literary interest.".[17] However, as Concha notes, "The 'Asiatic' . . . is much more than a picturesque reference in the conception of *Facundo*. . . . This element stands as a central component in the ideological landscape of the work. . . . It supplies a basic paradigm for the representation of barbarism [and] covers the entire artistic map of *Facundo*: the iconographic, the metaphoric, and the lexical registers among others."[18] Carlos Altamirano pinpoints despotism as the conceptual scheme behind Sarmiento's Orientalist imagery.[19] Ramos reads Sarmiento's invocation of European Orientalism as an attempt to insert himself into the European and civilized realm. Ramos astutely notes, however, that in Sarmiento's deliberately misquoting European sources and "badly" imitating established European discourses, he disrupts and manipulates the authority of the European model with his own barbarous subalternity. He uses European discourses to formulate a new place of enunciation for the subaltern and thereby to claim a new type of intellectual authority, an alternative way of knowing, implicit in his attention to the voice (forms of speech and oral narrative) of the gaucho Other.[20]

The examination of Sarmiento's conjuring of the Arab gaucho leads us to a parallel question: How does he manipulate the European construction of the Arab to establish this Argentine intellectual subject position?

He uses a deeply rooted European figure of the Other, the Arab, as an analogy or metaphor for the Argentine Other. However, it is unclear which term acts as the illustrative equivalent of the other, which term is known and which unknown. It might seem that Sarmiento is using the gaucho as a frame of reference for that which is unknown to him—the Arab—as he attempts to master European knowledge about the Other. But we could almost say that the gaucho and the Arab are equally unknown to him; certainly he visits Algeria before he visits the pampas. Actual contact aside, what he purports to know (the gaucho) is unknown to Europeans. Conversely what is unknown to Sarmiento (the Arab) is part of what Europeans have "mastered" as their "territory of knowledge." Since Sarmiento recognizes the Orient as a terrain that is known intellectually, it is the gaucho who must be mapped out.[21] Thus I would argue that Sarmiento is using the Arab to frame the gaucho in a comprehensible way for Europeans as well as for himself; he is using the gaucho-Arab to mark the "territory of knowledge" about the gaucho as his own, as an Argentine domain.

Therefore, rather than a straight analogy (the gaucho is to Sarmiento and the Argentine as the Arab is to the European), Sarmiento carries out a translation of sorts. Integral to the textual functioning of his pairing of the gaucho and the Arab is the desire to differentiate the Argentine from the European. Even the way Argentines know or master their Other is different from that of the Europeans. While the Arab is not accepted as part of the European (keeping in mind that, for Sarmiento, Europe does not include Spain), the gaucho, however subordinately, is constructed as part of the Argentine. Sarmiento uses the comparisons with the Arab and the invocations of the Orient as a way of translating what Europeans know (the Arab Other) and their means of knowledge (through overseas colonization) into a picture of the somewhat different relationship that exists between gauchos and Argentines. In this way, the Argentine, as Europe's alternative Other, cannot slip into the position of barbarian and can also stake out its own particular form of knowledge and establish its own cultural identity.

Viajes: Contact with "the Orient" and the Arab-Gaucho Self

Sarmiento's actual voyage to "the Orient" further elucidates his creation and deployment of the Other, whether Arab or Argentine barbarian. As a result of political tensions during his exile in Chile, Chilean Minister Manuel Montt suggested that Sarmiento go on a government-sponsored trip to Europe and North America to learn about educational systems, and entrusted him with a secondary mission: the study of French colonization methods in Algeria. Sarmiento's writings suggest that personal interest as well as official business motivated his trip. As Paul Verdevoye points out, Sarmiento's interest in going to Algeria stemmed from the desire to confirm his notions about the similarities between Arabs and gauchos and the possibility of "civilizing" the Argentine gaucho through immigration or colonization, as the French were attempting to do with the Algerians.[22] Indeed in his "Letter to Juan Thompson," the section of *Viajes* written in Algeria, Sarmiento continues to search for a way to solve Argentina's enigma.

In this text we can see the full extent of Sarmiento's fascination with the gaucho and the Arab and the dynamics that structure this fascination. Once again he describes the barbarian Other—this time actual North African Arabs—in a very ambiguous manner. Arabs are vengeful barbarians who do not know how to appreciate France's civilizing project, but they are also noble, elegant, and hardy horsemen. Although Sarmiento tries to find the features of his idealized barbarian of the pampas among the Arabs and thus arrive at a solution to the Argentine enigma, his efforts seem to end in disillusionment. Upon arriving at the desert camps of some Arab tribes, he sees the barbarism of the pampas and even worse. Everything and everyone— children, women, pitchers, water, and food—are in a state of uncleanliness that fills him with disgust: "My God!, My God!, So many are the false hopes dissipated in one blow, so much poetry, so many historical recollections, and above all, so many writers' descriptions ruined by the most prosaic and miserable reality that ever was seen!"[23]

Near the end of his letter, in a similar process, Sarmiento looks out at Oran and has a vision of the modernization that he thinks still might take place there. What is at first identical to passages written by European travelers in Latin America, which Mary Louise Pratt appropriately designates as "industrial reverie,"[24] becomes the horror of the colonies. As Sarmiento emerges from his vision of modernization, established and enjoyed by Europeans, he hears the news of an Arab attack against a group of French colonizers. He looks at one of the corpses and says, "Here we have—I said to myself—the reality of the situation! There is blood and crime! Here we have the only thing that is possible and feasible!" (274). His grand dream of modernization, like the literary images he evoked, becomes hollow and untenable before the dirty and chaotic reality he sees.

As Said points out, Romantic Orientalists often experienced such disillusionment: "There is disappointment that the modern Orient is not at all like the texts," this being "a common topic of Romanticism." Thus Sarmiento's images are well described by Said's formulation of Orientalism: "a generalized—not to say schizophrenic—view of the Orient."[25] Given that Sarmiento appears to mirror the Orientalism of many other writers and scholars, he might seem at first glance to be firmly entrenched within the Orientalist tradition denounced by Said.

However, we must take into account Sarmiento's particular uses of Orientalism and the cultural and political context from which he writes. Many of the ways he responds to Arabs and the Orient do not fit within the Romantic Orientalist tradition. At times he uses Orientalist imagery in order not only to describe what he considers the gauchos' positive traits but also to identify with them. In his travelogue, he similarly praises the Arab guides and trackers in Algeria: "The Arab *baqueanos* caught my attention because of their unique similarity to ours from the pampas. Like these, they smell the soil to orient themselves, taste the roots of grasses, recognize paths, and are attentive to the smallest circumstance of the ground, the rocks, or the vegetation. But the Arabs leave our gauchos very far behind in the amazing sharpness of their senses" (267). Thus, rather than dismiss the Arab as primitive, he relates these qualities to those of the gaucho with which he himself identifies.

This identification is evident in a significant episode of this travel narrative when Sarmiento describes his journey across the desert to the Arab camps that cause him such disillusionment. As he rides on horseback with his Arab guides he enjoys the freedom of riding through open terrain, going so far as to imitate and identify with the Algerians. It is not surprising that he mimicked and shared the voice of the gaucho in his *Facundo*, given that he positions the gaucho as an autochthonous figure emblematic of Argentina. It is striking, however, that in his exploration of the civilized, the barbarian, and the Argentine, he should engage in mimetic identification with the Arab world.

Sarmiento rides through the Algerian desert wearing an Arab burnoose and in doing so feels as though he were in the Argentine pampas. He enjoys "the pleasure of seeing [him]self on horseback on the rough, open range" and marvels at the newly awakened "gaucho instincts that sleep within so long as we have no other vehicle available but carriages, trains, or steam boats" (256). Rather than *riding* on horseback, Sarmiento phrases it as "verme a caballo"; that is, he *sees* himself on horseback, as a gaucho. Verdevoye considers this moment one of pure pleasure, free from theorizing, in which the intellectual, enamored with European civilization, indulges in unrestrained delight.[26] It is not, however, a scene of abandon but rather one of self-conscious pleasure. Sarmiento not only enjoys riding like a *gaucho moro*, but he also enjoys envisioning himself, finding himself, in the act of doing so.

Sarmiento then recounts his efforts at imitating his Arab guides in the way he wears his burnoose, wanting to look like an Arab prince or nobleman (265). Yet almost every previous mention of this hooded cloak worn by the local Arabs is laden with negative symbolism: it is "the dirty and torn burnoose" that disrupts his feeling of being in Europe, rises up against France, and "may conceal the fanatic's dagger or the prayer beads of the ascetic who go around calling for a holy war" (239–43). After recasting the burnoose as a positive symbol of Oriental grace and nobility, he tries to outdo his guides in their riding ability. He wants to go faster and, swearing by the Prophet Muhammad, tells them that he can ride to the last oasis of the Sahara without getting worn out—but nearly falls from his horse when it starts to gallop (256–57). It is an attempt on Sarmiento's part to prove to himself and to his Arab guides that he does have something of the barbarian in him. However, when he arrives at the camp and tries to sit on the ground as the Arabs do, he finds this position very uncomfortable, but then he sits with ease "the way our gauchos do" (258). Thus Sarmiento is ultimately successful in establishing that there is a noble barbarian within him.

In the Bedouin camp he appropriates the gaucho. In speaking of "our gauchos" he helps establish a "we": the Argentineans. And it is not only an outward connection. The gaucho is in him, a part of him, as he claims in his phrase "the gaucho instincts in us." By keeping up with the Arabs who outdo the gaucho, he is able to arrive at the gaucho—to become a gaucho—with and through the Arab. As González Echevarría suggests, "If the gaucho is the origin of Argentine culture, the deep stratum of the Argentine self, that origin is the solidly literary figure of a gaucho dressed in the garb of a Bedouin as described by French, German, and British travelers [to the Argentine pampas]."[27] Sarmiento is not the first to describe the gaucho in Oriental terms, but he is the first to mimic and identify with both figures—and to use the *gaucho-moro* in building a national "we."

Nevertheless it is at this point in his narrative, with his first experience of disillusionment, that he notices his surroundings and is repulsed by their extreme "barbarism." His disgust could be read as a failed attempt at identification with the barbarian Other (both Arab and gaucho), which leads to his definitive positioning alongside the civilized European. Such a reading, however, is countered by the fact that his imitation of Arabs did not end in Algeria. As he continues his travels he takes a nighttime gondola in Venice, wearing his burnoose and carrying his Arab pipe in order to make the ride more "piquant" (304). Along similar lines, in Argentina he was known to wear a *chiripá*, the loose pants worn by gauchos and peasants, under his frockcoat.

The idea that Sarmiento identifies exclusively as European can arise only from reading his text using a sharp division between colonizer and colonized. Such binary opposition obscures the truly complex position of this Latin American subject: Sarmiento is neither the colonized nor the colonizer, and yet he is both at once. The Algerian commentator Zeghidour eloquently describes Sarmiento's situation: "Sarmiento . . . seems to me to prefigure the intellectual of what would later be called the Third World. . . . The struggle between the barbarian and the civilized became, in him, an intimate tearing and a rupture."[28] Sarmiento inhabits an ambiguous, doubled, and ultimately in-between space in which he constructs his sense of self by identifying with various different subject positions. As with any gesture of imitation carried out by a subject in the ongoing process of self-constitution, Sarmiento's mimesis, his role-playing of Bedouins and gauchos, is of great significance. Mimetism is a way of exploring and defining subjectivity and thus of imagining a stable or coherent identity. In imitating another, the subject plays at being that Other. This impersonation is indicative of Sarmiento's search for an Argentine identity for both himself and his nation.

Given these different roles, we must consider the heterogeneous elements that shaped Sarmiento. He was born into an impoverished *criollo* family in a provincial town in western Argentina and thus was raised in contact with *mestizo* culture. Yet through self-education, he moved into a position among the urban elite of Buenos Aires. As Pratt points out, "The newly independent elites of Spanish America . . . faced the necessity for self-invention in relation both to Europe and the non-European masses they sought to govern."[29] Further, there was the need, in the wake of independence and in the process of demarcation of an Argentine territory out of heterogeneous provinces, to formulate a distinct national culture represented by an autochthonous type. For the *criollo* statesman, such a unified national identity was also potentially useful for governing the masses.

Sarmiento is between the pampas (the indigenous interior) and Buenos Aires (the Europe-oriented port), between Argentina and other Latin American countries, and between Latin America and Europe. His formulation of an identity suitable for himself and all Argentineans can be understood as a negotiation that maneuvers within the "foreign" without entering "foreignness." These two terms, used by Humboldt to describe great translation, are useful in describing identity formation in hybrid spaces:

> Translation should indeed have a foreign flavor to it, but only to a certain degree; the line beyond which this clearly becomes an error can easily be drawn. As long as one does not feel the foreignness [Fremdheit] yet does feel the foreign [Fremde], a translation has reached its highest goal;

but where foreignness appears as such, and more than likely even ob-scures the foreign, the translator betrays his inadequacy.[30]

This desire for a limited amount of foreign flavor with no sense of strange-ness is an apt explanation of the workings of *criollo* self-formation, par-ticularly in the case of Sarmiento. In *Recuerdos de provincia*, he himself describes the process of his formation as "translating the European spirit into the American spirit, with the changes that the different theater re-quired."[31] Sarmiento "translates" himself, carefully crafts himself as differ-ent yet not strange, in order to "act" on the Argentine "stage," to perform a particular identity. He strives to be different from the European (that is, somewhat of a barbarian) and different from, say, the Peruvian (a barbarian of a particular type), but not so different as to be too barbaric (or uncivilized). He displays both disdain and ambivalence toward barbarism. However, in his attempt to construct an identity by translating established types, Sarmiento not only goes so far as to view gauchos in a positive light but also approv-ingly regards gauchos as Arab-like and Arabs as gaucho-like.

The presence of this mimesis and identification in Sarmiento leads me to question Said's conceptualization of Orientalism. Sarmiento certainly fits, however obliquely, within Said's definition of Orientalism as a phe-nomenon that establishes the Orient as ontologically and epistemologi-cally different from Europe and as a discourse with close ties to imperialist power and colonialist tradition. Sarmiento builds his notions on the idea that Europe and the Orient are essentially dissimilar, and his project can be seen as an offshoot of colonialism. His construction of the Orient also fits with Said's description, "The Orient is less a place than a topos, a set of references, a congeries of characteristics, that seems to have its origin in a quotation, or a fragment of a text, or a citation from someone's work on the Orient, or some bit of previous imagining, or an amalgam of all these."[32] Yet Sarmiento's Orientalism goes beyond references and citations alone to instances of mimesis and identification, and it is certainly not disciplined in the way that Said's formulation requires.

As various critics have noted, Said's groundbreaking study tends to characterize Orientalism as a monolithic discourse that replicates itself throughout history. Although in *Culture and Imperialism* Said moves to-ward a more nuanced understanding of Orientalism and recognizes resis-tance to it, he does not account for more heterogeneous formations, such as those that arise from the relationship between Creole colonials of Span-ish descent and the Arab world. His Eurocentric conception of Orientalism does not allow for the manifestation of Orientalist discourses in different contexts or in conjunction with other discourses, such as those in *Facundo* and the epistolary account of Algeria.

Likewise Sarmiento's images of the Orient cannot be reduced to Barrenechea's characterization of them as Romantic poetics or evidence for geographic determinism. His images convey an essentialization of the Orient and the performance of certain roles, significant to identity formation, precisely because they pertain to a *criollo* writer. Lisa Lowe's approach in her study of French and British Orientalisms is particularly useful in understanding Sarmiento's discourse. Lowe focuses on "Orientalism as a tradition of representation that is crossed, intersected, and engaged by other representations." She argues for a new conception in which "Orientalism is not a single developmental tradition but is profoundly heterogeneous," involving "a plurality of referents" and producing versions of the Orient "engendered differently by social and literary circumstances at particular moments."[33] Her approach allows for the existence of interventions and resistance to such controlling discourses. This type of theorization of Orientalism also allows, beyond the strict East/West polarity, for other, third-party cultural positions, which are involved in imagining in their own various ways both Europe and the Orient, as well as their own cultural spaces. It is a concept well suited to the discursive practices of hybrid spaces and contact zones in different parts of the world.

I would like to take Lowe's formulation further in the direction of Creole cultural spaces by emphasizing the heterogeneous functions, as well as sites, of Orientalism. Not only is Orientalism interconnected with a variety of discourses, but it also takes place in a variety of settings. This interplay of discourses is particularly salient in cultural locations of marked heterogeneity, such as Latin America. A more fluid and multiple rather than fixed and binary theorization of Orientalism also allows for alternative cultural positions.

One of the most highly visible and significant discursive practices in Latin America, also at the core of Sarmiento's Orientalism and role-playing, is the definition and negotiation of the categories of self and Other. Since the nineteenth century, Roberto González Echevarría suggests, Latin American discourses "deal obsessively" with that "other within" who may be the violent source of Latin American difference: "The Latin American self both fears and desires that 'other within.'"[34] In struggling with (both fearing and desiring) the "Others within" (the gaucho and the European), Sarmiento turns to a more removed Other (the Arab). He passes through moments of identification as well as opposition and comes to understand his gaucho Other, and his gaucho self, through his Orientalism. His identity—and that of Argentina—remains a moving kaleidoscope, with personas shifting in and out of focus, in which the gaucho, the Arab, and the European are recurring figures.

Sarmiento's texts display the overrunning, intersecting enunciations of various discourses that arise out of his historical, social, and political position, including the legacy of the first European (particularly Spanish) image of the barbarian Other (the Arab); the dissemination of Orientalist works (as far as South America's Southern Cone); the effort to construct a manageable Argentine identity and thereby establish a national type (the figure of the gaucho); and the related drive to formulate an identity on the level of the elite *criollo* subject. Situated among these various discourses, Sarmiento likens gauchos to Arabs, engages in opposition to and identification with the Arab-gaucho, and struggles to come to terms with his gaucho Other and his gaucho self, through his Orientalism. In short, he uses the figure of the Arab as a graspable counterpart to the gaucho and as part of the translation, the crafting, of the Argentine.

Notes

Author's Note: This essay is adapted from two sections of *Between Argentines and Arabs: Argentine Orientalism, Arab Immigrants, and the Writing of Identity* (New York: State University of New York Press, 2006). In the book I analyze how Arab immigrants to Argentina respond to the Orientalist discourses of Sarmiento and others. I thank SUNY Press for permission to reprint some of this material.

1. The standard English equivalent for *criollo* is "Creole." However, although *criollo* refers to a person of Spanish or French descent born in the Americas, it does not have as strong a connotation of African-European racial mixture as "Creole." Additionally the term *criollo* has a particular valence in Latin American cultural history because *criollos* were first at odds with Spanish colonial administration and then with immigrants.

2. Benedict Anderson, *Imagined Communities* (London: Verso, 1991), 6.

3. Roberto González Echevarría, "A Lost World Re-discovered: Sarmiento's *Facundo*," *Sarmiento, Author of a Nation*, ed. Tulio Halperín Donghi et al. (Berkeley: University of California Press, 1994), 220–56; Solomon Lipp, "Sarmiento Revisited: Contradictions and Curiosities," *Sarmiento and His Argentina*, ed. Joseph Criscenti (Boulder, Colo.: Lynne Rienner, 1993), 7–16.

4. Nicolas Shumway, *The Invention of Argentina* (Berkeley: University of California Press, 1991), 112.

5. Félix Weinberg, "La dicotomía civilización-barbarie en nuestros primeros románticos," *Río de la plata* 8 (1989): 8–9.

6. Santiago Kovadloff, "España en Sarmiento," *Viajes por Europa, África y América 1845–1847 y Diario de gastos*, ed. Javier Fernández (Buenos Aires: Fondo de Cultura Económica de Argentina, 1993), 759–89.

7. Paul Verdevoye, "Viajes por Francia y Argelia," in Fernández, 707. In *Recuer-dos de provincia* Sarmiento traces his mother's surname, Albarracín, to a twelfth-century Saracen leader.

8. Domingo F. Sarmiento, *Facundo o civilización y barbarie* (Buenos Aires: Cen-tro Editor de América Latina, 1979), 8. Page numbers refer to this edition. Transla-tions are mine unless otherwise noted.

9. Shumway, 70.

10. Julio Ramos, *Desencuentros de la modernidad en América Latina* (Mexico City: FCE, 1989), 24–31.

11. Sarmiento quotes Volney's *Les Ruines de Palmyre*: "La pleine lune á l'Orient s'élevait sur un fond bleuâtre aux plaines rives de l'Euphrate" (27). (The full moon rose to the East over a bluish background on the brimming banks of the Euphrates.) Pal-myra, an ancient city whose ruins are in present-day Tadmur, Syria, once served as a desert way station for caravans.

12. Edward Said, *Orientalism* (New York: Pantheon, 1978), 39.

13. Jaime Concha, "On the Threshold of *Facundo*," in Halperín Donghi et al., 153n9.

14. Slimane Zeghidour, "Sarmiento y su viaje a Argelia," *La Gaceta* (Tucumán, Argentina), September 4, 1983.

15. Allison Williams Bunkley, *The Life of Sarmiento* (Princeton, N.J.: Princeton University Press, 1952), 211.

16. The French painter Monvoisin lived in Chile for three months in 1843 and held an exhibition that Sarmiento attended. It included the painting *Alí Pachá y Vasi-liki* (1833). Monvoisin taught painting while in Chile; among his pupils was Sarmien-to's sister Procesa. See Verdevoye (693); Ricardo Orta Nadal, "Presencia de Oriente en el *Facundo*," *Anuario del Instituto de Investigaciones Históricas* (Universidad Nacional del Litoral, Rosario, Argentina) 5 (1961): 93–122; Ricardo Rojas, *El profeta de la pampa, Vida de Sarmiento* (Buenos Aires: Losada, 1951).

17. Ana María Barrenechea, "Función estética y significación histórica de las cam-pañas pastoras en el *Facundo*," *Nueva Revista de Filología Hispánica* 15.1–2 (1961): 321.

18. Concha, 153n9.

19. Carlos Altamirano, "El orientalismo y la idea del despotismo en el *Facundo*," *Boletín del Instituto de Historia Argentina y Americana Dr. Ravignani* (Universidad de Buenos Aires) 3.9 (1994): 7–19.

20. Ramos, 21–25.

21. Altamirano, 9.

22. Verdevoye erroneously states that Sarmiento had no official business in Alge-ria (689–90).

23. Domingo F. Sarmiento, *Viajes por Europa, África y América* (1849; Buenos Aires: Editorial de Belgrano, 1981), 259–62. Page numbers refer to this edition. Trans-lations are mine unless otherwise noted.

24. Mary Louise Pratt, *Imperial Eyes: Travel Writing and Transculturation* (New York: Routledge, 1992), 150.

25. Said, 100–102.

26. Verdevoye, 697.

27. In Halperín Donghi et al., 238.

28. Zeghidour, n12.

29. Pratt, 112.

30. Wilhelm von Humboldt, "From the Introduction to His Translation of *Agamemnon*," *Theories of Translation*, ed. Rainer Schulte and John Biguenet (Chicago: University of Chicago Press, 1992), 58.

31. Domingo F. Sarmiento *Recollections of a Provincial Past* (1850), trans. Elizabeth Garrels and Asa Zatz (Oxford: Oxford University Press, 2005), 186.

32. Said, 177.

33. Lisa Lowe, *Critical Terrains: French and British Orientalisms* (Ithaca, N.Y.: Cornell University Press, 1991), ix. See also Michel Foucault, "Of Other Spaces," *Diacritics* 16.1 (1986): 22–27.

34. In Halperín Donghi et al., 223.

CHAPTER FOUR

Orientalism and Mexican Nationalism

Catarina de San Juan as the China Poblana's Asian Mother

Blake Seana Locklin

How is it that the same Asian woman could be pictured as an ascetic saint in Mexico in 1688 and a joyful national symbol today? The changing roles of Catarina de San Juan reflect the dynamics of Mexican self-fashioning through the centuries. Catarina de San Juan, originally named Myrra, was born in the early seventeenth century somewhere in Asia but lived in the city of Puebla, Mexico, for most of her life. Kidnapped as a girl, she was taken to the Philippines by pirates, sold, transported to Acapulco, and placed in the household of Don Miguel de Sosa in the city of Puebla; after Sosa's death, she was married to Domingo Suarez, a Chinese slave, survived him, and by the time of her own death was famous for her charity and her visions.

Catarina was a religious figure. The China Poblana, in contrast, represents to many the feminine essence of Mexican patriotism. She, or rather her red, green, and white costume (the colors of the flag), has become a national emblem, often pictured with Mexico's eagle and serpent on her skirt. What links these two figures is the legend, rather than any proof, that they are related; in popular culture, Catarina de San Juan is considered the first China Poblana. It is my intention to address the religious and nationalist versions of Catarina de San Juan's legend and the significance of her apotheoses as a Mexican saint and symbol. While the details can be fascinating in and of themselves, the repeated shifting between East and West and the changing significance of racial and sexual associations provide insight into the anxieties associated with the origins and character of a Mexican national icon and with Mexican identity itself.

There are a number of stages in the legend of Catarina de San Juan. Tracing the story from the historical Catarina through her seventeenth-century depiction as a devout mystic, from the origins of the China Poblana class in the nineteenth century to its adoption as a Mexican icon, and finally to the twentieth-century reinvention of Catarina de San Juan as the foremother of the China Poblana, will show how Catarina functions as a receptacle for fantasies of Mexican identity. Whereas Mexico has not come to terms with the social problems (brought to international attention by the Zapatista movement) hidden behind the myth of a powerful multi-cultural nation as represented by José Vasconcelos's ideal of "the cosmic race," in Catarina's case society attempts to assimilate a nonthreatening difference in a controlled fashion by celebrating an apparently harmless and simple woman.

It is difficult to penetrate the legend of Catarina de San Juan, since even official seventeenth-century accounts are mostly fantastical constructions. Beyond the basic facts of her Asian origin, her sale as a slave, and her death in 1688 in Puebla, her life has been represented in wildly different ways by biographers, historians, novelists, poets, and artists. Even the year of her arrival in Nueva España has been mistaken and at times contested. Despite the existence of colonial biographies, her life before setting foot in Acapulco has been the subject of diverse interpretations. The first published accounts are Francisco de Aguilera's funeral sermon (1688), Alonso Ramos's three-volume account of her "miracles" (1689–92), and José del Castillo Graxeda's summary of her "life and virtues" (1692).[1] In these three accounts, she is a saintly woman who adopts Catholicism with fervor, guarding her chastity until death, submitting to fasting and self-flagellation, living in poverty, and spending most of her time praying. For the authors, such virtues, along with her obedience to her confessors, make her a model for all women, whether maidens, wives, or widows. She has visions and conversations with Jesus, the Holy Family, and various angels, which she reports in detail to her confessors. Her relationship to Jesus allows her to become an "advocate" for the souls of the dead and the living, pleading for divine clemency. Ramos, whose biography makes a strong case for her sainthood, documents her visionary journey, in which she ministers to dying Spanish imperial soldiers, and details many other miracles. All three biographers agree that Catarina is a credit to her adopted home, already known for its mystics. When these priests discuss her life in Asia, they focus on signs of her future mysticism, such as the prediction by three men at her birth that she would achieve fame in a distant land for her virtue. Despite their differences, her biographers tell her story within a hagiographic discourse already standardized in the descriptions of previous generations of mystics.[2]

The Inquisition banned all pictures of Catarina de San Juan in 1691, and Ramos's biography was banned a year later.[3] Although Graxeda's biography was not banned, Mexicans lost interest in Catarina until the nineteenth and twentieth centuries. Although a short biographical entry appeared in 1855 in the *Apéndice al Diccionario Universal de Historia y Geografía*, her popularity is largely due to her association with the China Poblana, first suggested in print in 1896.[4] Before analyzing how her legend as the first China Poblana shapes and limits images of Catarina, it will be useful to examine the relationship between independence, sexuality, and patriotism in portrayals of the China Poblana.

The history of the China Poblana is more complex than her current iconic status suggests. The word *china* has been traced to a Quechua root meaning a female animal. According to Rodolfo Lenz, the word spread from Peru to the other Spanish American colonies, where it came to have a number of meanings, most often related to race or lower class status, sometimes with a sexual connotation. In general usage, *china* could signify a girl, an Indian woman, a servant woman, a nanny, or a *mujer pública* (prostitute).[5] Lenz points out that it made sense for one word to include these meanings, which correspond perfectly to the relations of the Indian woman as servant or concubine to the soldier of the Conquest. Although the specific definition of mistress or prostitute did not travel to Mexico, the association between a woman who worked and a *mujer pública* would remain a subtext to many descriptions of the China Poblana.

The word *china*, along with the masculine *chino*, also figures in colonial caste designations to describe children of mixed race. The word thus comes to have very specific racial meanings, but what it specifies varies depending on the source. In Peru, where the word originated, one source defines as *chino* children of an Indian father and a black mother, a mulatto father and a *mestiza* mother, or a mulatto father and a *china* mother.[6] Luis Castillo Ledón begins his description of the China Poblana with a reference to the colonial caste paintings in the Mexican Museo Nacional de Arqueología, Historia y Etnografía, which depict in portrait form the results of mixed marriage: *chino* or *china* was the caste or mix produced by an Indian father and a European mother, by a *morisco* father and a Spanish mother, and also by a *lobo* father and a Negro mother.[7] Ledón dismisses the categories in the paintings as "absurd" and "complicated" and goes on to define the China Poblana as simply a type of *mestiza* that formed more of a class than a caste. Few people associate the China Poblana with any of the specific caste designations found in colonial racial definitions or paintings, but certain connotations persist. For example, Fortino Ibarra de Anda traces the word *china* to the following definition, which combines racial and personal characteristics: "child of mulatto man or woman and Indian man or woman, an attractive-looking type, with wavy (not curly) hair, with a spirited character and passionate for love."[8] Ibarra de Anda concludes that their racial background, with its accompanying sexual characteristics, led many *chinas* to become prostitutes, giving the China Poblana a licentious reputation until the costume was eventually adopted by respectable women. The trajectory from loose woman to national symbol is fascinating in itself and as it relates to the legend of Catarina de San Juan, who becomes associated with the China Poblana through her clothes and through a linguistic coincidence.

Etymologies of the *china* in China Poblana emphasize that the word has nothing to do with the Chinese (Lenz 295; Ledón 192). In popular culture, however, the linguistic doubling of the words *china* and *poblana* becomes an important justification for linking Catarina de San Juan and the figure of the China Poblana. Catarina's confessor, Alonso Ramos, says that although she was not Chinese, she was still known as "la China," because she was one of the people who came from Asia by way of the Philippines, the designation for which in Puebla was *Chinos naturales de la India* (1:11). Although Ramos does not use the phrase, since Catarina lived in Puebla, she would be a "China de Puebla" or "China Poblana."[9] Antonio Carrión, usually cited since 1897 as promoting the legend of Catarina as the original China Poblana, says Catarina was affectionately known as "la China de Puebla" (160).

Even at the level of linguistic coincidence, the correspondence between Catarina de San Juan and the China Poblana has racial and sexual connotations. Before examining how this applies to Catarina, I will trace its role in portrayals of the China Poblana. Even before she becomes a national symbol, the China Poblana is hailed as authentically Mexican. In the years between Mexico's independence from Spain and the French intervention, there is a desire to privilege local culture over that imported from Europe. In 1855 José María Rivera contrasts the China Poblana favorably with women who rely on artifice and foreign styles to look beautiful.[10] The China Poblana is so authentic that he compares her to the Mexican landscape itself, calling her "daughter of Mexico as pretty as her blue sky, as fresh as her flowery gardens, and as happy and smiling as the delicious mornings of this land blessed by God and his saints" (89). In this description, the China Poblana's authenticity, beauty, and sensuality are inextricably linked, and the landscape, by extension, is seductive as well. Rivera goes on to tell the story of a China Poblana named Mariquita who embodies the qualities of natural innocence and irresistible sexuality, the latter causing trouble among her jealous admirers.

A foreign visitor, writing of his travels in Mexico between 1829 and 1834, also blends the China Poblana, the landscape, and a certain lack of seriousness bordering on licentiousness. Discussing the China Poblana costume, Carlos Nebel, a German, notes that Mexicans spend an inordinate amount of money on frivolous clothing, a luxury permitted by their comfortable climate.[11] The equation of the China Poblana with Mexico will eventually lead to the sublimation of the China Poblana's sexuality into the more acceptable love of country.

Later accounts draw more explicit connections between the China Poblana and Mexican independence from Spain. One historian attributes to the transition from colony to nation the privileging of popular culture that lay behind nineteenth-century interest in writing about the China Poblana: "Rita Eder says that the stage on which the China Poblana appears is the advent of Mexico as a free nation; that in the culture, there is consequently an anxious search for national heroes arising from the people and with their own characteristics; that local color, during Romanticism, also prevails; everything is prepared for the exaltation of the China Poblana."[12] Eder, analyzing the China Poblana from the perspective of the late twentieth century, focuses on the effect of Independence on the priorities of those who chose to praise the China Poblana in their writings. Other writers link the China Poblana to social transformations brought about by Independence.

In Mexico, working outside the home is a risky business for a woman's reputation.[13] In the case of the nineteenth-century China Poblana, her work in public places contributes to visions of her as dangerously sensual, even as her financial independence is seen to parallel the Independence of Mexico.[14] One 1873 economic analysis of the rise and fall of the China Poblana as a class claims that, before industrialization, many weavers in Puebla worked at home, with the assistance of their wives and daughters, the *chinas*, whom they took special pleasure in dressing well.[15] Most chroniclers prefer to emphasize the China Poblana's own industry. Rivera, in his story of Mariquita, makes the point that she lives alone, despite being pretty enough to attract a man to support her (92). Many writers refer to the China Poblana as a woman who works in a restaurant or sells drinks. Abraham Sosa in 1926 eulogizes her in a poem but goes on to compare her to the sweetness of the fruit she sells, suggesting—despite her characterization as a good daughter, loyal wife, and reliable servant—the kind of associations that could lead to suspicions about the China Poblana's morals.[16] Sosa is writing during a nostalgic period, after the disappearance of the China Poblana as a class. Yet in the same year, Joaquín García Icazbalceta connects the China Poblana's independent attitude and her finances as "a woman of the town who lived without serving anyone and in some comfort, at the expense of a husband or a lover, or even by her own industry."[17] He claims that the China Poblana's costume and attitude were so provocative that if she had reappeared on a public street in the 1920s, she would have been arrested.

Ledón acknowledges that nineteenth-century descriptions of the China Poblana praised her morals, but he insists that her public life led to her decline to the point that it was considered scandalous: "She possessed, it is true, the moral qualities of which those who knew her speak, but by her very way of living she degenerated, and her costume ended up being the dress of simple vendors of caresses" (19). The China Poblana has fallen down the slippery slope from selling food to selling herself. In the process, there is a slippage that often occurs in writing about the China Poblana, between the woman and the dress. Presumably, women of good morals nevertheless caused, through their suspect behavior, the adoption of their outfit by prostitutes.

Yet the same liberty seen as licentious is also associated with the Independence of the nation. Ledón says that the China Poblana appeared when Independence relaxed the rules that had bound colonial Mexican society: "It is almost certain that the 'type,' if we can call her that, began to form during the war of independence, due to the relaxation that it came to produce in religious and social austerity. The *china* reached her greatest peak in the first years of independent Mexico" (17). Unlike most who associate the China Poblana with the Independence of Mexico, Ledón sees such political change as morally suspect in itself. Even as the China Poblana arose during a period of moral laxity, she disappeared not from economic changes in society but as a result of her own sinfulness: "Precisely because of her degeneration, the China Poblana finally disappeared around 1870" (20). Nevertheless, despite Ledón's criticism of her past, even for him the China Poblana makes a successful transition to national symbol. Despite changes to her original (authentic) costume and association with what he deems a ridiculously inauthentic dance, the *jarabe tapatío*, she evokes the same *trémula emoción* (tremulous emotion), now figured as a patriotic feeling, as the historical China Poblana did.

Another writer who, looking back, associates the China Poblana with Mexican Independence is Ibarra de Anda, who declares in 1942 that although some trace the typical costume to the 1840s, it must have become popular after 1821, because its colors match the green, red, and white of the Mexican flag, which was established then (87). He also mentions a theory that the invention of the legend linking the China Poblana to Catarina arose due to patriotic sentiment on the hundredth anniversary of the Revolution in 1921. The hypothesis is incorrect in that 1921 actually marks the publication of Nicolas León's attack on the legend, but his perception of the nationalist motive is telling. It seems that the association of the China Poblana with national Independence is a given, whether it be interpreted positively or negatively.[18]

The letters of Fanny Calderón de la Barca, wife of the Spanish minister to Mexico, offer a glimpse of the image of the China Poblana in the mid-nineteenth century: a symbol of the people, but not yet morally acceptable to the elites.[19] When Fanny decided to wear a China Poblana costume to a ball held on January 6, 1840, the affair became "a matter of state" (126). "The Secretary of State, the Ministers of War and of the Interior, and others" made a visit on January 5, during which "they assured [her] that all Poblanas were *femmes de rien* . . . that they wore no stockings, and that *la Ministra de España* should by no means wear, even for one evening, such a dress" (125). A delegation of "the chief ladies of Mexico" gave her husband a similar message, and Don José Arnaiz sent him a note informing him the costume was that of "una muger . . ." (a . . . woman; ellipses in the original). The China Poblana's character is so far from acceptable that the gentleman cannot even specify it in a respectable letter; in her published letters, Fanny translates Arnaiz's phrase as "a woman of no character" (691n3, 126). Fanny had already been surprised when the Poblana who helped her with the costume told her that "everyone" was happy that she would be wearing the costume; she saw no reason why "everyone" should care one way or another (125). It was suggested that the official disapproval arose out of fear that her wearing the costume would strengthen the hand of her husband, who had suggested it "in compliment to the Mexicans" (112, 126). In the end, Fanny wore a less controversial dress, but in one of the many twists in the story of the China Poblana, Ibarra de Anda claims that the costume became acceptable after the "Condesa" Calderón de la Barca wore it to a charity ball (87).

If it was not Calderón de la Barca who made the costume respectable, how did it come to be worn to express patriotism on special occasions by girls of the upper classes? While associations with various types of independence left the China Poblana with a suspect reputation, another period of national struggle contributed to her rehabilitation. Not surprisingly, the China Poblana is most closely associated with the resistance in Puebla to the French invasion. In January 1862 British, French, and Spanish troops landed at Veracruz. The British and Spanish went home, but the French proceeded to occupy Mexico. On May 5 Mexicans held back the French at Puebla. The following year, the French besieged Puebla, which fell to the invaders on May 17, 1863. Conservative Mexicans and the French installed Maximilian as emperor in 1864. The French intervention in Mexico ended in 1867, with the departure of French troops and the execution of Maximilian by Benito Juarez.

In a poem published in 1899 as a response to a request for "national verses," Amado Nervo describes the wife of a *chinaco*, or soldier who fought against the French.[20] Nervo calls her "Guadalupe (la chinaca)," presumably because the China Poblana is also known as the companion of the *chinaco*. Albert Pill includes in his bilingual children's book about the China Poblana a picture of a woman dancing while a soldier plays a harmonica, with the explanation, "During the French intervention (1861–1867), the costume was changed slightly and it was worn by the wives and girlfriends of the soldiers of Benito Juarez ('Los Chinacos')."[21]

Alfredo Cuéllar traces a lineage from the colonial period to the present in which the China Poblana's association with resistance against the French is the term that mediates between her decline into prostitution and the costume's adoption by respectable women,

> those women who, from the princess Myrra, later Catarina de San Juan, were passing through all of our history, first as maids in the convents, later as peasants, restaurateurs, vendors of fruit drinks, and then as loose women, finally becoming during the French invasion the symbol of the woman of the Republic, the companion of the *chinaco* who defended with his machete the land that had given him birth, until coming, in our days, to be the representative costume of the woman of Central Mexico.[22]

This genealogy not only provides a direct link from Catarina to the China Poblana but also shows how involvement with nationalist resistance moved the China Poblana from the economic and social margins to the mainstream of Mexican society. At the end of the trajectory, the subject changes from "those women" to "the representative costume," indicating that not only is it items of clothing that link Catarina de San Juan to the China Poblana, but the China Poblana "in our days" (1928) is embodied in her clothes. There is no longer a China Poblana, only a national costume, which becomes more standardized as it is worn only by women who want to assume, on certain occasions, the role of Mexicanhood.[23]

The French intervention provides, in retrospect at least, a symbolic transformation in the image of the China Poblana. Respectable girls adopt the costume as a symbol of patriotism. Thus a 1930 poem begins "¡Soy mexicana!" and describes a young woman, proud to be both a Mexican and the granddaughter of a Spaniard, dressing up as a China Poblana on September 16, Mexican Independence Day. There is no hint of scandal in the costume, only a comparison between its colors and those of the Mexican flag.[24]

In 1941 Luis Andrade praises the China Poblana as an emblem of virtuous and self-sacrificing Mexican womanhood. He proclaims that the China Poblana "with only her presence makes us see and feel, within or outside our country, the beating heart of our soil, the intense love for the native land, the irreplaceable tradition of our race, the gallantry of our people, like the soul and beauty of our self-sacrificing Mexican women." The China Poblana is no longer associated with historical women who worked and danced in Puebla, but rather with a patriotic "archetype of the Mexican woman." The origin of this symbol is traced directly back to "la filantrópica y noble dama, la princesa Catarina de San Juan."[25] The same type of respectable women who were once sent to advise Fanny Calderón de la Barca to avoid the China Poblana costume are now enlisted to promote it.

Andrade's simplification of Catarina de San Juan's life story to a one-line summary reflects the change in her significance, which now resides in her ability to provide the China Poblana with a foremother rather than in the religious experiences detailed by her colonial biographers. Catarina's new secular role is evident in the packaging of her story in the twentieth century. The 1950 publication of Rafael Carrasco Puente's indispensable *Bibliografía de Catarina de San Juan y de la China Poblana* is justified in González Peña's "Prólogo" not simply as an important scholarly resource but by the significance of the China Poblana in Mexican society. González Peña lauds Carrasco Puente as a patriot. As Andrade and others mention, the China Poblana represents Mexico at home and abroad. Pill indicates that her dress is an aspect of Mexican folklore that should appeal to Chicano children, affirming cultural identity and possibly educating other children about Mexican culture.

When Catarina de San Juan and the China Poblana are linked through legend, a cross-fertilization occurs: Catarina contributes respectability to the China Poblana's image even as her own becomes more sexual in the process. A splitting of the Asian Myrra from the colonial Catarina de San Juan facilitates the exchange. Enrique Cordero y Torres exemplifies this process when he states that "the beautiful Mirrha" decided to enter a convent in Puebla, after which "she relinquished her erotic name and clothing, which tradition says the people inherited."[26] In this version, the Asian Myrra is figured as sexual before she is assimilated into the colonial institution of the convent. Contact with the nobleman Miguel de Sosa, who frees the slave and teaches her Christianity, leads Myrra to become Catarina de San Juan and leave behind her "erotic" identity, defined by her name and clothes. The frequent rewriting of the legends about Sosa's role, from that of Myrra's purchaser to that of her liberator, sets up a contrast between a humanistic Nueva España and a despotic East, eliding the history of slavery in Mexico. The sexuality associated with Myrra actually comes from two directions, although it is entirely attributed to the Asian princess. First, her name is erotic, it seems, simply because it is exotically Asian. Her clothes, on the other hand, are sensual precisely because they are equivalent to the typical China Poblana costume. The sexuality of the China Poblana is thus displaced onto the Asian Myrra, while the domesticated Catarina de San Juan provides a virtuous origin for what has become a national icon.

Illustrations of the Asian princess before she arrives in Mexico appear in Cordero y Torres's *Leyendas*, accompanying a poem by León Sánchez Arévalo titled "La China Poblana" (which is mostly praise for Miguel de Sosa). Three drawings show a ship, a demure Asian woman in something slightly resembling the China Poblana costume, and a sexy Asian female pirate reclining in her cabin, wearing a large sword and an outfit that reveals her legs and cleavage (153). This last image is gratuitous, since neither the poem nor any other version of the story includes female pirates, much less Myrra acting or dressing like one.

In his retelling of the legend, Salazar Monroy similarly eroticizes "the seductive Myrra, with her slanted sparkling eyes, her cheekbones that emphasized her splendid youth and oriental beauty."[27] Even Pill, writing for children, begins his description of Myrra not simply with her beauty, but the way she drew attention to herself by wearing "fancy clothes."

In contrast, when Ramos praises Catarina's beauty, he frames it as a reflection of her virtue: she asks Jesus to make her ugly so that men will not bother her (1:123). There is a suggestion of disrepute in the colonial biographies of Catarina, which mention that she was originally destined to be a slave of the viceroy, who presumably did not want to buy beautiful Chinese women simply to baptize them (Graxeda 33–34; Ramos 1:29). The

Nao de China, which sailed between Manila and Acapulco until 1815, was known to bring concubines to Mexico along with its merchandise.[28] Given that Ramos and Graxeda have a professional interest in the transformative power of Catarina's conversion to Catholicism, they do not describe her Asian life in erotic terms but rather look to it for signs of her future devotion. To Ramos, an Asian origin provides a basis for comparison with Saint Catherine of Egypt rather than a sinful prelude to conversion.

Religion as it appears in the legends of Catarina de San Juan as the first China Poblana is notably less complex than in the colonial biographies. Where Ramos and Graxeda describe Catarina's mysticism in strikingly sexual terms, if conventional for the time, the Catarina of China Poblana legends, in contrast, expresses her religious devotion through simple good works. In the most widely repeated version of the legend, Ramón Mena (1907) describes Catarina as a charitable lady whose clothing was imitated by the grateful populace: "With the disappearance of the China Poblana [Catarina de San Juan], the disenfranchised classes of Puebla de los Angeles lost their good angel, but the people, always grateful, always noble, and always grand, preserved the memory of their saint, imitated her dress, and thus originated the *chinas*."[29] Vito Alessio Robles specifically cites this legend as an attempt to provide the national costume with a less sinful progenitor than the historical China Poblana.[30] In Mena's story, the China Poblana's clothing, which is so often described as provocative, becomes associated with gratitude and saintliness, a direction of influence opposite to that in Cordero y Torres's formulation. Together these and other versions of the legend demonstrate not a consistent relationship but an ongoing transfer of sin and virtue.

Clothing is an essential element in the exchanges, since aside from the linguistic doubling of the words *china* and *poblana*, the primary connection posited between Catarina and the China Poblana is in their dress. Those who study the history of the China Poblana costume, without trying to force it into supporting the legend, usually identify its origins in either a Spanish or an indigenous model. Nicolás León (1921) discounts any connection to indigenous styles and insists that if we compare the costume of a Spanish *Manola* from the beginning of the nineteenth century with that of a *China*, "they are almost identical" (68–70). Nevertheless Solís (1942) declares that the China Poblana's costume came from Oaxacan indigenous women's clothing.[31] Ibarra de Anda, reviewing the debate between Solís and other members of the Mexican Sociedad de Geografía y Estadística, uses pictorial evidence to support the view that the costume has its roots in Spain (86–87). Chía Bolaños Montiel supports the theory of a

Spanish origin (16). Both Ibarra de Anda and Bolaños Montiel view the costume as a national symbol and emphasize the unique Mexican development of the clothing in their discussions of its Spanish history. Ibarra de Anda believes that the *china's* costume dates to the colonial period and for that reason is an invention of New Spain, but with its foundation in a typical costume of Old Spain (87).

Ibarra de Anda dismisses the idea of a Chinese princess as the origin of the China Poblana's dress (86). León severely criticizes attempts to connect Catarina de San Juan's clothing and the China Poblana's, calling them a "tangle of inventions and fantasizing" and the legend itself a "ridiculous old wives' tale" (45, 9). Yet neither the Spanish nor the indigenous model has captured the nation's imagination as the story of the Chinese princess has. Some authors, including Bolaños Montiel, focus on the importance of the legend as a manifestation of "the soul of the people" (1). For Bolaños Montiel, there is an essential cultural value to the legend that goes beyond its historical inaccuracy. José Manuel López Victoria similarly prefaces his retelling of the story of Catarina de San Juan and the China Poblana with the definition of legend as a "source of the basic principles of nationality."[32] This same sense of the importance of the legend has led other authors to make some far-fetched associations between various items of Asian clothing and parts of the China Poblana costume.[33]

Two children's books from the United States have different versions of the story. Perhaps anticipating that young audiences would be quick to spot the difference between traditional Chinese or Indian clothing and the China Poblana costume, the authors invent explanations. In *The Pirate's Doll*, the young Meenah decides to cut her Chinese robes and sew them into a skirt so that she will be less conspicuous in Puebla and not scare the servants; a nice local girl named Catarina de San Juan then teaches Meenah how to sew.[34] Pill says that Catarina de San Juan changed her Hindu clothing for dresses that were typical of colonial New Spain, which were then given her nickname, China Poblana, and copied after she died. In contrast, an adult historical romance from the United States about Catarina de San Juan, *La China Poblana*, mimics the Mexican stories in attributing the China Poblana costume directly to an Asian culture from the Mekong Delta.[35]

Theories of an indigenous or Spanish origin for a national costume seem more sensible than appeals to an exotic Asian source. However, Nancy Vogeley's article "Turks and Indians: Orientalist Discourse in Postcolonial Mexico" sheds light on the dynamics at work here.[36] Vogeley shows how Mexicans viewed Italian Orientalist opera from the perspective of citizens of a newly independent country trying to form a national identity while rejecting both sides of their ancestry: the Spanish oppressors and the abject Indians. The operas about distant Turks and Christians helped Mexican elites recast the terms *civilized* and *barbaric* in a way that allowed them to avoid the task of reconciling their anti-Spanish glorification of ancient American cultures with their oppression of contemporary indigenous peoples. A similar anxiety is evident in the legend of Catarina, whose supposedly green, white, and red clothes allow Mexicans to locate their identity outside Spanish or indigenous traditions.

Catarina's history and legend parallel the historical links between Asia and Mexico, which by imperial decree mediated all Asian-Spanish trade, required to go to the Philippines, then by sea to Acapulco and overland to Veracruz, before reaching the Iberian Peninsula. The role of Chinese immigrants in Mexico is linked from the beginning to domestic racial issues. According to Maza, in colonial Mexico "Chinese" slaves were preferable to Indian ones because they could not run away and return to their homes (12). The first large wave of Chinese immigration to Mexico in the nineteenth century came from Cuba, which had originally brought in Chinese indentured laborers when the slave trade became difficult, but which in 1871 expelled many Chinese who had worked off their indenture, out of fear they would support anticolonial movements.[37] In the various portrayals of Catarina/Myrra, however, such connections fade away as the historical woman becomes an empty vessel filled by Mexican fantasies. Asia is merely an exotic background in stories where a one-sided representation allows no space for a dialogue between Asia and Spanish America or between Mexicans and the Asians in their midst.

The greatest popularity of the China Poblana and of the legend of Catarina as her ancestor coincides with a strong anti-Chinese movement in Mexico in the first half of the twentieth century. Ironically, the same type of *proyecto nacionalista* that adopts Catarina de San Juan as the foremother of the China Poblana excludes Chinese immigrants. Perhaps because the lineage between Catarina and the China Poblana is not a biological one, nobody objects to an Asian origin for the national symbol that embodies, as Andrade said, "nuestra raza." In contrast, attacks on Chinese workers in the early twentieth century portrayed them as a threat to the Mexican race. Catarina also has the advantage, as a long-dead woman, of representing less of a threat to modern Mexican men. Whereas the twentieth-century version of Catarina's legend helps to sublimate the China Poblana's sensuality into the allure of patriotism, the male Chinese immigrants posed a sexualized danger to Mexico. In emotional attacks that often masked economic reasons for anti-Chinese sentiment, Chinese mixing with Mexican women was a frequent theme: "They spread disease . . . encouraged vice . . . and debauched Mexican womanhood. . . . Thus, they prostituted the Mexican 'race.' Images of tentacular octopuses and corrupt blood, of contagious disease and exotic perversion, accompanied the anti-Chinese campaigns."[38] Stealing Mexican women constituted an attack on the Mexican race as a whole.

Moreover, according to Alan Knight, the Chinese, who were supposed to provide cheap labor, instead moved into competition with Mexicans as businessmen, were allied with U.S. mining companies, and had many poor and resentful Mexicans as customers. Also, after the financial crisis of 1929, the United States sent many Mexican laborers home, where jobs were also scarce, a problem that they blamed on Chinese immigrant labor. Thus while the ideal of "the cosmic race" glorified *mestizaje* in theory, in practice this did not include Asians. A tension between valuing *mestizaje* and fearing the Chinese is evident from a local history of Soconuso, a coastal region in Chiapas bordering Guatemala, the site of much Chinese immigration and anti-Chinese activity. After discussing the contributions of past foreign residents of Soconuso, Mario García criticizes Chinese immigrants. Aside from their economic competition and dirtiness, what most provokes anxiety is the prospect of an unsavory racial mixture. Even when expelled, the Chinese heritage somehow remains a threat: "It appears that their mission was only to accumulate fortunes . . . and transport them to the legendary China, as well as to propagate their race."[39]

According to José Jorge Gómez Izquierdo, elites in independent Mexico manipulated negative stereotypes of Asians inherited from the Spaniards to blame scapegoat Chinese immigrants for national problems and to build national unity in opposition to the Asian Other (8–12). Legal and propaganda campaigns culminated in the Chinese expulsion of the early 1930s. Meanwhile, in 1928 Alfredo B. Cuéllar was describing a direct link from Catarina de San Juan to the China Poblana as a symbol of patriotic resistance (125). The juxtaposition of anti-Chinese violence and Catarina as China Poblana occurs at the intersection of three centuries of evolving representations of Catarina de San Juan and the history of a nation seeking to define itself with reference to an acceptably autonomous past.

The historical Catarina was culturally hybrid; the historical Chinas Poblanas were lower class and most likely mestizas. In legend, both are assimilated into a simpler image with less troubling resonances. Both Catarina de San Juan and the China Poblana are empty vessels. Gender and race shape their reinvention as outlets for Mexican anxiety about national identity and sexuality. These female figures provide mannequins who can be made to represent in simple form the complexity of the nation. The manipulation of difference in their legend has a number of ramifications. If tradition embodies the soul of the people passed down from parents to children (as Bolaños Montiel insists), in this case it seems dysfunctional rather than empowering. The myth cannot hide the reality of racial and cultural conflict in Mexican society. Chinese in Mexico did not benefit from Catarina's fame. Some tried. Salazar Monroy's *La verdadera China Poblana*, published in 1942, after most Chinese had been expelled, contains a frontispiece in Chinese, translated on the following page into Spanish, in which members of the Asociación Fraterna China de Puebla declare "que nuestro cariño por México acrezca con entusiasmo y fervor al recuerdo de Mirra" (that our love for Mexico grows with enthusiasm and fervor with the memory of Myrra).[40] While the legendary Catarina became the repository of positive associations, Chinese immigrants suffered from stereotypes and violence that were the negative complement of Catarina's safe difference. The legend may serve as a source of strength for some (as in Pill's book), but this comes at the cost of denying the complexity of the society and its history.

Notes

1. Alonso Ramos, *Prodigios y milagros de Catharina de S. Joan*, 3 vols. (Puebla: Fernández de León, 1689–92); Francisco de Aguilera, "Sermón en que se da noticia de la vida admirable, virtudes heroicas y preciosa muerte de la Venerable Señora Catarina de San Juan" (1688), in Ramos, 95–113; José del Castillo Graxeda, *Compendio de la vida y virtudes de la venerable Catarina de San Juan* (1692; Puebla: Secretaría de Cultura, 1987).

2. Jean Franco, *Plotting Women: Gender and Representation in Mexico* (New York: Columbia University Press, 1989), 21.

3. Francisco de la Maza, *Catarina de San Juan: Princesa de la India y visionaria de Puebla* (Mexico City: Libros de México, 1971), 131–35; Chía Bolaños Montiel, *Recopilación de la vida y leyenda de Catarina de San Juan y la China Poblana* (Puebla: Comité de la Feria de Puebla, 1993), 122.

4. Antonio Carrión, *Historia de la Ciudad de Puebla de los Angeles: Obra dedicada a los Hijos del Estado de Puebla* (Puebla: Centro de Estudios Históricos de Puebla, 1970), 165.

5. Rodolfo Lenz, *Diccionario etimológico de voces chilenas derivadas de lenguas indíjenas americanas* (Santiago de Chile: Cervantes, 1904), 94–99, 294–96; José Rogelio Álvarez, ed., "China Poblana," *Enciclopedia de México*, 4th ed. (Mexico City: Enciclopedia de México, 1978), 3:387.

6. J. J. von Tschudi, *Travels in Peru during the Years 1838–1842: On the Coast, in the Sierra, across the Cordilleras and the Andes, into the Primeval Forests*, trans. Thomasina Ross (London: David Bogue, 1847), 114.

7. Luis Castillo Ledón, "La China Poblana" (1924), *Bibliografía de Catarina de San Juan y de la China Poblana*, ed. Rafael Carrasco Puente (Mexico City: Secretaría de Relaciones Exteriores, 1950), 16–20.

8. Fortino Ibarra de Anda, "¿Será española la china poblana?," *Hoy*, December 5, 1942, 86–87.

9. The *Enciclopedia de México* complicates the issue by suggesting that the *poblana* in China Poblana may not be related to Puebla but rather to another, more general meaning: "The interpretation of Poblana from Puebla, applied to the *china*, appears debatable: *poblano*, in Spanish America, is equivalent on occasions to provincial, peasant, local, neighborhood resident. This meaning is still conserved in Yucatan. It is possible that the convergence of poblano as provincial and *poblano* as a name for people from Puebla has created a confusion" (388).

10. José María Rivera in Carrasco Puente, 88–98.

11. Carlos Nebel, *Viaje pintoresco y arqueológico sobre la parte más interesante de la República Mexicana, en los años transcurridos desde 1829 hasta 1834* (1840; Mexico City: Porrúa, 1963), xvi.

12. Bolaños Montiel, 14.

13. See Debra A. Castillo, *Easy Women: Sex and Gender in Modern Mexican Fiction* (Minneapolis: University of Minnesota Press, 1998), 3–17.

14. According to her seventeenth-century biographers, Catarina de San Juan worked to support herself all through her life in Puebla. Ironically the legends that link her with the China Poblana highlight her royal origins, eliding her much longer working life.

15. See Carrasco Puente, 130–31.

16. Ibid., 109.

17. Ibid., 29–30.

18. Nicolás León, *Catarina de San Juan y la China Poblana: Estudio etnográfico-crítico* (Puebla: Ediciones Altiplano, 1971).

19. Fanny (Frances Erskine Inglis) Calderón de la Barca, *Life in Mexico: The Letters of Fanny Calderón de la Barca, with New Material from the Author's Private Journals*, ed. Howard T. Fisher and Marion Hall Fisher (Garden City, N.Y.: Doubleday, 1966).

20. In Carrasco Puente, 84–86.

21. Albert S. Pill, *La China Poblana* (Fullerton: California State University Press, 1976).

22. Alfredo B. Cuéllar, "El relato verbal de una verdadera China Poblana," *Charrerías* (Mexico City: Azteca, 1928), 124–25.

23. On the variety of nineteenth-century China Poblana clothing, see Bolaños Montiel, 67–79. Images and basic information on the China Poblana and Catarina de San Juan are readily available by Internet search.

24. See Bolio in Carrasco Puente, 129.

25. Ibid., 5.

26. Enrique Cordero y Torres, *Leyendas de la Puebla de los Ángeles* (Mexico City: Leo, 1972), 4.

27. Salazar Monroy, *La verdadera China Poblana* (Puebla: Imprenta López, 1942), 12.

28. William L. Schurz, *The Manila Galleon* (Manila: Historical Conservation Society, 1985), 220.

29. In Carrasco Puente, 85.

30. Vito Alessio Robles, *Acapulco en la historia y en la leyenda* (Mexico City: Mundial, 1932), 156.

31. In Carrasco Puente, 108.

32. José Manuel López Victoria, "La China Poblana," *Leyendas de Acapulco: Tradición Porteña* (Mexico City: Ediciones Botas, 1944), 48.

33. See Mena in Carrasco Puente, 81.

34. Eula Long, *Pirate's Doll: The Story of the China Poblana* (New York: Knopf, 1956), 56–57.

35. Louise A. Stinetorf, *La china poblana* (Indianapolis: Bobbs-Merrill, 1960), 9, 206, 249.

36. Nancy Vogeley, "Turks and Indians: Orientalist Discourse in Postcolonial Mexico," *Diacritics* 25.1 (1995): 3–20.

37. José Jorge Gómez Izquierdo, *El movimiento antichino en México (1871–1934): Problemas del racismo y del nacionalismo durante la Revolución Mexicana* (Mexico City: Instituto Nacional de Antropología e Historia, 1991), 44–45. From 1847 to 1874 Cuba and Peru were the destinations for most coolie labor; the 1871 Cuban decree repeated an earlier one forbidding the importation of Chinese to Cuba in 1859, which had been ignored (35–37).

38. Alan Knight, "Racism, Revolution, and *Indigenismo*: Mexico, 1910–1940," *The Idea of Race in Latin America, 1870–1940*, ed. Richard Graham (Austin: University of Texas Press, 1990), 96.

39. J. Mario García S., *Soconusco en la Historia* (Mexico City: N.p., 1963), 85–86.

40. Secretaría de Relaciones Exteriores, Departamento de Publicidad, *La China Poblana (Síntesis de su origen y evolución a través de los tiempos)*, Ts. 193-, Bancroft Library, University of California, Berkeley, 2–3.

CHAPTER FIVE

Journeys and Trials of the Fu Family

Transpacific Reverberations of the Anti-Chinese Movement in Mexico

Julia María Schiavone Camacho

Fu Gui emigrated from Guangdong Province in southeastern China around the turn of the twentieth century. He settled in the northern Mexican border state of Sonora, where he adopted the name Roberto M. Fu, learned Spanish, and became part of local society. In 1919 he married Ana María Domínguez in the town of Aconchi, central district of Arizpe, and they had seven children. His wife died a short while after their last son was born, during the Great Depression. A Mexican Chinese compatriot would later write from Portuguese Macau that the cruelty and viciousness of the anti-Chinese movement had caused her great stress and was a factor in her premature death. Sonoran officials expelled the widower and his seven young children within months of the death of the wife and mother. Fu and the children entered U.S. territory as "Chinese refugees from Mexico" in 1933 but were soon deported to China. They settled in Macau, where Fu worked to support his family amid trying economic circumstances. Later in the decade, as the Sino-Japanese War broke out, President Lázaro Cárdenas's administration orchestrated a repatriation in an effort to repudiate the anti-Chinese movement and rescue Mexican women and Mexican Chinese children who were stranded in China. The repatriation barred Chinese men, causing the Fu family great heartache. Owing to their unstable economic situation, they decided it was best for the older children to return to Mexico. Roberto M. Fu and his youngest son, Maximiliano, too young to make the voyage without his father, remained in Macau. The other children worked for two decades to bring their father and youngest sibling to Mexico, but they encountered unforeseen obstacles and tragedies along the way.[1]

Years earlier, just before Fu's marriage to Domínguez, a group of Mexicans elsewhere in Sonora began to sow the seeds of the events that would lead to the family's departure from Mexico. In 1916 in the northern Sonora town of Magdalena, José María Arana organized the country's first anti-Chinese campaign. Although it would take years for the movement to gain traction, it eventually succeeded in expelling the vast majority of Chinese from the state. The Fus were among many Mexican Chinese families to face inordinate trials for decades as a direct result of anti-Chinese organizing and exclusionary nationalist policies. But their story begins decades before the anti-Chinese movement began, when men like Roberto M. Fu became part of Sonora.

The Chinese in Sonora

The Chinese arrived in the late nineteenth century and early twentieth into a fluid, culturally diverse Sonoran society, stratified by class and ethnicity. Situated on the border with the United States, Sonora drew influence from both central Mexico and the United States. A number of marginalized indigenous groups, including the Yaqui, Tohono O'odham, Seri, Apache, and Mayo, occupied the state. Throughout the nineteenth century, its export economy had attracted foreigners interested in mining and trade. French, British, German, and American immigrants had married into wealthy Mexican families. Between 1860 and 1900 the state gained more newcomers from the United States, Europe, the Middle East, and Asia as its border economy took shape. Mexicans from other parts of Mexico also migrated north during this time in search of work in the mines, haciendas, and nascent border towns. Isolation from markets in central Mexico increased Sonora's economic dependence on the United States, such that foreign investment came to dominate the economy by the turn of the twentieth century. New border towns eventually led to a complicated Mexican-U.S. economic interdependence, although vast inequality characterized the burgeoning relationship. Owing to Mexico's Spanish colonial past and the persistent presence of foreigners since Independence in 1821, people in Sonora often viewed themselves as ethnically distinct from other Mexicans, and their notions of race explicitly privileged the lighter skinned.[2]

The Chinese influx added to Sonora's complexity. Owing to Chinese gender norms and exclusionary policies in the Americas, Chinese migration to Sonora was overwhelmingly male.[3] By the early twentieth century they constituted the largest foreign group in Sonora and one of the largest Chinese settlements in Mexico. Nonetheless they composed less than 2 percent of Sonora's population between 1910 and 1930. Concentrating in particular towns and communities, however, they eventually gained disproportionate attention.[4]

The Chinese were crucial to local communities. They participated in the traditional rural economy by becoming landowners or laboring on the haciendas, ranchos, and fields of Mexican as well as Chinese landowners. Yet they also helped Sonora modernize by becoming the first petit bourgeois class. Catering to a variety of needs, they brought merchandise and services to towns across Sonora. They drew on transnational economic networks in a way that other local residents could not. Brethren in China and the diaspora contributed capital and inexpensive merchandise to the Chinese in Sonora. This helped them prosper and eventually establish a monopoly on low-end consumer goods. As in other areas where the Chinese settled, they took on the roles of peddlers and merchants, as the local population remained tied up in a traditional, rural social hierarchy, in which some Chinese also participated. As the growing border economy led to the Americanization of northern Mexico and there was no local petite bourgeoisie, the Chinese found an important economic and social niche.

Street peddling earned the Chinese enormous visibility in local communities. Selling vegetables and other goods on carts they pushed from house to house and neighborhood to neighborhood, Chinese peddlers formed daily relationships with their clientele. North American and European immigrants—many of whom were also businessmen, though they had far more capital—were simply absent from the daily lives of Sonora's working people. Chinese peddlers, laborers, and small shopkeepers, on the other hand, were in view on a daily basis.

The Chinese maintained diasporic overseas connections and formed bonds among themselves while at the same time integrating into Sonoran society, as their compatriots did elsewhere in Latin America.[5] As Sonorans accepted them into existing social and economic networks and the Chinese created new ones, they became deeply incorporated into local communities. While the businesses they established became critical to Sonora's modernization, the relationships they formed with Mexicans became culturally important in the state, as a new Chinese Mexican identity took shape. Chinese immigrants made local communities their second home.

They often died there, never to see China again. For decades Chinese cemeteries in towns throughout the state have been a testament to the men who contributed to Sonora's growth.

The Mexican Revolution of 1910 and the Anti-Chinese Movement

Chinese immigrants experienced prejudice from their arrival in Sonora. Negative attitudes and jokes abounded and, for a period, an anti-Chinese newspaper circulated. Some Mexicans perceived them as unwanted foreigners. Nevertheless anti-Chinese sentiment was neither widespread nor organized in Sonora until the revolutionary era.[6]

The Revolution fueled immense social change in Mexico.[7] Revolutionary momentum and Mexican emigration, partly due to U.S. labor shortages during World War I, set notions of race, citizenship, and *mestizaje* in flux. Revolutionaries renounced the conservative Porfirian tradition of privileging foreigners and fair-skinned Mexicans. In this climate, resentment against the Chinese and perceptions of their purportedly undeserved economic success became more and more pronounced. At the height of the Revolution, some twenty people led by José María Arana founded the Junta Comercial y de Hombres de Negocios (Commercial Association of Businessmen) of Magdalena, a small northern mining town. The group vowed to defend "Mexican" merchants and rid the state of Chinese business owners.

It is significant that the anti-Chinese movement began so close to the U.S. border. Men left Magdalena to work in the United States or fight in the Revolution. Pointing to the shortages, some local people grumbled that Chinese men had filled the void, acquiring both capital and women that rightfully belonged to Mexican men. Anxiety over the gender imbalance fueled anti-Chinese sentiment. Spreading quickly, anti-Chinese campaigns in Sonora, like those in California during the 1860s and 1870s, portrayed the Chinese as dangerous outsiders who had infringed on the domain of Mexicans.[8]

The people who organized the campaigns were working-class and middle-class Mexicans, just like those who had formed bonds with the Chinese over the previous decades. *Antichinistas* (anti-Chinese proponents) focused on Mexican-Chinese relationships, romantic unions, and marriages, arguing that they threatened the integrity of the Mexican race and nation. They chastised Mexicans who maintained ties with or were kind to the

Chinese, labeling them *chineros*. This term appeared in Arana's speeches and communications and in his newspaper *Pro-Patria* as early as 1917. Spending much time and resources on their struggle, anti-Chinese activists recruited people, organized protests and boycotts, drew vivid images, wrote manifestos, and printed newspapers. The astonishingly hateful nature of the Sonoran movement against the Chinese—and any Mexicans who accepted them into their communities—reverberated in the sheer abundance of *antichinista* propaganda and its elaborate ideology of hate. For instance, one drawing depicted an enormous dragon emerging from Asia and stretching across the Pacific, one of its claws reaching menacingly toward Mexico. Another portrayed Arana appealing to his followers: "Mexicans: out of every dollar you spend at a Chinese store, fifty cents go to Shanghai and the other fifty serve to keep you in chains and prostitute the women of your race!!!" *Antichinistas* bred hatred through a highly racialized and gendered polemics that played on people's fears by invoking images of invasion and domination by a threatening alien force.[9]

Revolutionaries developed the ideology of *indigenismo*, the belief that the nation needed to honor and embrace its indigenous and mestizo character. Yet while Mexico continued to marginalize indigenous peoples, the discourse of *mestizaje*, the ideology of the nation's heritage of racial and cultural mixture that emphasized its indigenous spirit, became the centerpiece of modern Mexican nationalism. The vision of a *raza cósmica* (cosmic race), which held that racial and cultural mixture (mainly European and indigenous) had enhanced the Mexican people and nation, took shape during this time. These new ideas of Mexicanness largely excluded or denigrated Chinese and other Asians, as well as Africans.[10]

The Chinese Expulsion

The anti-Chinese movement eventually infiltrated state and national politics. Plutarco Elías Calles, governor of Sonora (1915–19), became an avowed anti-Chinese ideologue, despite his Middle Eastern heritage. Arana, who quickly praised the governor's anti-Chinese agenda, himself served as mayor of Magdalena from 1918 until his death by poisoning two years later. In 1919 Adolfo de la Huerta, backed by Calles, became governor and publicly endorsed anti-Chinese policies. The anti-Chinese leaders Alejandro Villaseñor and José Angel Espinoza became elected officials in Sonora during the following decade. Sowing the seeds for a national campaign, the 1925 Anti-Chinese Convention in Hermosillo created the Liga Nacionalista

Pro-Raza, an umbrella organization for anti-Chinese committees emerging throughout the nation. With the Liga's support, congressmen from the northern states of Sonora and Sinaloa, as well as territorial Baja California, became an anti-Chinese voting bloc. Congressman Espinoza established the Anti-Chinese Campaign Steering Committee as a branch of the Partido Nacional Revolucionario. Meanwhile Calles became president of Mexico (1924–28) and ruled as *jefe máximo* of the Revolution for another six years (1928–36) over three succeeding puppet presidencies. A sign on the presidential palace reputedly read, "The President lives here; the man in charge lives across the street." Family members who shared his anti-Chinese hatred continued to control Sonora: his uncle Francisco Elías was governor (1929–31), succeeded by his son Rodolfo Elías Calles (1931–34), who would enact the massive Chinese expulsion.[11]

Anti-Chinese policies nonetheless were more significant at the regional and local levels than in the national arena. In 1919 Governor Huerta of Sonora passed a labor law mandating that businesses owned by foreigners, implicitly aimed at the Chinese, had to employ 80 percent native Mexicans. In 1923 Congressman Villaseñor introduced two anti-Chinese bills that passed unanimously: Law 27 set out to create Chinatowns (although they never materialized), and Law 31 banned marriages and unions, which *antichinistas* called "illicit friendships," between Mexican women and "individuals of the Chinese race, even if said individuals obtain a Mexican naturalization certificate." Municipal officials were responsible for enforcing the ban and fining violators.[12]

Despite *antichinista* efforts in Sonora, Mexicans maintained economic, social, and romantic ties with the Chinese for at least a decade and a half after the start of Arana's campaign. In some communities where the Chinese were deeply entrenched, anti-Chinese laws and ideology held little sway. But the Great Depression and the consequent U.S. deportation of Mexicans invigorated *antichinista* organizing.

In 1930 the Sonoran state government began to pressure municipal governments to consistently enforce anti-Chinese laws. A governor's edict compelled local officials of the civil registry to report "illicit unions" and birth certificate applications for children born of Chinese fathers. Then, in 1931, the Sonoran government set *antichinismo* into full swing. Local and state authorities began to forcibly remove Chinese men and their families, sending them north through Arizona or south through Sinaloa. Governor Elías Calles further entrenched the process of expulsion. He nationalized local commerce, closed Chinese businesses, and legally dissolved Mexican-Chinese marriages. He ordered local authorities to apprehend and jail Chinese individuals who maintained or reopened businesses or continued their relationships with Mexican women.[13]

Within a few years, under Elías Calles, the central government fully implemented anti-Chinese laws and rid Sonora of the vast majority of Chinese. Authorities, aided by vigilantes, drove out the Chinese with mob violence, arrest and deportation, and exit deadlines. The method of expulsion varied from town to town, from month to month and year to year. The *Arizona Daily Star* reported that people in towns around Sonora broke into Chinese homes and businesses, looted, and forced them and their families into the street.[14] In some instances, local and state authorities or mobs simply rounded up Chinese men and their Mexican wives or companions and mixed-race children and pushed them out of the state. Expelled Chinese reported to U.S. immigration agents that Mexicans had treated them harshly, barred them from working, and stripped them of their possessions.

Some Chinese Mexicans remained, hiding in Sonora with the support of family and friends. Some defended their businesses and rights in federal court.[15] Others became vagabonds wandering the streets and communities for months, hoping to find respite. A few of the wealthiest returned to China, and others relocated to the border territory of Baja California Norte and the border state of Chihuahua, where anti-Chinese movements never matured enough to carry out widespread evictions.[16] Sonora and Sinaloa, in turn, defied the federal government's official stance in carrying out the mass expulsions. Many entered the United States surreptitiously, given the U.S. Exclusion Laws (1882–1943). Some remained there without incident, while immigration agents apprehended others. Soon they would constitute a refugee crisis for Mexico's northern neighbor.

Mexican women and Mexican Chinese children accompanied Chinese men out of Sonora and Sinaloa during the expulsion era for a number of reasons, whether by force or by choice. Women opted to go along out of love, to keep their families together, and for fear that they would be unable to support their family without their husband or that anti-Chinese zealots would direct their hatred at their racially mixed children. *Antichinistas* portrayed Mexican women who formed relationships with Chinese men as traitors to the race and their children as degenerates. The dominant gender ideology and citizenship policy, moreover, defined women's status by that of their husbands. Indeed in 1930 the Mexican Census Bureau began listing women who had civilly married Chinese men as "Chinese" rather than "Mexican."[17]

Even though only Sonora and Sinaloa carried out mass expulsions, many Chinese elsewhere in Mexico also were driven out. Their population fell dramatically, from close to 18,000 in 1930 to fewer than 5,000 by 1940. The decline was most dramatic in the two northern states: from 3,571 to 92 in Sonora and from 2,123 to 165 in Sinaloa.[18]

Crossing into the United States as Refugees

During the expulsion period, Mexican authorities confiscated Roberto Fu's assets. Seeing officials treat her husband with such contempt and brutality deeply affected his wife, Ana María Domínguez de Fu, who died shortly after the birth of their son. Fu was a widower by the time Sonoran officials expelled the family. He and his children, Roberto, Manuela, Jacinto, Tomás, Ventura, Amelia, and Maximiliano, entered U.S. territory; the eldest was thirteen, and the youngest was only a few months old. Immigration agents apprehended the Fus and jailed them in southern Arizona, documenting their expulsion from Mexico and passage through the United States. In October 1933 the Immigration and Naturalization Service (INS) put them and other "refugees" on a train to San Francisco for ultimate deportation to China.[19]

Several thousand Chinese men and their families entered the United States illegally and became refugees from Mexico between 1931 and 1934, complicating U.S.-Mexican relations during the Depression. U.S. officials at first perceived Mexican Chinese families through the decades-old lens of the Chinese Exclusion Act, but after hearing testimony, classified them as refugees whom the agency could neither send back to Mexico nor allow into the United States because of the exclusion laws. U.S. immigration agents employed a gendered rubric of Chinese exclusion as they labeled even the Mexican women, whether married or not, and Mexican Chinese children as "Chinese refugees from Mexico," ultimately deporting them to China. Although the INS and the State Department labeled them refugees, nations in the prewar era had not yet adopted this classification as a regular practice or attached any special treatment to it. Indeed the United States usually referred to "illegal" Chinese immigrants as "contraband" or "smuggled." The term *refugee* pointed to the complexity of the case and the diplomatic issues it raised.[20] This was further complicated by the fact that the United States had itself already begun the forced "repatriation" of hundreds of thousands of Mexicans and Mexican Americans in the post-Depression era.[21]

U.S. immigration agents took testimony from few Mexican women, although they interviewed hundreds of Chinese men. The ideology of men's control over women under the notions of coverture and "the femme covert" legitimized the deportation to China of entire Mexican Chinese families. Gender ideology and citizenship policy commonly upheld around the world during this time stripped women of their citizenship when they married or formed unions with foreigners, defining their citizenship status as that of their husband or companion. Mexican women would fall deeper into the interstices of the nation-state once they reached China, where in some cases Chinese men's previous marriages removed the possibility that local authorities would consider them Chinese citizens either.

The INS took testimony from Chinese entrants in part to try to determine if Mexican authorities in Sonora and Sinaloa had in one way or another forced them to cross the border illegally, and in doing so had violated U.S. immigration law. Although the United States had created the Border Patrol in 1924, the border region was still quite porous. Mexican officials used the same networks for illegal entry that Mexicans, Chinese, and Americans had already established, since the cross-border smuggling of people (namely, Chinese) as well as goods, narcotics, and alcohol had become a profitable business by the turn of the twentieth century. Immigration officials tried the Sonoran authorities in Arizona courts for allegedly coordinating refugee smuggling efforts or acting as "coyotes."[22] The INS and the State Department concluded that in executing the eviction of Chinese from Sonora, Mexican authorities had violated U.S. sovereignty and damaged relations between the two nations. Sonora's actions, American officials warned, could have serious international repercussions and were inconsistent with the neighborly friendliness that had characterized the relationship between Arizona and Sonora and the two countries as a whole.[23]

In the summer of 1932, after apprehending hundreds of Chinese who had crossed the Arizona-Sonora border, the INS began to compile a comprehensive record of the cases and ensuing costs to the agency. By then U.S. officials perceived the situation as an unfolding refugee crisis. Immigration inspectors in charge at the border towns of Douglas, Naco, and Nogales and the city of Tucson compiled lists of refugees and sent them to their superiors in Washington, D.C. After completing the first register of Chinese refugees deported to China for fiscal year 1931–32, twenty "supplementary lists" documented further apprehensions and deportations between 1932 and 1934. Handling 4,317 cases in all, the INS spent $530,234.41 to detain and deport the refugees. This included at least 574 people who were members of 114 Mexican Chinese families traveling as units.[24]

Congregating in Portuguese Macau

After deportation to China, the Fu family, like other Mexican Chinese, was drawn to the port that had long been a foreign enclave. Situated on the southeastern edge of Guangdong Province on the South China Sea, Macau was under the control of a Portuguese colonial administration. Mexican Chinese found Macau attractive for a number of reasons: many had extended families in Guangdong Province; having been for centuries an important economic center and a kind of "borderland" between China and the West, Macau had drawn diverse people and developed a distinctly cosmopolitan flavor; the culturally and racially mixed Mexican Chinese found space to blend in and in time create a dynamic, cohesive community; and the deeply Catholic atmosphere provided them with a certain sense of familiarity. Churches and other Catholic institutions, moreover, offered ways to meet compatriots and build ties; they also provided jobs, services, and food in tough economic times.

Life in Macau, however, became ever more difficult as refugees from China poured into the colony during the era of Japanese aggression. Macau's population doubled, from about 75,000 in the early 1900s to 150,000 by the early 1930s. A host of economic and political problems besieged the republic after the Sino-Japanese War broke out in 1937 and 50 million refugees fled the northern war zones within a few years, some reaching Macau. The Portuguese colony's population reached 350,000 by the end of the decade.[25]

In the midst of the growing population and insecurity due to war in the mainland, the Fu family remained in Macau. The father worked as a porter at the San José Catholic Seminary, but his meager wages were insufficient during this very difficult time. When the family learned about the Cárdenas repatriation program, they considered returning to Mexico. But they would have a painful decision to make.

The Cárdenas Repatriation Program

After President Lázaro Cárdenas (1934–40) came to power, the anti-Chinese movement in Mexico began to lose momentum as he tried to remedy some of the wrongs the *antichinistas* had committed. The repatriation program would serve his larger goals of strengthening the central government and bolstering Mexico's foreign relations. Focusing on national interests and revolutionary ideology, Cárdenas continued to divest foreigners of their power in the nation. Mexico sought international legitimacy for the Revolution, in part by drawing on connections with similar struggles against imperialism around the world. Moving in this direction, Mexico accepted refugees from Spain during the Spanish Civil War (1936–39), officially supported China, and, like other nations, denounced Japanese aggression.[26]

As armed conflict loomed in East Asia, Cárdenas learned that Mexican women and children were stuck in China. Most had separated from or been abandoned by their Chinese husbands. Mexicans urged the authorities to take action, and newspapers began publishing pleas to the government to "rescue" its citizens in China in the months before the start of the Second Sino-Japanese War. Eduardo Miller, a member of a distinguished Mexican family and a businessman in China, helped disseminate news of the plight of hundreds of Mexican women who begged for charity in the streets of Shanghai and elsewhere. Failing to mention the expulsions, he believed that Mexican women and children had left Mexico in search of a better life, only to find misery, desperation, and death in China. Newspapers reported that Chinese men had forsaken their Mexican spouses in China with "Asiatic indifference." The Mexican government began to plan a major repatriation. In the spring of 1937 officials remitted 94,000 pesos to the Mexican consul in Yokohama to feed and repatriate approximately four hundred Mexican women and hundreds of Mexican Chinese children. The repatriates began arriving in Mexico later that year and resettled mainly in Sonora and Sinaloa.[27]

When they saw that the repatriation focused on Mexican women and children and that Chinese men were officially barred, Roberto M. Fu and his children were devastated. Few Chinese men had remained by their Mexican families, but that did not matter to the authorities, and neither did the fact that as a widower, Fu was quite exceptional in this regard. The repatriation program's exclusionary policies forced the family to weigh staying together under dire circumstances in Macau against separating for the sake of greater economic and social stability for the children in Mexico.

The Fu family decided to separate in order to survive. The father and his youngest son remained in Macau while the six older children returned to Mexico, vowing to sponsor their father and brother. At first the Fu children lived in Hermosillo, Sonora, where they opened a neighborhood grocery store. They later moved to the border city of Mexicali, Baja California Norte, which was home to a large Chinese community. Torn apart during the Cárdenas repatriation, the family would forge new transpacific ties over the following two decades.[28]

The older Fu children worked for years to secure the papers for their father's and youngest brother's repatriation. They could never have foreseen that a world war would prolong their separation. But once World War II ended, there was hope again. After liquidating their store in Hermosillo, the children at last obtained the necessary documents and permissions to bring their father to Mexico. Since their youngest brother was born on Mexican soil, his entry was less problematic. The Fus shared the good news with their contact in Macau, Ramón Lay Mazo, a leader in the Mexican Chinese community: "We are poor, but happy, as we have succeeded in securing Dad's entry." Regrettably their father's documents took a very long time to arrive in Macau. When they finally did, the Mexican permit had nearly expired, and Fu was unable to obtain a Chinese passport or passage on a ship. Upon hearing this, Lay Mazo appealed to the Mexican Embassy in Nanking, Nationalist China's capital, to have the permit extended. But shortly thereafter, in the spring of 1949, Communist forces in the Chinese Civil War took over the city, and Mexican diplomatic representation in China ceased.[29]

The youngest sibling, Maximiliano, became very sad and distraught after this last disappointment. Some people in Macau had cruelly ridiculed him for unknown reasons, adding to his trauma. He experienced angry fits over the situation and the inability to return to Mexico. Like his father, he worked at San José during this time. In June 1953, when he was around twenty, authorities arrested him at the seminary and interned him in a mental institution after a violently angry episode. The next morning, in a furious rage against the Mexican government and people over the family's hardships, he hit his head against the cell so hard that he died immediately. The death of his youngest son added great depth to the father's suffering. After waiting more than a decade to reunite with his older children, Roberto M. Fu was now left with no family in Macau. More than ever he wanted to return to Mexico. But he was still in Macau five years later, when Lay Mazo wrote on his behalf to Carlos Gutiérrez-Macías at the Mexican Embassy in Manila. Pleading with the Mexican ambassador to repatriate the poor man, Lay Mazo relayed that Fu worked day and night simply to have enough to eat and lived a lonely and sorrowful life.[30]

Lay Mazo's 1958 letter to Ambassador Gutiérrez-Macías was the last time Roberto M. Fu appeared in the record. What became of him is unclear. One possibility is that his children in Mexico were finally able to sponsor him with the ambassador's assistance. Or he may have returned during the second official repatriation in 1960; unlike Cárdenas, President Adolfo López Mateos allowed Chinese men to be repatriated with their Mexican families. But Fu could also have died in Macau in the interim.

Although Lay Mazo had written letters on his behalf, Fu was absent from his list of Mexican residents in Macau who wished to return to Mexico under the second repatriation. Lay Mazo also advocated for Mexican women who wanted their Chinese husbands to travel with them to Mexico. Ultimately his pleas were successful, but there was no further mention of the Chinese widower and his special status. Fu would have been at least sixty by this time.[31]

Had the Cárdenas administration appreciated the uniqueness and complexity of their reality rather than maintaining a narrow and punishing view of who belonged in the nation, the family's trajectory would have been different. The ensuing tragedy was owed not only to *antichinismo* but also to the limits of Cárdenas's attempt to redress its wrongs.

The Fu family's story illustrates the long-lasting international and transpacific reverberations of the anti-Chinese movement and the insufficient and belated response of the Mexican nation. Even though the Fus were unusual in that the father was a widower, they were not uncommon in their deep integration into local Mexican society before the anti-Chinese movement. Nor were their experiences uncommon as they went through expulsion from Mexico, U.S. detention, deportation to China, settlement in Macau, and eventual separation; war, revolution, and exclusionary repatriation policies severed other families as well. Nor were they the only family to bury loved ones before their time.

The anti-Chinese movement and its mass expulsions have yet to be assimilated into the Mexican national psyche. Even less well-known are the partial repatriations to Mexico and the transpacific ties that some families maintained as they worked to be reunited, as well as the lost hopes and traumas that followed, at a time of economic instability and political chaos for China and the world. The Mexican Chinese experience ought to be more widely understood, if only so that it may never be repeated.

Notes

Author's Note: I thank Erik Camayd-Freixas, Mae M. Ngai, Robert Chao Romero, the William P. Clements Center for Southwest Studies at Southern Methodist University, the Macau Foundation, the Macao Association for the Promotion of Exchange between Asia-Pacific and Latin America, and the Comadres Writing Group at the University of Texas at El Paso. This chapter draws on material from my book *Chinese Mexicans: Transpacific Migration and the Search for a Homeland, 1910–1960* (Chapel Hill: University of North Carolina Press, 2012).

1. National Archives, Washington, D.C., Immigration and Naturalization Service (INS), Records of the Central Office, Record Group 85, Subject Correspondence, 1906–32, boxes 514–15, folders 718 A–D, file 55771; Archivo General de la

Nación, Mexico City, Fondo Adolfo López Mateos, caja 714, exp. 546.2/1. All translations are mine unless otherwise noted.

2. On Sonora, see Cynthia Radding, *Wandering Peoples: Colonialism, Ethnic Spaces, and Ecological Frontiers in Northwestern Mexico, 1700–1850* (Durham, N.C.: Duke University Press, 1997); Ramón E. Ruiz, *The People of Sonora and Yankee Capitalists* (Tucson: University of Arizona Press, 1988); Miguel Tinker Salas, *In the Shadow of the Eagles: Sonora and the Transformation of the Border during the Porfiriato* (Berkeley: University of California Press, 1997); Josiah M. Heyman, *Life and Labor on the Border: Working People of Northeastern Sonora, Mexico, 1886–1986* (Tucson: University of Arizona Press, 1991). On the border region and "contact zones," see José David Saldívar, *Border Matters: Remapping American Cultural Studies* (Berkeley: University of California Press, 1997).

3. Lucy Salyer, *Laws Harsh as Tigers* (Chapel Hill: University of North Carolina Press, 1995); George Peffer, *If They Don't Bring Their Women Here* (Urbana: University of Illinois Press, 1999); Judy Yung, *Unbound Feet: A Social History of Chinese Women in San Francisco* (Berkeley: University of California Press, 1995); Eithne Luibhéid, *Entry Denied: Controlling Sexuality at the Border* (Minneapolis: University of Minnesota Press, 2002).

4. When the Chinese first migrated to Sonora during the last quarter of the nineteenth century, they concentrated in Guaymas, a port of entry, and Hermosillo, the state capital. They later moved to other areas. See Evelyn Hu-DeHart, "Coolies, Shopkeepers, Pioneers: The Chinese of Mexico and Peru (1849–1930)," *Amerasia* 15 (1989): 98–99, and "Immigrants to a Developing Society: The Chinese in Northern Mexico, 1875–1932," *Journal of Arizona History* 21 (1980): 275–312.

5. Evelyn Hu-DeHart, "Latin America in Asia-Pacific Perspective," *What Is in a Rim? Critical Perspectives on the Pacific Region Idea*, ed. Arif Dirlik (New York: Westview, 1994) 251–82; Sucheng Chan, *Asian Americans: An Interpretive History* (Boston: Twayne, 1991); Madeline Yuan-yin Hsu, *Dreaming of Gold, Dreaming of Home: Transnationalism and Migration between the United States and South China, 1882–1943* (Stanford: Stanford University Press, 2000).

6. The anti-Chinese newspaper *El Tráfico* was published in Guaymas (1889–96) and Nogales, Sonora (1896–1905). See Gerardo Rénique, "Anti-Chinese Racism, Nationalism and State Formation in Post-Revolutionary Mexico, 1920s–1930s," *Political Power and Social Theory* 14 (2000): 95–102; Evelyn Hu-DeHart, "Racism and Anti-Chinese Persecution in Sonora, Mexico, 1876–1932," *Amerasia* 9 (1982): 1–28; Robert Chao Romero, *The Chinese in Mexico, 1882–1940* (Tucson: University of Arizona Press, 2010); Charles C. Cumberland, "The Sonora Chinese and the Mexican Revolution," *Hispanic American Historical Review* 40 (1960): 191–211; Phillip A. Dennis, "The Anti-Chinese Campaigns in Sonora, Mexico," *Ethnohistory* 26.1 (1979): 65–80.

7. Katherine Elaine Bliss, *Compromised Positions: Prostitution, Public Health, and Gender Politics in Revolutionary Mexico City* (University Park: Pennsylvania State University Press, 2001), 12; Erika Lee, *At America's Gates: Chinese Immigration During the Exclusion Era, 1882–1943* (Chapel Hill: University of North Carolina Press, 2003), 152–61, 187; Alan Knight, "Racism, Revolution, and *Indigenismo*: Mexico, 1910–1940," *The Idea of Race in Latin America, 1870–1940*, ed. Richard Graham (Austin: University of Texas Press, 1990).

8. Gerardo Rénique, "Race, Region, and Nation: Sonora's Anti-Chinese Racism and Mexico's Postrevolutionary Nationalism, 1920s–1930s," *Race and Nation in Modern Latin America*, ed. Nancy P. Appelbaum et al. (Chapel Hill: University of North Carolina Press, 2003), 219–26. See also Alexander Saxton, *The Indispensable Enemy: Labor and the Anti-Chinese Movement in California* (Berkeley: University of California Press, 1971). Sonora had the largest Chinese population of all Mexican states for every census year from 1900 to 1930 except 1927, when it had the second largest. Chinese men in Sonora numbered 850 in 1900; 4,486 in 1910; 3,639 in 1921; 3,571 in 1930. See José Jorge Gómez Izquierdo, *El movimiento antichino en México (1871–1934): Problemas del racismo y del nacionalismo durante la Revolución Mexicana* (Mexico City: Instituto Nacional de Antropología e Historia, 1991), 77–78, 109, 127, 150. A report by the Mexican Department of Labor recorded 6,078 Chinese in 1919. See Hu-Dehart, "Latin America in Asia-Pacific Perspective," 265–67. See also Kif Augustine-Adams, "Making Mexico: Legal Nationality, Chinese Race, and the 1930 Population Census," *Law and History Review* 27:1 (2009) 113–44. These figures pale in comparison to those in the United States. Chinese in the U.S. numbered 71,531 in 1910, compared to 13,203 in Mexico, and 61,659 in 1920, compared to Mexico's 14,498 in 1921 (Lee, *At America's Gates*, 238).

9. Papers of José María Arana, Special Collections, University of Arizona Library, Tucson.

10. On the formation of the dominant ideology of *mestizaje* during the Mexican Revolution, see Knight, "Racism, Revolution, and *Indigenismo*"; Rénique, "Anti-Chinese Racism"; José Vasconcelos, *La raza cósmica: Misión de la raza iberoamericana* (1925; Mexico City: Aguilar, 1976).

11. Rénique, "Anti-Chinese Racism," 102–18; Rénique, "Race, Region, and Nation," 228–29; Erika Lee, "Orientalisms in the Americas: A Hemispheric Approach to Asian American History," *Journal of Asian American Studies* 8 (2005): 248.

12. Archivo General del Estado de Sonora, Hermosillo, año 1927, caja 362, tomo 1166, asunto: "problema chino"; see also José Angel Espinoza, *El problema chino en Sonora* (Mexico City: N.p., 1931).

13. Gómez Izquierdo, 137–41.

14. *Arizona Daily Star* (Tucson), September 5, 1931, cited in Dennis; *Nogales Daily Herald* (Nogales, Arizona), February 25, 1932, in folder IV-211-2, Archivo Histórico Genaro Estrada, Secretaría de Relaciones Exteriores, Mexico City.

15. On the use of the federal court system by the Chinese, see Chao Romero, *The Chinese in Mexico*.

16. Evelyn Hu-DeHart, "The Chinese of Baja California, 1910–1934," *Baja California and the North Mexican Frontier: Proceedings from the Pacific Coast Council on Latin American Studies*, vol. 12 (San Diego: San Diego State University Press, 1985–86). My book *Chinese Mexicans* explores the diverse paths of the expelled.

17. Augustine-Adams, 21–23, 30–31.

18. Gómez Izquierdo, 150, 161; Rénique, "Race, Region, and Nation," 230.

19. INS file 55771; Archivo General exp. 546.2/1. See note 1.

20. Mae M. Ngai, *Impossible Subjects: Illegal Aliens and the Making of Modern America* (Princeton, N.J.: Princeton University Press, 2004).

21. Francisco E. Balderrama and Raymond Rodríguez, *Decade of Betrayal: Mexican Repatriation in the 1930s* (Albuquerque: University of New Mexico Press, 1995);

Mercedes Carreras de Velasco, *Los Mexicanos que devolvió la crisis, 1929–1932* (Mexico City: Secretaría de Relaciones Exteriores, 1974).

22. Records of the National Archives, Pacific Region, Laguna Niguel, California, cases 6381, box 143, and 6461–62, box 145, District of Arizona, Tucson Division, Criminal, Case Files, 1914–47.

23. INS file 55771.

24. Ibid.

25. Founded by merchants in the sixteenth century, Macau was a Portuguese colony that bore some similarity to nearby British Hong Kong. In 1976 Macau became a Chinese territory with a Portuguese administration. It came under China's sovereign control in 1999. See R. D. Cremer, ed., *Macau: City of Commerce and Culture* (Hong Kong: UEA, 1987); Steve Shipp, *Macau, China: A Political History of the Portuguese Colony's Transition to Chinese Rule* (Jefferson, N.C.: McFarland, 1997).

26. Friedrich E. Schuler, *Mexico between Hitler and Roosevelt: Mexican Foreign Relations in the Age of Lázaro Cárdenas, 1934–1940* (Albuquerque: University of New Mexico Press, 1998); Thomas G. Powell, *Mexico and the Spanish Civil War* (Albuquerque: University of New Mexico Press, 1981).

27. *El Universal* (Mexico City), January 7 and March 10, 1937; *Excélsior* (Mexico City), March 10 and 29, 1937.

28. Exp. 546.2/1. See note 1.

29. Chen Jian, *Mao's China and the Cold War* (Chapel Hill: University of North Carolina Press, 2001), 17–41.

30. Exp. 546.2/1.

31. My book *Chinese Mexicans* explores the stories of other families. While some waited decades to be reunited after separation by expulsions or repatriations, others never saw each other again. See also Schiavone Camacho, "Crossing Boundaries, Claiming a Homeland: The Mexican-Chinese Transpacific Journey to Becoming Mexican, 1930s–1960s," *Pacific Historical Review* 78.4 (2009): 545–77.

CHAPTER SIX

Narrating Orientalisms in Spanish American Modernism

Ivan A. Schulman

*The interpretation of our reality through patterns not our own serves only
to make us ever more unknown, ever less free, ever more solitary.*
GABRIEL GARCÍA MÁRQUEZ, "THE SOLITUDE OF LATIN AMERICA"[1]

In desultory notes, paralleling Jules Michelet's statement that "the Orient
advances, invincible, fatal to the gods of light by the charm of its dreams,
by the magic of its chiaroscuro," José Martí declared that "the Orient in-
vades the West" not merely in the context of nineteenth-century discursive
practice but as a sign of hybridity in the evolution of East-West thought.[2] In
reexamining Spanish American Modernist texts that span the years 1880 to
1930 and in which the Orient is inscribed, I argue that there is a need to
question the perpetuation of previous critical positions with regard to the
meaning of Orientalism in Modernist literature, and that the revision of
Modernism's Orientalisms implies a fundamentally dynamic project in
which the nineteenth century's desire for the Orient should be viewed not
simply "as an *intertextual* phenomenon but . . . as a social phenomenon"
that is scripted into a network of heterogeneous cultural representations
generated by the forces of both authority and aesthetics.[3] Furthermore, if I
prefer to speak of Orientalisms rather than Orientalism, it is because of the
heterogeneous, polyphonic nature of a discourse referring to both Near
and Far East whose basic operational meaning I appropriate from Edward
Said. "Orientalism," he insists, "is the discipline by which the Orient was
(and is) approached systematically, as a topic of learning, discovery, and
practice" (73).

In the course of this process of learning, discovery, and practice, the
Spanish American Modernists were drawn to the representations of

the Orient they encountered in their readings of classical and nineteenth-century texts, principally French. An insight into their contemporary archive of readings can be gleaned from a narration by Abel Morán, the protagonist of Efrén Rebolledo's short novel *Hojas de bambú* (Bamboo Leaves). Morán had read "the *Book of Wonders* in which the master Marco Polo spoke for the first time of distant Cipango, goading, with his vivid descriptions, the studies of wise men, and at the same time feeding the greed of the conquerors; the studies on Japanese Art of Edmund de Goncourt and Gonse; the novels of Loti; the *Japanese Histories*, by the magnificent Lafcadio Hearn, each one of whose lines is a gem of literature." Inspired by these and other cultural readings, instead of directing his steps toward the more traditional choice of exploring Europe, Morán preferred to feast his eyes, firsthand, on prototypical Oriental visions: "cricket cages and dwarf pines, houses made of paper, and *geishas* with colorful *kimonos* and dark hair buns, temples of red lacquer, the graceful Fujiyama, and Japanese natural settings of blue skies and twisted trees."[4]

This particular predilection for Japanese themes over Chinese or Near Eastern themes is prevalent in Spanish American Modernism and may be understood in a sociohistorical context.[5] Given the familiar Arabic influence in Spain issuing from the Moorish occupation (711–1492), it is understandable that Spanish Americans should look to the more exotic Far East. Yet during the rise of Western Orientalism in the nineteenth century, China was in social and political turmoil, which may have caused travelers, whether French or Spanish American, some apprehension about visiting the country. The year 1839 marks the beginning of a period of revolutionary changes with decades of rebellion. Western presence begins in the late 1860s as China grants permission to foreign merchants and missionaries to set up residence in various cities. Later came the Tientsin Massacre (1870) and the Boxer Rebellion (1898), whose purpose was to rid the country of foreigners, the so-called foreign devil. In contrast, Japan's opening to the West in 1853 was much less problematic since Japan had a deeply rooted tradition of learning from foreigners.[6] Indeed for centuries the Japanese adopted and transformed many elements of Chinese civilization. Thus the incursion of Western economy and culture was less disturbing than in China, such that one might surmise that due to this cultural hybridity, Westerners— travelers, readers, and writers—felt more comfortable identifying with a Japanese Orient. The European early nineteenth-century enthusiasm for China was replaced by a midcentury "Japanism," a cultural transference that coincided with Japan's opening to the West and, in Spanish American countries, with the beginning of socioeconomic modernization. Japan represented a cultural novelty, and it was the principle of "the new" that defined the experiments and transformations of Spanish American Modernist culture.

Whether in its Chinese, Japanese, or Mediterranean modalities, Orientalism as a source of knowledge, as an institution, or as literary expression coincided with the expansion of imperialism and Western colonialism in the "period from 1815 to 1914 when European colonial domination became extensive to 85 percent of the world's surface."[7] Thus it was not only the lure of the exotic but also the sense of an ending that moved Spanish American Modernists and their protagonists to examine the Orient, that is, the awareness that tourism and European colonialism had already turned what was exotic into the familiar. As Behdad notes, the belated travel writers and literary artists of the nineteenth century, filled with the desire to explore alternative horizons, other cultures, and cognitive systems, frustrated in their desire to capture an authentic Other, produced melancholy discourses, texts signifying an absence, frequently taking as present what in fact had already vanished (92).

This loss of the past is inserted in many forms in Modernist texts; we find it, for example, in José Martí's *Versos sencillos* (poem XLII, *Obras completas* 16:120), framed in the symbolic statement of Agar's frustrated search for her lost pearl, or in Enrique Gómez Carrillo's polarized vision of Damascus, which, much to his chagrin, he discovers is a modern city. However, a visit to the old part of the city where he finds houses are hermetic, hostile, and mysterious intrigues him in his search for the traditional, paradigmatic Orient.[8] There is in his writing a splitting or diffraction of Orientalist discursive authority, that is, an ambivalence and uncertainty evident in his search for the true Orient, on the one hand, and the discovery of its absence, on the other, as he slowly realizes the past is irretrievable. In spite of these contradictions, characteristic of the hegemonic Orientalist discourse, or perhaps because of them, his Orientalism is frequently lacking in cultural distortion or fanciful idealizations. It contains what Said would term an unrepresentative "natural" depiction (21), evidenced, for example, when he writes that the Orient is on the cusp of modernization or that China is a working, industrial country. And as he travels from Near East to Far East his gaze is not that of the colonizer but of a Westerner who chronicles the steps taken by the Orient in its process of industrialization. Thus he notes that Shanghai is the most Western of the Chinese ports (178) in a country that only a few years before was where the production of anything other than products of ivory, lacquer, silk, or porcelain seemed impossible (176–77). In the face of modernity's displacement of tradition, his, like that of other

Modernists, is a search for value in the face of the rationalization and sec-
ularization of society from the time of the French Revolution and the spread
of the market system in capitalist societies. Traditional societies with fixed,
frequently hierarchical social constructions had no need to search for value;
value became visible and significant only at the point at which it ceased to
exist, that is, with the advent of modernity. "In the passage from the traditional to the rationalized, value is at once lost (as reality) and gained (as
abstraction)."[9] And so, together with other Modernists, he cultivates an ex-
oticizing strategy by selecting and focusing on Oriental visions such as the
mysterious *musmé* he glimpses as he leaves the train station in Tokyo, an
embodiment of the orientalized Orient, the stereotypical sensual, seductive, eccentric, impenetrable, and fatalistic reconstruction of the voids of
the present.[10] The *musmé*'s eyes are

> not big but long, very narrow and very long, [and] have a voluptuous
> sweetness that explains the enthusiasm of those ancient Japanese poets
> who composed *tankas* in which women's pupils are compared to filters
> of enchantment. . . . And this spirit does not wear the gray unadorned
> dress of my female traveling companions, but a pale yellow kimono
> covered with white lilies which makes her appear to be a deity of spring
> of this nation, smaller and more splendid than that of Botticelli, but no
> less seductive. I contemplate her entranced. (185)

Rubén Darío alluded to this fascination in his prologue to Gómez Carrillo's *De Marsella a Tokio* (From Marseilles to Tokyo): "This poet, I say,
comes from the country of dragons, of rare things, of awesome landscapes
and of people who seem to have fallen from the moon. . . . He was attracted by all things strange or unknown, and demonstrated a violent se-
duction for a young girl who knew nothing of Western nations or other
ways of thinking."[11]

Why, we may well ask, this transfixion with orientalized Orients in
Modernist discourse? What lies beneath the more obvious textual surfaces
of these "exotic" appropriations? What are the modalities of its discourse?
Is it, as Abdeslam Azougarth has suggested, a counterdiscursive mechanism for dealing with a developing mercantilist society whose newly insti-
tuted norms and values nineteenth-century Latin American writers found
to be at odds with their cultural, social, and aesthetic ideals? Or is it a case
of the writers' protesting against the values of an economic modernity that
denied art its previously accepted role as a determinant of truth and spirituality?[12] In response, did the Modernists, in their conflictive relationship
with modernity, choose the path of evasion and geographical displace-

ment, which the Orient, among other imagined spaces and communities, provided with its voluptuous visions of sultans, peris, Scheherazades, Aladdins, pagodas, temples, kimonos, and cherry blossoms? In engaging these issues, Iris Zavala posits the notion that among the Modernists the utilitarianism and disintegration of established social paradigms encouraged the creation of supernaturalisms, the experience of the occult and the esoteric. It also heightened subjectivities beyond the boundaries of reason and "acted as a mechanism for dealing with or mediating social contradictions."[13] However, the question of hegemonic authority uppermost in Said's perception of Orientalism "as a sign of European-Atlantic power over the Orient [rather] than . . . a veridical discourse about the Orient" (6) is called into question by Julia Kushigian, for example, whose view is that Hispanic Orientalism, unlike its French or British models, is not repressive or manipulative but an open and welcoming means of exploring the self through a gaze upon the Other.[14] If, in the face of these multiple and conflicting tenets, we proceed from theory to praxis by analyzing the alternative spaces of Modernism's Orientalism in Julio Herrera y Reissig's exemplary poem "Odalisque" (*Las clepsidras*, 1910), we may succeed in clarifying the function and meaning of exoticism, so essential to the concept of Orientalism and the nature of its discursive operation:

ODALISQUE

To bewitch me, houri of marvels,
you startled me with oriental pomp,
with earrings, slippers, veils and corals,
with bangles and astral necklaces.
On regal carpets, on hands and knees,
you smoked the houkah with ritualistic opiums,
while to the sound of guzlas and drums
the aromatic incense burned.
Your body, undulating in the Turkish manner,
slipped into a mystical mazurka. . . .
Then in a waltz of strange gyrations
you vanished in a miraculous haze,
carried away by chimeras of smoke
above the glory of the censer.[15]

Herrera y Reissig's exploration of Oriental plastic beauty constitutes a displacement in space in which the narrator is entranced and overpowered by the ravishing houri. In a prototypical representation his gaze is centered on the female body, which in the final tercet dissolves into the smoke and fumes of the incense pot. In examining Herrera y Reissig's exoticism Said's two methodological devices seem particularly appropriate: *strategic location*, that is, "the author's position in a text with regard to the Oriental material he writes about," and *strategic formation*, "the relationship between texts and the way in which groups of texts, types of texts, even textual genres, acquire mass, density, and referential power among themselves and thereafter in the culture at large" (20). In "Odalisque," as in other Orientalist poems by Herrera y Reissig ("Óleo indostánico," "Unción islamita"), the poet reinscribes the Orient as part of a process of description and definition of both self and the universe. Emphasis is on the visual, which is conveyed through creative, experimental metaphors. The female body, the center of his focus, rises to the level of a metaphor of the Orient and suggests a strategic formation that is not only self-referential but socially mediated, a reconceptualization dynamically formed and frequently de-formed. Herrera y Reissig's representation of women in enticing idealized poses—a prototype of the stereotyped Modernist enunciation of the Oriental female body—is not "an innocent depiction of the beauty of exotic peoples but an ethnographic alibi arising from the desire to create a sexual text that can be manipulated, interpreted, and exchanged between artist, exotic subjects, and spectators."[16] The poet's exoticism is not simply an aesthetic exercise; it is tied to his role as a voyeur; it reflects hierarchical social and culturally generated positions of masculine and feminine values. And in privileging difference it serves to explore what is both threatening and necessary to male subjectivity (Charnon-Deutsch 254). A progression of generative factors, based on Mario Praz's ideas, would seem to be operational here: curiosity and desire to fathom the unknown leads to exoticism; the desire for distant cultures produces a flight from self and ultimately eroticism (Tanabe 43). In its broader social connotations, the Orient, metaphorized in the female body, is perceived as a sexually unstable, mysterious, impenetrable space, and as such, its representations are not only cultural or aesthetic but political. Kabbani says the insistence on the portrayal of women is linked to the dominant culture's patriarchic values and its racism. The female other is seen as a member of a subgroup in patriarchal society, and Oriental women were doubly demeaned—as women and as Orientals—while at the same time they were sublimated (67).

Revisionist analyses of so-called Modernist escapist discourses, Orientalist or otherwise, have taught us that when examined as a corpus they constitute social texts that through a strategy of geographic or cultural displacement are linked to a social and political discourse in spite of the fact that as individual texts they can be, and frequently are, (mis)read as mere aestheticizing enunciations of idealized visions conjured up by the writer's creative spirit. A binary strategy, aesthetic and sociocultural, of reading texts can be applied in "Odalisque" to the stereotypical artifacts of the houri's slippers, earrings, or veils. The veil in particular attracts the eye and forces us to speculate about what is behind it. It hides the woman but heightens the voyeur's desire for penetration and knowledge. The inscription of the veil turns the Oriental woman, a synecdoche of Oriental culture, into an enigma. Julián del Casal's sensuous Salomé comes to mind, dancing, bejeweled, to the sound of sweet music with a white lotus in her hand.[17] "In Western eyes, the Orient is always *more and other* than what it appears to be, for it always and everywhere appears in a veiled, disguised, and deceptive manner": the veil not only hides but it also reveals; travelers, writers, and poets establish via the veil an imaginary anchor in order to assert individual subjectivity and authority.[18] Authority for Latin American writers, notes Zavala, was different from European figurations, which sought to construct the Orient as Other while establishing national identities. Rather than a discourse of power to create, incorporate, or control Oriental spaces, Latin Americans sought to affirm their own identities through discourses against power (85), created through creolized visions and polyphonic hybridized strategies. In Herrera y Reissig's poem this pluriculturalism is evidenced in the houri's dancing of the mazurka and the waltz, the latter characterized by the narrator as a waltz of strange—that is, foreign—gyrations. The orchestration and juxtaposition of these non-Oriental objects and artifacts are linked to a strategy of appropriation and reinscription whose desired end product is the affirmation of self and the liberation of the social community from center-imposed cultural and sociopolitical systems during the period of emerging national cultures in nineteenth-century Latin America.

Reinscription need not follow the self/other modality as in Herrera y Reissig's work. It can also be inscribed from within, either through "natural" (Said's term) enunciations such as those in Martí's chronicles or in aesthetic formulations such as those of José Juan Tablada's appropriated haikus. In the case of Martí's writing, the hand of the revolutionary is evident in his reporting of the upheavals and rebellions in Egypt in the 1880s sparked by the Egyptians' longing to free themselves of the presence of the English and the threats of the French: "Egypt finds that it has paid too dearly for the civilization and the support which it asked of the Europeans and it wants to shake off the yoke of its civilizers" (23:158). Indochina has similar aspirations. He writes in one of his children's stories published in *La edad de oro* (The Golden Age):

We wear pigtails, pointed hats, wide breeches, colored shirts, and we are yellow, short, frail and ugly; but we work with both bronze and silk: and when the French came to take away our Hanoi, our Hue, our cities with wood palaces, our ports with their houses of bamboo and boats made of reeds, our storehouses of fish and rice, in spite of our almond-shaped eyes, we knew how to die, thousands and thousands of us died in order to close off their approach. Now they are our masters; but tomorrow, who knows! (18:461–62)

Martí's is an internalized Oriental discourse of the colonized; a discourse generated not by hegemonic authority but by the Orient's search for authenticity in a projected, liberated, and reconstructed sociopolitical community. It is, in addition, a discourse that exemplifies the open, welcoming Orientalism described by Kushigian (11–12). It frequently seeks guidance from the East: "From the Arabs we should take two things at least: their daily prayer in which they ask Allah to help them choose an unswerving course" and their proverb that asserts that "he who turns his head when dogs thwart his path will not reach the end of his journey" (3:117). The appropriation of these Oriental adages is inserted into Martí's political discourse and his revolutionary project for Cuba's liberation from Spanish rule. But his can also be a decorative, aesthetic discourse, evident in the incorporation of decorative art objects in his novel *Lucía Jérez* (18:205), in his insistent use of the metaphor of Arab steeds (e.g., 17:270), in his reference to the "mushma" in *Versos sencillos*, and in lines from an erotic poem that conjures up parallel visions of *ukiyo-e* prints:[19]

Over her delicate ear
Her voluptuous hair falls
Like a curtain
Which rises near her neck.
The ear is a heavenly creation
Of Chinese porcelain. (16:121)

But it is Tablada rather than Martí who among the Modernists is most consistently and ardently identified with the Oriental. Tablada was not the first Spanish American Modernist to cultivate Oriental themes. That distinction rests with Julián del Casal, especially in his celebrated poems "Sourimono" and "Kakemono," whose original title was "Pastel japonés" (A Japanese Pastel), signaling the significant role that painting, ceramics, and sculpture were to play in the creation of an Oriental literary discourse in nineteenth-century Spanish America. It has been said that Tablada's Orientalism, gleaned from French readings and the plastic arts, as well as firsthand from his travels in the East, conceived of the Orient as a literary circumstance, a formalist disfigurement lacking in hybridity, correlation, or affinity vis-à-vis national or regional cultural identities.[20] Those who fault Tablada for his lack of a national sensibility point out the futility of his attempting to use an Oriental form, the *haikai*, in a Western idiom, but Tablada was aware of the tensions of his cultural preferences. In the poem "Exégesis" he elucidates the nature of the doubleness of his discourse:

My soul, a hieroglyphic, is both Mexican and Asian.
....
Perhaps my mother when she bore me in her womb
Looked at many Buddhas, lotuses, the magnificent
Nippon art and everything those strange boats
Off-loaded on the native shores of the Pacific!
That's why I love jades, smaragdine stones,
The light green *chalchihuitl*, with its double mystery,
For it decorated monarchs of Anahuac and China
And it germinates only in Mexico and the Celestial Empire.
Wrapped in the sumptuous brocades of the Seres
And adorned with jades, my poetic inspiration is American,
And in the onyx vessel that is my heart,
Endowing my blood with its esoteric vigor,
Flowers a miraculous
Japanese cherry tree![21]

The Mexican poet who described himself as a "servant of the Mikado" and a bonze of the Orient's pagodas was a life-long devotee of Japanese culture, which he wove into his texts from his first volume of poetry, *El florilegio* (1899), but most especially the second, 1904 edition, with its section of "Poemas exóticos" (Exotic Poems) and his "Musa japónica" (Japanese Muse).[22] The 1904 edition also includes translations of *utas* and a section titled "Cantos de amor y de otoño" (Songs of Love and Autumn), which paraphrase short texts of the *Kokinshifu*, a collection of ancient and modern Japanese odes. In prose he is known for his journalistic pieces, written while in Japan, which were later collected under the title *El país del sol* (The Land of the Sun). If in the first period of his work (1890–1900) there is an attraction to exotic themes, French-learned and -inspired, in the second (1900–1910) there is a movement toward authenticity in place of exoticism. The third period (1911–20), when he travels to France and expands his knowledge of the Orient, also includes his stay in New York, where he internationalizes his creative and cultural insights, befriends the Japanese scholar Frederick Starr, and publishes his essay on the Japanese painter Hiroshigue, whose art had an overwhelming influence on Tablada's most significant and original Japanesque poetry, including his experiments in melding rhythm and spatial dimension with poetic discourse. First came the *haikais* in a steady stream:

> Bits of mud
> On the darkened path
> Frogs jump . . .
> > (*Los mejores poemas* 54)

Then came more daring innovations, inspired by Japanese calligraphy, by the transfer of techniques from print media, especially those of Hiroshigue. Through his experiments Tablada succeeded in creating visual rhythm—before its use by either Vicente Huidobro or Octavio Paz. In Japanese calligraphy and art he discovered transferable techniques to produce poetry that would simplify, symbolize, and synthesize impressions and voices. In his book on Hiroshigue, writes Tanabe, Tablada indicated he used "Japanism as a springboard to awaken among Mexican artists an interest in popular national art. He was not an exoticist, clear and simple, as other Modernists" (138). This emphasis on the plastic arts—calligraphy and Hiroshigue's prints—suggests, as I noted at the start, the need to reconsider previous critical positions that have identified the genesis of Hispanic Orientalism with literary texts, especially with those of Edmond and Jules de Goncourt and Pierre Loti. But the plastic arts were equally significant in creating a Latin American Oriental discourse. Tablada, for example, explained that before his trip to Japan he collected Japanese paintings in reproductions, including *Fugaku Hiakei* by Hokusai. His interest in erotic poetry was stimulated by viewing *ukiyo-e* prints, representations of sexual union in which the male organ was drawn in an incredibly exaggerated size and female faces expressed complete ecstasy.

Tablada's ties to art were both visual and literary; he read Edmond de Goncourt's works on Utamaro (1891) and Hokusai (1896) and admired their paintings (Tanabe 37). Utamaro's influence was especially notable, not only on Tablada but on other Modernists whose texts evidence a transference of pictorial elements to literary imagistic systems. In general, the Modernists were captivated by an art form that in the Orient was considered unorthodox and decadent, that is, the art of painters who represented Oriental women as we find them in so many Modernist texts: with white faces, eyes narrow as threads, small mouths like a cherry tree leaf, inexpressive and indolent but with the suggestion that behind their mysterious impassivity was an insatiable passion.[23] And while it is true that most Modernists were not as well acquainted with Oriental art as Tablada, we know, for example, that Julián del Casal's Orientalism, in the case of the sonnets of *Mi museo ideal* (My Ideal Museum), was inspired by reproductions he viewed in Havana of Gustave Moreau's biblical motifs and that he was moved in "Japonerías" (Japanese Bibelots) by the sight, one morning, of the splendor of a Japanese ceramic.[24] And we know that Martí was fascinated by Oriental art to the point of translating an essay by E. Bergerat on Japanese painting that reviews the different forms of art cultivated by the Japanese and their historical development (19:321–26). In short, it can be said that the engendering sources of Modernist Orientalisms were the written word of literary texts and art criticism (principally French), paintings, and the decorative arts. And while exoticism stands out as the sharper of their discursive modalities, it should not be taken at face value. A detailed revisionist study of Modernism's Oriental *strategic formations*, along the lines suggested in this essay, will confirm ever-present emancipatory projections and epistemological concerns linked to the reconstruction of the self, the nation, and the universe through the visioning of an alternative cultural space.

Notes

Author's Note: This essay was first published in Malva E. Filer, Dominick L. Finello, and William M. Sherzer, eds., *A Celebration of Brooklyn Hispanism: Hispanic Literature from Don Quijote to Today* (Newark, Del.: Hispanic Monographs, 2004).

1. "The Solitude of Latin America," quoted by Rana Kabbani, *Europe's Myths of the Orient* (Bloomington: Indiana University Press, 1986), x.

2. Michelet quoted in Edward Said, *Orientalism* (New York: Pantheon, 1978), 73; José Martí, *Obras completas*, 28 vols. (Havana: Editorial Nacional, 1963–73), 19:359. In addition to the authors cited below, the mainstream of Spanish American Modernist Orientalism is amply represented by Rubén Darío, *Obras completas* (Madrid: Aguilar, 1950); Leopoldo Lugones, *Obras poéticas completas* (Madrid: Aguilar, 1959); Amado Nervo, *Obras completas* (Madrid: Aguilar, 1962); and Guillermo Valencia, *Obras poéticas completas* (Madrid: Aguilar, 1955).

3. Ali Behdad, *Belated Travelers: Orientalism in the Age of Colonial Dissolution* (Durham, N.C.: Duke University Press, 1994), 136.

4. Efrén Rebolledo, *Obras completas*, ed. Luis Mario Schneider (Mexico City: Ediciones de Bellas Artes, 1968), 178. All translations from the Spanish are mine.

5. For this sidebar on the histories of China and Japan I have consulted Kenneth S. Latourette, *The Chinese and Culture,* 4th ed. (New York: Macmillan, 1967); Patrick Smith, *Japan: A Reinterpretation* (New York: Pantheon Books, 1997); Edwin O. Reischauer, *Japan: The Story of a Nation* (New York: Knopf, 1970). I have also consulted personally with Dr. Thomas Breslin, a historian at Florida International University.

6. On the adaptability of the Japanese, see Reischauer (123):

> The Japanese also had another advantage over the Chinese, whose age-old assumption that theirs was the only land of true civilization made it extremely difficult for China to adapt herself to outside ideas. The Japanese, because of their old pattern of borrowing from China and their continuing awareness that things could usefully be learned from abroad, had no difficulty in realizing that the strong nations of the West offered valuable economic and political models. They quickly seized on the idea that the best way to make their country secure from the West was to modernize it along Western lines, and they were willing to do anything necessary to achieve this goal.

7. Fred R. Dallmayr, *Beyond Orientalism: Essays on Cross-Cultural Encounter* (Albany: State University of New York Press, 1996), xvi.

8. Enrique Gómez Carrillo, *Páginas escogidas II: Impresiones de viaje* (Guatemala City: Biblioteca de la Cultura Popular, 1954), 152–53.

9. Chris Bongie, *Exotic Memories: Literature, Colonialism, and the Fin de Siècle* (Stanford: Stanford University Press, 1991), 8.

10. Rana Kabbani observes that the traveler in travel literature "travels to exercise power over land, women, peoples. It is a commonplace of Orientalism that the West knows more about the East than the East knows about itself; this implies a predetermined discourse, however, which limits and in many ways victimizes the Western observer. It is as if the imagination of the traveler, in order to function, has to be sustained by a long tradition of Western scholarship, by other Western texts." Thus the Orient is often reduced to a cliché. Rana Kabbani, *Europe's Myths of the Orient* (Bloomington: Indiana University Press, 1986), 10.

11. In Atsuko Tanabe, *El japonismo de José Juan Tablada* (Mexico City: Universidad Nacional Autónoma, 1981), 27, n37.

12. Abdeslam Azougarth, "Martí orientalista," *Casa de las Américas* 210 (1998): 13–14.

13. Iris M. Zavala, *Colonialism and Culture: Hispanic Modernism and the Social Imaginary* (Bloomington: Indiana University Press, 1992), 127.

14. Julia A. Kushigian, *Orientalism in the Hispanic Literary Tradition: In Dialogue with Borges, Paz, and Sarduy* (Albuquerque: University of New Mexico Press, 1991), 12.

15. Julio Herrera y Reissig, *Poesías completas* (Buenos Aires: Losada, 1942), 280.

16. Lou Charnon-Deutsch, *Culture and Gender in Nineteenth-Century Spain* (Oxford: Clarendon, 1995), 252. Charnon-Deutsch borrows the term *ethnographic alibi* from Mark Alloula, *The Colonial Harem* (Minneapolis: University of Minnesota Press, 1956), 28.

17. Julián del Casal, *Poesías completas y pequeños poemas en prosa* (Miami: Ediciones Universal, 1993), 173.

18. Meyda Yegenoglu, *Colonial Fantasies: Towards a Feminist Reading of Orientalism* (Cambridge: Cambridge University Press, 1998), 48.

19. Japanese representations of sexual union.

20. Schneider in Rebolledo, 9.

21. José Juan Tablada, *El florilegio*, 1st ed. (Mexico City: Imprenta de Ignacio Escalante, 1899); 2nd ed. (Mexico City: Librería de la Viuda de Ch. Bouret, 1904). The quote and the reference to the bonze is from "Japón," *El florilegio* (1904), 121.

22. José Juan Tablada, *Los mejores poemas* (Mexico City: UNAM, 1971), 45.

23. For the information on Tablada and his links to the plastic arts I am indebted to Tanabe's informative work.

24. In his prose poem "Japonerías," dedicated to María Cay, Casal wrote, "He visto esta mañana, al salir de paseo, un búcaro japonés digno de figurar en tu alcoba blanca ¡oh espiritual María! donde no se han oído nunca las pisadas de tus admiradores o el eco sonoro de los besos sensuales" (As I went for a walk this morning I gazed upon a Japanese vase worthy to be featured in your white bedroom—oh, spiritual María!—where the steps of your admirers or the sonorous echo of sensual kisses have never been heard; 145).

CHAPTER SEVEN

Enrique Gómez Carrillo's Japan and Latin American (Peripheral) Orientalism

Zoila Clark

The chronicles on Japan written by the Guatemalan Modernist Enrique Gómez Carrillo are an example of the peripheral Orientalism that emerges from the encounter between two formerly colonized societies, in this case, the Japanese and the Latin American. As Kazue Nakamura reminds us, Japan has a hybrid culture that resulted from both the adoption of Chinese writing characters before the Meiji Restoration in the mid-nineteenth century and the influence of the Western world when Meiji Japan opened itself to Euro-American standards at the end of that same century.[1] Furthermore these two hybrid cultures are similar in ideology. On the one hand, the Japanese have created an original culture with the assimilation of the religious philosophy of Chinese Buddhism; on the other, Amerindian religious principles, which have some characteristics in common with Buddhist doctrine, have pervaded and survived Spanish evangelization. A good example of both cultures' similarity is that they have continued to worship the Sun god until modern times within their religious syncretism.[2]

Set in the periphery, Latin American Orientalism is supposed to be different from that of Europe and North America, which in its search for territorial expansion see the Other as an inferior object of domination, thereby creating a distorted, stereotyped, and self-serving representation of the Oriental Other.[3] Hence my interest in the chronicles of Gómez Carrillo, whose visit to Japan may have meant something more than the imitation of a French trend at the end of the nineteenth century. This study seeks to analyze the author's travelogue, *El Japón heroico y galante* (Heroic and

Gallant Japan), in order to find out how these chronicles depart from Western Orientalism and to help define a Latin American brand.

I refer in my analysis to Said's methodology for questioning the authority of narrative voice from the standpoint of an author's *strategic formation* and *strategic location*, as well as to such concepts as *mimicry, ambivalence, hybridity,* and *stereotype,* as defined by Homi K. Bhabha, whose "theoretical anarchy," as he calls it, sets out to reevaluate colonial identity. Said's strategic formation "is a way of analyzing the relationship between texts and the way in which groups of texts, types of texts, even textual genres, acquire mass, density, and referential power among themselves and thereafter in the culture at large" (20). It is the ideological background that the author brings to his text. The strategic location is not a place but "a way of describing the author's position in a text with regard to the Oriental material he writes about. . . . This location includes the kind of narrative voice he adopts, the type of structure he builds, the kinds of images, themes, motifs that circulate in the text—all of which add up to deliberate ways of addressing the reader, containing the Orient, and finally, representing it or speaking on its behalf" (20). Mimicry is for Bhabha the imitation of the colonizer by the colonized. This concept tends to divide the natives between the "good," who imitate white civilization, and the "bad," who resist assimilation. Nevertheless mimicry may also be a threat to colonial authority because of its ambivalence, for as it demands similarity and difference at the same time, the colonized may produce their own identity as an assertion of difference. In Bhabha's words, "Mimicry is, thus, the sign of a double articulation; a complex strategy of reform, regulation, and discipline, which 'appropriates' the Other as it visualizes power [and] poses an imminent threat to both 'normalized' knowledges and disciplinary powers."[4] In this sense, Bhabha's hybridity is textually similar to Bakhtin's heteroglossia.[5] In ambiguous colonial discourse, the voice of power is affected by the appropriation of the colonized as a sign of its difference. As Bhabha describes it, "Hybridity is a problematic of colonial representation and individualization that reverses the effects of the colonialist disavowal, so that other denied knowledges enter upon the dominant discourse and estrange the basis of its authority—its rules of recognition. . . . It is now a partial presence, a strategic device in a specific colonial engagement, an appurtenance of authority" (114). Stereotype is the mechanism through which the representation of the Other is fixed, visible, and cognizable as social reality. It is ambivalent for it has the qualities that the colonizer hates in himself. These constitute a kind of negative identity and, at the same time, a projection upon the Other of his most intense desires. Stereotypes generate racial prejudice, such as prejudging the Black as lascivious or the Asian as deceitful (Bhabha 70–75). Any colonial discourse is ambivalent because the native is simultaneously the object of desire and of rejection. This ambivalence describes simultaneous processes of denial and identification with the Other. The colonizer and the colonized are trapped in this paranoiac dynamics of identification. Thus, to say that colonial identity is ambivalent is to say that it is also potentially subversive (112).

I will start by inquiring into the ideological background of Gómez Carrillo, who is remembered as a Francophile intellectual because he studied and resided in Paris, where he wrote his chronicles and sent them to Latin American journals. According to Juan M. Mendoza, he was born to a humble family in Guatemala, had a Spanish grandfather, and defined himself in contrast to his father, a simplistic, pragmatic, and conservative man with a weak character. In his diary, the young Enrique confesses that he did not like the serious texts his father wrote: "I find a list of philosophers, chroniclers, and historians in my family. . . . Had my good father been a skeptical psychologist instead of a grave historian, he would have opened [Balzac's] *La Comedie Humaine* before my eyes."[6] This may explain that even though he dedicated himself to writing chronicles in his adult life, his mimicry does not follow the formality of those texts; rather he does his best to delight his readers in a creative way, and he might even have added social interest to his texts.

His mother was a Belgian, and he inherited some of her physical features. He was very lazy from childhood, and in France he ended up being a spendthrift, womanizing, and bohemian intellectual. He joined the Parnassians, Symbolists, Impressionists, and other French trends but ended up "proclaiming absolute artistic freedom . . . a type of literature cast in a new mould with fresh nuances and cured from all sectarianism" (Mendoza 56). His modernist works resulted from making foreign ideas his own and looking for a new way of expressing his individuality.

In Paris he adopted the ideas of Darwin, Spencer, Carlyle, Nietzsche, Taine, Renan, and Ruskin. He faithfully applied to Spanish American Modernism one of the Ruskin's concepts: that art reveals universal beauty and must be constantly reestablished. Moreover among his readings of late nineteenth-century authors, we find Pierre Loti, who visited Japan in 1885, and Rudyard Kipling, who visited that country in 1889. Loti analyzed the subjugation of Japanese women by European money in his novel *Madame Chrysanthème*; Kipling published letters about Japan's industrialization and the domination of its race by capitalistic interests from England and the United States. Gómez Carrillo selected and used these two Western images of Japan as a model for contrasting his own personal experience in that country in 1905. After reading these authors, he constantly repeats in his chronicles that Japan is not as Europeanized as Europeans say. As we can see, here a counterdiscourse is created, for Gómez Carrillo breaks loose from the European canon represented by Loti and Kipling, and although he considers himself a Westerner, he feels he has enough authority to give his own version of the state of affairs in Japan. His strategic position is ambivalent because he regards himself as a European by genealogy and education but disapproves of the Westernization of Japan. Araceli Tinajero shares this opinion in *Orientalismo en el modernismo hispanoamericano*:

> In his journey, Gómez Carrillo does not show much pleasure either toward the North Americans he runs into. It seems as though the travelers, disappointed at the sight of the Americanization/Europeanization of the Far East, wished in some cases to avoid other contemporary travelers. . . . Those changing times in which such travelers lived also allowed them to see how power roles in the relation between the Oriental and the European were reversed. Both the Chinese and the Japanese stand out [in the travel narratives] for their innovations and abilities.[7]

Gómez Carrillo's standpoint makes it evident that the Guatemalan traveler tacitly compares the process of Westernization and "modernization" of both Japan and Latin America. He begins to value Eastern achievements not for their mimicry of Western elements but as Japan's own accomplishments and triumphs compared to those of the Europeans. According to Joan Torres-Pou, these chronicles' idealized representation of Eastern delicacies, craftsmanship, artistic and architectonic production, and moral values "represents what Spurr calls the trope of resistance; that is, a trope that attacks colonial ideology."[8] This standpoint is consistent with Spanish American Modernism's rejection of Western utilitarian imperialism and the concomitant reassessment of colonized societies.

Another way of recognizing the value of Japanese culture is by writing a travelogue using Japanese literary texts and quoting Japanese scholars to show the reader an admirable world whose culture is not exactly like that of the West. For example, Gómez Carrillo translates poems, stories, legends, and historical data, adding to them a positive interpretation to highlight the value of their folkloric elements. Even though he ends up creating Modernist images of Japanese landscapes and scenery, what they reveal about the character of Japan's inhabitants draws his attention too. Kage-Fumi Ueno points out that "Gómez Carrillo's most brilliant notes were those he wrote about Japanese worldview, literature, and poems. . . . These were nothing short of his homage and admiration for Japanese animistic (polytheistic) sentiment or spirituality."[9] In appreciating Japanese animism, it might be said that he also validates Latin American indigenous syncretism, which survives since colonial times as a folkloric and religious substrate to the superimposed European Christianity.

It is also worth pointing out that Gómez Carrillo was sent to Japan as a correspondent for two important newspapers, *La Nación* of Buenos Aires and *El Liberal* of Madrid. This means that he wrote for Latin American and Spanish readers who, after seeing how the United States took control of Cuba, Puerto Rico, and the Philippines in 1898, began to fear North American imperialist expansion. This sociohistorical actuality makes Latin Americans feel both rejection from and attraction toward the modern mercantile world. On the one hand, Modernist writers seem delighted with the new luxury items arriving from all over the world, especially from China and Japan, which they find refined and exotic and which inspired aestheticism in their own work. On the other hand, these very same writers and artists became displaced by modern society as they lost their patrons and were forced to make a living and market their skills like any other worker; therefore they were depersonalized within the homogenizing mercantilist system.

Ángel Rama remarks that the growing democratization that took place alongside Modernism greatly impacted the artistic production of bourgeois and working-class bohemians, among whom Gómez Carrillo might be placed. In his view, "they were characterized by an adventurous and provocative air that had to do with the social models established by the powerful of the day"; yet when they introduced their own worldview, they succeeded in modifying the new order.[10] In this context, it would appear that these chronicles may have actually set out to prove that tradition had survived in Japan despite the rapid modernization it underwent during this early globalizing period. Latin American countries were at a similar juncture: trying to consolidate their postcolonial identity after independence, while at the same time finding themselves immersed in the mercantilist progress of the United States.

Considering that Gómez Carrillo must have been influenced also by Latin American thinkers, we cannot overlook José Enrique Rodó's *Ariel* (1900). Rodó's landmark essay was written partly in response to the U.S. intervention in the Cuban War of Independence in 1898 (redubbed "The Spanish-American War"), whereby it gained control over the last Spanish colonies in the Caribbean and became the new colonizing empire of the twentieth century. Rodó sought to boost the self-esteem of Latin Americans, who felt they were being recolonized. To that effect, as an antithetical symbol to North American cannibalistic greed and materialism, he invoked the airy spirit of Ariel (from Shakespeare's Tempest) as the embodiment of Latin America's disinterested virtue and generous humanistic values. Moreover Rodó links Latin American humanistic heritage to the classical rationality of ancient Apollonian Greece worthy of imitation (as opposed to the Roman Empire), in the same way that Gómez Carrillo considers Japan a place of moral excellence. Thus in *El Japón heroico y galante* we find chapters devoted to such subjects as the worship of the *musumes* of Yoshiwara by their parents and lovers, the heroism of the samurai avengers, the honor of swords, the religiosity of the temples, aesthetic contemplation, the concealment of misery out of respect for others, the *bushido* code of conduct linked to bravery, loyalty, patriotism, and piety, and finally, common Japanese courtesy and good humor.

As Lila Bujaldón de Esteves observes, many of Gómez Carrillo's books "are the result of compilations from among the thousands of articles he published in Spanish and Latin American newspapers."[11] Hence it is important to stress that the articles selected for *El Japón heroico y galante* in 1912 are those that help to create an idyllic and positive vision of Japan, while in the previously published collection, *El alma japonesa* (The Japanese Soul, 1907), there are also articles about the Japanese attack on the Russians in 1904, as well as their imperialist policy toward the Koreans, whom they eventually colonized in 1910. *El Japón heroico y galante* also includes rosy travel articles about Japan taken from *De Marsella a Tokio* (From Marseille to Tokyo, 1906), where Gómez Carrillo promises to write a book "that will be like the complement of this one, entitled *El alma japonesa*").[12] Curiously the chapters taken from previous editions vary only in the title, if at all. For example, the first chapter of *El alma japonesa*, titled "Los jardines" (The Gardens), is exactly the same as the eleventh chapter of *El Japón heroico y galante*, titled "Paisajes" (Landscapes), and the same is true of seven others.

Considering the structure of his books about Japan, we can see how meaningful the title *El Japón heroico y galante* truly is. These chronicles show Japan as a country admirably heroic and gallant despite the mercantilist influence of the United States. Japan is heroic for it defeated Russia after modernizing its army along Western technological lines, but it is also gallant for it maintains its Japanese soul with the traditions explained in every chapter of the book. Consequently it is a model that gives hope to Latin America, which fears losing its historical past to Western neocolonization in the twentieth century. Gómez Carrillo fashions a Japan as ideal as Rodó's Ariel. Yet his gaze is not that of the imperial traveler, and his report to the Hispanic readership is neither orientalizing nor Westernizing in any partial or manipulative way. Rather, as a Latin American, he approaches that ideal brand of Hispanic Orientalism as "a spirit of veneration and respect for the Orient."[13]

Gómez Carrillo's admiration for Japan, however, cannot produce the open and horizontal dialogue Julia Kushigian wishes for, insofar as his intention is to find an idealized Japan. Even its heroic behavior before Russia comes from the ancient samurai, and although it has adopted some superficial Western features, it is still profoundly Japanese. Writing Japan means for Gómez Carrillo an act of negotiation between intentions and expectations, on one hand, and experience, on the other:

> Undoubtedly everything is just like I imagined, but with a bit less vividness, or rather, with a bit less poetry, color, flair, rarity. . . . What is missing in this Japan, where I have lived for some hours now, for it to be the Japan of my dreams? . . . Modern books, on the contrary, had prepared me to find an Americanized Japan. And yet, this one I see, and which is very Japanese, this one I see through my window, is not my delicious, ideal Japan.[14]

Gómez Carrillo creates an ambivalent discourse about a stereotyped Japan because in his view it is neither as Americanized nor exactly as traditional as he had imagined from the pictures he had seen. It seems to him that it is a combination of both, which he represents by the smiling *musume*, proud of her Western-like beauty. She is "thin, pale, of a light, transparent amber color. She wears a pale yellow kimono, covered with white lilies, which makes her look like an allegory of spring from this land, more petite and less splendorous than Botticelli's, but no less seductive. I gaze at her enraptured, and an admirable Japan appears before my ecstatic eyes" (12–13).

Given Gómez Carrillo's Western background, beginning with his childhood in Guatemala, it comes as no surprise that he should represent Japan by a Japanese Venus. In Jacinto R. Fombona's view, "Gómez Carrillo's encounter produces an object that fits into his (and the audience's) expectations of the Japanese . . . an aesthetic encounter."[15] It is also what Stephen McKnight would call an encounter with the materialization of the divine, for "when she appears to man, she awakens in him the love of divine beauty and truth."[16] Gómez Carrillo finds the ideal of beauty and truth in a *musume*, as Rodó finds them in his ethereal Ariel. Undoubtedly he has mimicked the Western colonizing process of stereotyping, and yet, with the ambivalence of his discourse, he has also overthrown the Western Venus, given that the humanized *musume* is no less seductive and may even surpass her by virtue of her majestic, real-life exoticism. This comparison of equality reassesses the Orientalist stereotype by creating a hybrid Venus that may look Western but with a difference that accentuates her otherness. Moreover so powerful is her exotic seductiveness that in the next chapter Gómez Carrillo is compelled to go to the Yoshiwara red-light district to sleep with an *oiran*.

Gómez Carrillo narrates his meeting with the princess of his dreams in the first-person plural, as though he is inviting the voyeuristic reader to join him in a ménage à trois or become an unidentified friend who accompanies him on this adventure. In dwelling on the sweet and sensual ritual, he shares a similarly sensual experience with his readers: "The young girls stripped us of our most intimate garments. Once naked, the ritual demands that we let ourselves be bathed and perfumed, so that we may be admissible under the linen bed sheets. That is fine. The innocent hands of the *maikos* dry us. . . . What infinite series of difficulties to eventually be able to embrace the doll we chose from the lacquered showcase!" (24). Gómez Carrillo has created in his chronicles what Mary Louise Pratt would call a "contact zone" or, in Bhabha's words, a "third space of enunciation," where transculturation between Japan and Guatemala takes place.[17] Ania Loomba acknowledges that "literature is also an important means of appropriating, inverting, or challenging dominant means of representation and colonial ideologies."[18] This gendered encounter between cultures (which could be read as a parody of Malinche and Cortés) seems to express a desire to symbolically blend and identify with a non-Western Other as a mechanism of self-affirmation.

Concerning the author's preconceived imaginary, Bujaldón de Esteves points out that Japanese painting, which spread throughout France at the time, not only focused on the geisha but also on the samurai, who represents the heroic, warlike spirit of the small Japanese David that has just defeated the Russian Goliath (55). The samurai is the stereotype of the warrior vanquished by Japan's modernization in 1854. This figure of the ancient, feudal Yamato (Japan's old popular name) is recuperated at this moment to indicate the coexistence of old Japanese traditions and honor with Western modernization and utilitarianism, supposed to have already merged into cultural hybridity by the beginning of the twentieth century. Thus the Japan that Gómez Carrillo experiences is still heroic and gallant like the samurai, but it also has its Westernized Japanese Venus. The Guatemalan expatriate in Paris, a bohemian and a *flâneur* now traveling in the Orient, identifies with the Japanese and calls them brothers, for as in Bakhtin's carnival, there are no colonizers or colonized, and all are free to feel the joy of life:

> Oh, sake drinkers, people of Yamato, my yellow brethren! Could it be pos-
> sible perchance that in some previous existence we harvested grapes to-
> gether, and under the Latin grapevines our wine glasses touched? This I
> ask you because, in truth, it would seem you hesitate about our vintage jo-
> vial inebriation. And believe you not this bacchanal merriment to be only
> a vexing way of the populace. The gods themselves, like their brethren
> from pagan Olympus, sure know how to drink, laugh and dance. (203)

Pagan carnival—that great equalizer—is revalued, as its participants are compared to Greek and Roman gods. Undoubtedly this hybrid condition is shared by Latin Americans, as Westerners who at the same time keep elements from indigenous peoples, Blacks, Asians, and other human groups that form our community. In this case, the same colonial discourse that marks us as different to make us inferior also calls us equal to make us conform to the European model. The ambivalence of this discourse allows the colonized to meet the colonizer on an equal footing and form a hybrid to produce a national identity in constant transculturation. Therefore it is necessary to continue to analyze the ambivalence of mimetic stereotypes in all cultural expressions from the standpoint of both the colonizer and the colonized in order to understand the processes by which our identity is defined and which are potentially the basis for future social structures.

Notes

1. Kazue Nakamura, "Colonizer Colonized: A Critical Study of Colonialism and Modern Japanese Literature in the Light of South Pacific Literature in English," *Colonizer and Colonized*, ed. Theo D'haen and Patricia Krüs (Amsterdam: Rodopi, 2000), 27.

2. Examples of similarity between Japanese and Mesoamerican religious syncretism can be found in the following works: Madanjeet Singh, *The Sun: Symbol of Power and Life* (New York: UNESCO, 1993); Octavio Paz, *Conjunctions and Disjunctions* (New York: Arcade, 1990); and Miguel León Portilla, *Aztec Thought and Culture: A Study of the Ancient Nahuatl Mind* (Norman: University of Oklahoma Press, 1963). In his monograph on Hiroshige, the Mexican Modernist José Juan Tablada announced that he would draw a book to be titled *Aztecas y Japoneses*, but he never went through with this project.

3. Edward Said, *Orientalism: Western Conceptions of the Orient* (New York: Pantheon, 1978), 3. In the sixteenth and seventeenth centuries, whenever Europeans traveled to Asia, America, or Africa, they carried with them the expansionist spirit of the Renaissance. Their travelogues created an Orientalist discourse to justify colonization. The West appeared superior in opposition to an inferior Orient, while America was viewed as an Other, often represented by a naked woman who needs to be civilized. According to Hernán Taboada, it was thought that the moral superiority of the Indians over the Orientals stemmed from their ability to adopt European civilization: they were capable of imitating, and therefore of adopting the Christian faith. Hernán G. H. Taboada, *La sombra del Islam en la conquista de América* (Mexico City: FCE, 2004), 182. This process of redemption through the Westernization of an Orientalized America produces an identity crisis among the hybrid populations of Latin America. Such is the case of Gómez Carrillo, who, in a letter to Ramiro de Maeztu, states, "Yo no soy americano, sino español" (I am not American, but Spanish), meaning that he was more European than Native American. Quoted in Humberto Jaramillo Ángel, "Gómez Carrillo: Cuatro glosas intemporales," *Boletín Cultural y Bibliográfico* 13.1 (1970): 82.

4. Homi K. Bhabha, *The Location of Culture* (New York: Routledge, 1994), 86.

5. Mikhail M. Bakhtin, *The Dialogic Imagination* (Austin: University of Texas Press, 1998).

6. Juan M. Mendoza, *Enrique Gómez Carrillo* (Guatemala City: Tipografía Nacional, 1946), 52–53. All translations are mine.

7. Araceli Tinajero, *Orientalismo en el modernismo hispanoamericano* (West Lafayette, Ind.: Purdue University Press, 2004), 65, my translation.

8. Joan Torres-Pou, "El discurso colonial en las crónicas sobre el Japón de Enrique Gómez Carrillo," *Bulletin of Hispanic Studies* 82 (2005): 186–94; David Spurr, *The Rhetoric of Empire: Colonial Discourse in Journalism, Travel Writing, and Imperial Administration* (Durham, N.C.: Duke University Press, 1993).

9. Kage-Fumi Ueno, "Japón y Guatemala," *La Hora* (Guatemala, Weekly Cultural Supplement), December 27, 2003–January 3, 2004, 7.

10. Ángel Rama, *Las máscaras democráticas del modernismo* (Montevideo: Fundación Ángel Rama, 1985), 15.

11. Lila Bujaldón de Esteves, "El modernismo, el Japón y Enrique Gómez Carrillo," *Revista de Literaturas Modernas* 31 (2001): 56.

12. Enrique Gómez Carrillo, *De Marsella á Tokio, sensaciones de Egipto, la India, la China y el Japón*, with a prologue by Rubén Darío (Paris: Garnier, 1906), 208; *El alma japonesa* (Paris: Garnier, 1907); *El Japón heroico y galante* (Madrid: Renacimiento, 1912).

13. Julia A. Kushigian, *Orientalism in the Hispanic Literary Tradition: In Dialogue with Borges, Paz, and Sarduy* (Albuquerque: University of New Mexico Press, 1991), 3.

14. Enrique Gómez Carrillo, *El Japón heroico y galante* (Guatemala City: Editorial del Ministerio de Educación Pública, 1959), 11–12. Page numbers refer to this edition.

15. Jacinto R. Fombona I., "Writing Europe's 'Orient': Spanish-American Travelers to the 'Orient,'" *Between Languages and Cultures: Translation and Cross-Cultural Texts*, ed. Anuradha Dingwaney and Carol Maier (Pittsburgh, Pa.: University of Pittsburgh Press, 1995), 15.

16. Stephen A. McKnight, *The Modern Age and the Recovery of Ancient Wisdom: A Reconsideration of Historical Consciousness* (Columbia: University of Missouri Press, 1991), 96.

17. According to Bhabha, "it is that Third Space, though unrepresentable in itself, which constitutes the discursive conditions of enunciation that ensure that the meaning and symbols of culture have no primordial unity or fixity; that even the same signs can be appropriated, translated, rehistorized, and read anew." See Homi K. Bhabha, "Cultural Diversity and Cultural Differences," *The Post-Colonial Studies Reader*, 5th ed., ed. Ashcroft et al. (New York: Routledge, 2001), 208. *Transculturation*, a term coined by the anthropologist Fernando Ortiz in *Contrapunteo cubano del tabaco y del azúcar* (*Cuban Counterpoint*, 1940), results when subordinate, peripheral, or marginal groups select or create from materials transmitted to them by a dominant culture. See Mary Louise Pratt, *Imperial Eyes: Travel Writing and Transculturation* (New York: Routledge, 1992), 6.

18. Ania Loomba, *Colonialism/Postcolonialism* (New York: Routledge, 2002), 70–71.

CHAPTER EIGHT

The Tao of Mexican Poetry

Tablada, Villaurrutia, Paz

Erik Camayd-Freixas

The Tao that can be named is not the eternal Tao; Nameless is the origin of heaven and earth.

LAO TZU

A mapping of Asian influence on twentieth-century Mexican poetry shows three well-defined moments—early, middle, and late century—represented by the works of José Juan Tablada, Xavier Villaurrutia, and Octavio Paz. In varying degrees and styles, these poets explored a cultural approach to the East and incorporated Orientalist elements they saw as fecund for the renewal of Latin American poetry in their generations. In considering their work, I seek to illustrate the evolving nature of this influence and, I would also argue, their deepening understanding of Latin American affinity with the East.

The origins of Far Eastern Orientalism in modern Latin American poetry can be traced to the French Parnassians of the mid-nineteenth century, whose influence on Latin American *modernismo* is well documented.[1] One need only browse through the poetry of such *modernistas* as Rubén Darío or Julián del Casal to perceive their rather decorative use of Oriental elements, chosen mainly for their plastic or pleasing value: silks, lacquers, stones, porcelain, ivory, and, let us not forget, exquisite gardens, landscapes, and aristocratic beauties dressed in traditional attire and striking symbolic poses. Thus the fleur-de-lis became conjoined with the lotus flower. But beyond the surface, what *modernismo* really sought in the East was an exotic ideal of cultural refinement. Moreover the thrust of that ideal was the attainment of a heightened sensibility, a connectedness of senses and emotions whereby the *modernista's* poetic persona could be sent into deep turmoil by the slightest change in his surroundings: the color of a room, a perfume, a melody, a furtive look from the beloved.[2] Underlying the *modernista* creed was a rejection of Western rationality. Their favorite poetic device, synesthesia, or the fusion of the senses, had a remote correlation in Eastern mysticism. All this, however, may not be enough to exonerate the *modernistas* from the charge of superficiality raised against them by later poets, such as the Mexicans Enrique González Martínez and Xavier Villaurrutia himself.[3] Certainly Eastern *thought* was largely ignored or diluted, given the prestige that trendy doctrines of Western irrationalism, theosophy, occultism, and Kardacian spiritualism enjoyed among the *modernistas*.[4] Rarely too did their poetics incorporate formal or structural aspects of Eastern art and aesthetics.

José Juan Tablada (1871–1945), the first poet who will occupy our attention, was an exception within *modernismo*.[5] This is perhaps because while the rest of the *modernistas* were flocking to Paris, Tablada made his pilgrimages to Japan in 1900 and 1910. As a result, his Orientalism was less removed and exotic, more immediate and genuinely felt. The trips had a lasting effect on Tablada's poetry. His Orientalism would mature during two decades of careful reflection that led him beyond *modernismo*. In fact the next generation would include Tablada in anthologies of young Mexican poets, even though he was already in his sixties. His youthful renewal of Latin American poetry was not, like others', the product of a shift to European avant-garde aesthetics but of a slow maturation of his Asian influences. In fact he always remained a *modernista* at heart. But while decorative Orientalism declined with *modernismo*, Tablada's construction of a Mexican-Asian affinity would influence later generations.[6]

Tablada's poetry of his early period (1892–1900) sang Hindu, Arabic, East Asian, European, as well as American themes. It reflected a preoccupation with being universal which, to my mind, is one of *modernismo's* most significant contributions to Latin American poetics, marking such greats as Octavio Paz (influenced by Tablada) and Jorge Luis Borges (influenced by his Argentine *modernista* compatriot Leopoldo Lugones). Two poems from Tablada's early period are worth considering here. The first one, "La venus china," depicts an exquisitely manicured woman sipping tea from a jade cup behind her ivory fan, but "the enchantment dissipates" when the woman stands up and reveals the horrible prison of her bound feet. The second poem, titled "Japón," begins to move away from decorative Orientalism in favor of cultural substance. It sings the landscapes, artists, and warriors of the "Empire of the Rising Sun" but also its cosmogony and mythology, whose figures Tablada begins to use with the adeptness of a European poet's Greek mythological allusions: "I love your strange mythology, the unusual monsters . . . your rituals. . . . I am the bonze [Buddhist priest] of your pagodas!"[7]

The poetry of his middle period (1901–18), after his first trip to Japan, begins to discover a close affinity between Mexico and the East. Particularly the poem "Exégesis," ostensibly an interpretation of his own self, already contains the major themes of this affinity:

> Of Mexico and Asia is my soul a hieroglyphic.
> Perhaps my mother, when she bore me in her womb,
> gazed all too much at Buddhas, lotus flowers, magnificent
> Japanese art, and all that strange ships brought
> to native Pacific shores!
> That is why I love jade . . . for its dual mystery,
> for it adorned the monarchs of Anahuac and of China,
> and is only born of Mexico and the Celestial Empire.
> Bejeweled in jade, my spirit is American,
> And in the onyx vessel of my heart,
> Infusing my blood with esoteric virtue,
> Blooms a miraculous cherry tree from Japan![8]

As we can see, Tablada's initial reaction to Japan was emotional, asserting a sentimental link. But in time his poetry will become more cerebral and the intercultural link more abstract. In his poem to the Japanese painter Hokusai (1760–1849) Tablada writes:

> Hokusai painted everything.
> . . . Plant and animal
> now live upon the paper
> by the magic of his brush.
> The insects' antennae,
> the cloud, the wave, the flame,
> . . . from star to shell,
> from pearl to mud frog,
> Hokusai painted everything,
> from the larvae to the sun!
> . . . Everything you painted lived,
> be it an image or a hieroglyph. (46)

The poems of his late period (1919–30) incorporate Eastern aesthetics, structures, and forms, not just themes or decor. It was then that Tablada introduced (and adapted) the Japanese haikai into Spanish verse.[9] The haikai is a string (*renga*) of ultracompact poems, whose most popular form is the three-verse haiku. Although its tripartite form is similar to that of the syllogism in Aristotelian logic, with a premise (thesis), a predicate (antithesis), and a conclusion (synthesis), the haiku actually seeks to defy logic and reason. In the tradition of the Zen koan, each haiku presents a riddle designed to promote an illumination or sudden understanding. Its solution or meaning is not to be found in the poem itself but in the meditative silence that follows. Here are some examples from Tablada's collection, *Un día . . . Poemas sintéticos* (1919):

LA TORTUGA

Aunque jamás se muda,
a tumbos, como carro de mudanzas,
va por la senda la tortuga.

THE TURTLE

Even though she never moves,
stumbling, like a mover's cart,
down the path the turtle goes.

HOJAS SECAS

El jardín esta lleno de hojas secas;
nunca vi tantas hojas en sus árboles
verdes, en primavera . . .

DRY LEAVES

The garden is full of dry leaves;
never did I see the trees so full
of leaves, all green, in springtime . . .

LA ARAÑA

Recorriendo su tela
esta luna clarísima
tiene a la araña en vela.

THE SPIDER

Running through its web
this very bright moon
keeps the spider awake.

And from *El jarro de flores* (1922):

SANDÍA

¡Del verano, roja y fría
carcajada,
rebanada de sandía!

WATERMELON

Summer's laughter,
red and cold,
a wedge of watermelon!

In many poems, Tablada actually applies Japanese aesthetics to elements of Mexican nature. Like Hokusai, Tablada paints everything. In fact the Japanese painter becomes a model for his poetry. In such minimalist depiction of small animals and nature's species, though seemingly lighthearted, there is no simple decorative intent nor any Western moral, allegorical meaning, or fable. Underlying this aspect of the haikai is actually the Taoist and Zen tradition of seeking illumination through the contemplation of nature from a nonanthropocentric perspective—a principle that, as we shall see, would acquire new meaning in Octavio Paz.

Tablada's Orientalist masterpiece is the "Li-Po" series (*Li-Po y otros poemas*, 1920). Here his "lyrical dissociations" and "synthetic poems" are graphically reconfigured as a concrete composition where Western alphabetic writing metamorphoses into pictorial ideograms (see figs. 8.1-8.3).[10]

Xavier Villaurrutia (1903–50), the second poet to be considered, shows an indirect and rather subtle influence of Orientalism, which is typical, and therefore representative, of his generation. He belonged to a poetry group called the Contemporáneos, a group that valued the old Tablada and sponsored the young Octavio Paz.[11] Asian influences on Villaurrutia are filtered in two ways: first, he received them indirectly from Western sources like Nietzsche and Gide; second, he received them critically and selectively, because he was above all a great skeptic. Like most Contemporáneos, he abhorred all theories, systems, and schools of thought, even eclecticism.

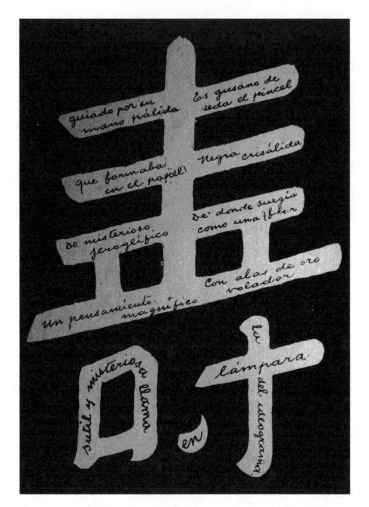

Fig. 8.1 Tablada, *Li-Po:* Guided by his pale hand / a silkworm is his brush / that formed upon the paper / the black chrysalis / of a mysterious hieroglyph / whence like a flower sprung / a magnificent thought / with wings of flying gold. / Subtle and mysterious flame / in / the lamp of the ideogram.

He was a severe critic of *modernismo* and reacted with impatience and irony toward Surrealism and other avant-garde programs. Tablada's pure Orientalist devotion would be inconceivable in Villaurrutia. Instead he internalized, digested, and transformed influences into a deeply personal style. His Contemporáneos were a group, not a school. They were not interested in either Mexican or foreign folklore, and therefore were neither regional nor universal like the *modernistas.* Instead they were accused of

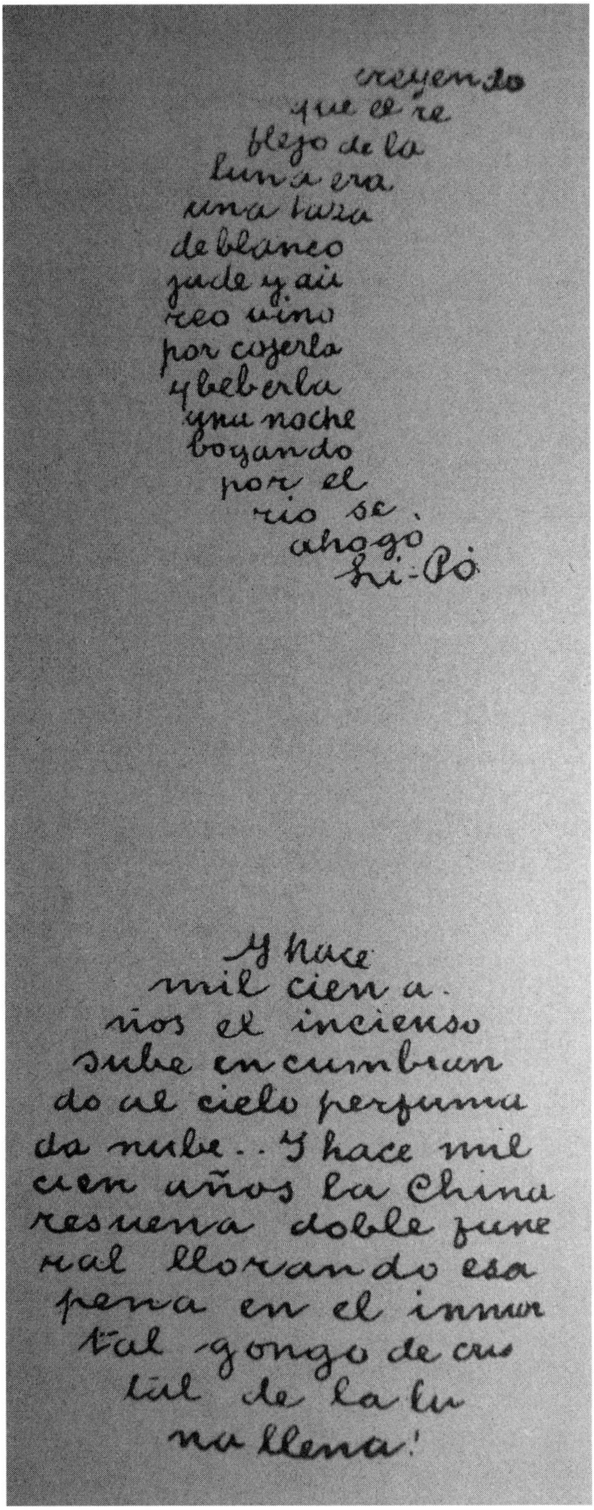

creyendo
que el re
flejo de la
luna era
una taza
de blanco
jade y au
reo vino
por cojerla
y beberla
y una noche
bogando
por el
río se
ahogó
Li-Pó

Y hace
mil cien a.
ños el incienso
sube en cumbran
do al cielo perfuma
da nube.. Y hace mil
cien años la China
resuena doble fune
ral llorando esa
pena en el inmor
tal gongo de cris
tal de la lu
na llena!

Fig. 8.2 Tablada: Li-Po, the divine, who drank the moon one night in his glass of wine . . . / Thinking the moon on the water a cup of white jade and gold wine, and wanting to reach it and drink it one night as he sailed down the river, Li-Po was drowned. / And for one thousand one hundred years incense climbs hanging on top of the sky a perfumed cloud . . . And for one thousand one hundred years China mourns its sorrow resounding a funeral twice on the timeless glass gong of the full moon!

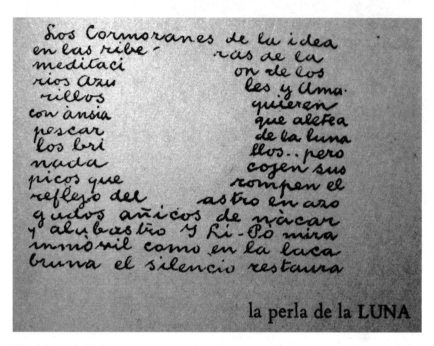

Fig. 8.3 Tablada: The cormorants of an idea at the shores of meditation on the rivers blue and yellow want with fluttering yearning to fish out the moon shine . . . but they pick up nothing in their beaks that break the heavenly reflection into quicksilvered smithereens of shell and alabaster, and motionless, Li-Po watches how, on the dark lacquer, silence restores the pearl of the MOON.

being decadent and cosmopolitan. They were connected not by ideas but by a similar sensibility: to be independently modern, to find a personal, intimate expression, where solitude and inner exile were often necessary elements.[12]

As Octavio Paz rightly observed, Tablada's lighthearted haikai become grave in Villaurrutia. And, I might add, he also departs freely from the haiku's strict metrical form while maintaining an almost Oriental conciseness. The following selections belong to a chain of poems entitled "Suite del insomnio" (74–75).

RELOJ

¿Qué corazón avaro
cuenta el metal
de los instantes?

CLOCK

What greedy heart
counts the metal
of the moments?

AGUA

Tengo sed.
¿De qué agua?
¿Agua de sueño? No.
De amanecer.

WATER

I am thirsty.
For what water?
Water of sleep? No.
Of dawn.

ALBA

Lenta y morada
pone orejas en los cristales
y en la mirada.

DAWN

Slow and purple
it places ears on window panes
and on the gaze.

Moreover Paz points out that Villaurrutia's poetry proceeds in constant dualities. Does he exaggerate Villaurrutia's Orientalism? Perhaps, but certainly the "mirror" and the "echo" were the *contemporáneos'* favorite images, for theirs was a poetry of reflection:

ECO

La noche juega con los ruidos
copiándolos en sus espejos
de sonidos.

ECHO

The night plays with the noises
copying them in its mirrors
of sounds.

ESPEJO

Ya nos dará la luz
mañana, como siempre,
un rincón que copiar
exacto, eterno.

MIRROR

It will eventually give us light
tomorrow, as always,
a corner to copy,
exact, eternal.

"The poet's sphere," said Villaurrutia, "is not only the sphere of logic, nor that of magic, but the combination and transcendence of these two potentialities of language" (113). But Villaurrutia is above all a poet of silence, concerned with the unnamed. "He taught me to distrust words," Octavio Paz recalls. In a poem entitled "Poesía" (Poetry) Villaurrutia says:

Eres la compañía con quien hablo
de pronto, a solas.
Te forman las palabras
que salen del silencio
y del tanque de sueño en que me ahogo
libre hasta despertar.

You are the company with whom I speak
suddenly, alone.
You are formed by words
that come out of silence
and from the sleep tank in which I drown
free until awakening. (76)

In "Nocturno Eterno" (1938) Villaurrutia shows that words and silence are the true protagonists of poetry.

Cuando un polvo más fino aún que el humo
se adhiere a los cristales de la voz
y a la piel de los rostros y las cosas
. . . cuando la vida o lo que así llamamos inútilmente
y que no llega sino con un nombre innombrable
. . . y es tan grande el silencio del silencio
que de pronto quisiéramos que hablara
o cuando de una boca que no existe
sale un grito inaudito
. . . o cuando todo ha muerto
tan dura y lentamente que da miedo
alzar la voz y preguntar "quién vive"
dudo si responder
a la muda pregunta con un grito
por temor de saber que ya no existo
porque acaso la voz tampoco vive
sino como un recuerdo en la garganta
. . . y porque acaso el grito es la presencia
de una palabra antigua
opaca y muda que de pronto grita
porque vida silencio piel y boca
y soledad recuerdo cielo y humo
nada son sino sombras de palabras
que nos salen al paso de la noche.[13]

When a dust finer still than smoke
adheres to the glass of the voice
and to the skin of faces and of things
. . . when life or what we uselessly so call
arrives but with an unspeakable name
. . . and the silence of the silence is so vast
at times we wished it spoke
or when a nonexistent mouth
lets out an unheard scream
. . . or when all has died
in ways so harsh and slow we fear
to raise our voice and ask "who lives"
I hesitate to answer
the mute question with a scream
for fear of finding out that I exist no more
because perhaps our voice too lives no more

but as a memory in our throat
. . . because perhaps the scream is just
an ancient word's return
that, mute, opaque, suddenly cries
because life silence skin and mouth
and solitude remembrance sky and smoke
are nothing but shadows of words
that cross our path at night.

The Nobel laureate Octavio Paz (1914–98) completes the triad, our brief haiku of Mexican poets. His early works echo Villaurrutia in compositions such as "Silencio" (1944):

Así como del fondo de la música
brota una nota
que mientras vibra crece y se adelgaza
hasta que en otra música enmudece,
brota del fondo del silencio
otro silencio
. . . y sube y crece y nos suspende
y mientras sube caen
recuerdos, esperanzas,
las pequeñas mentiras y las grandes,
y queremos gritar y en la garganta
se desvanece el grito: desembocamos al silencio
en donde los silencios enmudecen.[14]

Like from the bottom of music
springs a note
that vibrating grows and narrows
until it quiets down into another music,
so springs from the bottom of silence
another silence
. . . that rises and grows and suspends us
and as it rises down fall
memories and hopes,
small lies and big.
We feel like screaming, but in our throat
our cry's extinguished:
we end up in the silence
where silences grow mute.

Building on his predecessor, Paz's distrust of language is first the realization that in the very act of naming we shatter the primordial Oneness of reality:

Todos eran todo
Sólo había una palabra inmensa y sin revés
Palabra como un sol
Un día se rompió en fragmentos diminutos
Son las palabras del lenguaje que hablamos . . .
Espejos rotos donde el mundo se mira destrozado.

All was whole
There was only one huge word and without opposite
A word like a sun
One day it burst into minute fragments
The language that we speak, words . . .
Broken mirrors that reflect the world in pieces. (*Libertad* 90)

Thus poetry can reflect reality only by reestablishing the silent relations behind the words. As with the haiku, the music is not in the notes but in the silence that sustains them. Like his friend the American Zen musicologist John Cage, Paz would always remain "committed to the nothing in between."[15] In his commentary to his 1967 book-length poem *Blanco* (White/Target), where the text and the pages are arranged in the form of a mandala, Paz notes that he wanted to emphasize "not so much the presence of the text but that of the space which sustains it."[16]

Husserlian phenomenology and the Heidegger of *Being and Time* are also among Paz's early influences.[17] His early poetry conceives Time as a duality of movement and stasis, with images like "sudden statue," "petrified spiral," "idle vortex," and "cruel pupil, still, at the height of the vertigo" (*Libertad* 53). He also distrusts the rigidity of language that widens the distance between words and things, name and being, language and reality, a distance that grows as we lose the immediacy of childhood:

Como en la infancia cuando decíamos "ahí viene un barco cargado
   de . . ."
Y brotaba imprevista instantánea la palabra convocada
        Pez
           Alamo
              Colibrí
Y así ahora de mi frente zarpa un barco cargado de iniciales
ávidas de encarnar en imágenes.

Like in childhood when we used to play "there comes a ship loaded
with . . ."
And instantly sprang, unforeseen, the invoked word
>
> Fish
>
> Elm
>
> Hummingbird

And yet now leaving my forehead is a ship loaded with characters
yearning to incarnate into images. (*Poemas* 151)

In this poem entitled "Semillas para un himno" (Seeds for a Hymn) the
three notes, like glyphs rising from the silence of the stone, are held together by the hidden relations that abide in the empty space around them:
the "Fish" is water and movement; the "Elm" is earth and firmness; and
the "Hummingbird" is air and the conjunction of opposites: movement
and stillness at once.

Paz discovered Tablada early on, together with his haikai and his preoccupation with hieroglyphs and with the painted word:

CRUZ CON SOL Y LUNA PINTADOS

Entre los brazos de esta cruz
anidaron dos pájaros:
Adán, sol, y Eva, luna.

CROSS WITH PAINTED SUN AND MOON

Between the arms of this cross
two birds have nested:
Adam, the sun, and Eve, the moon.

PLENO SOL (EN UXMAL)

La hora es transparente:
vemos, si es invisible el pájaro,
el color de su canto.

FULL SUN (AT UXMAL)

The hour is transparent:
we see, if the bird is invisible,
the color of his song.

But Paz has also discovered Tablada's conjunction of Asia and Mexico, jade and onyx. In fact these haikus from the collection *Piedras sueltas* (Loose Stones, 1955; *Poemas* 153–56), composed after Paz's trip to India and Japan in 1952, attempt to reconstruct ancient Mexican thought with Eastern means. He writes the following haikus to Tláloc (Aztec god of rain), to the Mayan city of Uxmal, and to the Aztec mother goddess Coatlicue:

MÁSCARA DE TLÁLOC GRABADA EN CUARZO TRANSPARENTE

Aguas petrificadas.
El viejo Tláloc duerme, dentro,
Soñando temporales.

MASK OF TLÁLOC ENGRAVED IN TRANSPARENT QUARTZ

Petrified waters.
Old Tláloc sleeps, inside,
dreaming storms.

MAS TARDE (EN UXMAL)

Se despeña la luz,
Despiertan las columnas
y, sin moverse, bailan.

AFTERNOON (AT UXMAL)

The light cascades
the columns awaken
and, without moving, they dance.

DIOSA AZTECA

Los cuatro puntos cardinales
regresan a tu ombligo.
En tu vientre golpea el día,
                    armado.

AZTEC GODDESS

The four cardinal points
return to your navel.

The day pounds on your belly,
armed.

In Paz's time Mexico's ancient link to Asia began to be substantiated. Since the rise of Mesoamerican archaeology in the 1930s, evidence for such a link began to mount. Four hundred years earlier, when European cartographers still thought that the New World was but a vast peninsula of Asia, the Spanish chronicler of Mexico, Fray Bernardino de Sahagún, wrote that American Indians had migrated from the Orient by land. Today it is generally accepted that during the last Ice Age, Mongoloid tribes walked across the Beringia land bridge and populated the Americas. Once the sea level rose to form the Bering Strait, further contact may have been sparse, as Asian fishermen followed migrant seals in the ocean currents down the Pacific coast. This link is considered too early to account for cultural similarities and influences. But archaeological evidence points to much later transpacific contacts from the East, before Columbus, among already advanced civilizations. Ancient Chinese records tell of the merchant Nu Sun's voyage 2,500 years ago to a land that may well have been America. A Ming Dynasty map depicts a "ring continent" east and west of the Old World, possibly reflecting mariners' reports, trade, and explorations. All this suggests that early civilizations were more active, daring, and capable than we give them credit for. It suggests the fascinating prospect of centuries of contacts and cultural diffusion previously unaccounted for, which would force us to reconsider the whole of ancient history.

I wonder if this is what Tablada had in mind when he wrote the verses "and all that strange ships brought to native Pacific shores." The interpretation of this archaeological evidence is very much debated, as it should be. Some scientists and historians dismiss it, but for a Mexican poet wanting to justify his Orientalist poetics, it is quite enough. Moreover, in the late 1950s, new evidence for the fundamental dualism of Nahuatl (Aztec) thought came from the Mexican anthropologist Angel María Garibay and his pupil Miguel León-Portilla. León-Portilla's influential thesis, *La filosofía náhuatl* (1956), argued that what the Europeans thought were different gods, the Aztecs saw as the different manifestations of a supreme deity: Ometéotl/Omecíhual (Our Lord/Lady of Duality), male and female, creator and destroyer, a concept that resembles certain traditions in Hinduism (Rudra-Shiva) and Tibetan Buddhism.[18]

Then, in the late 1960s and early 1970s, after his return from a diplomatic post in India, Paz became deeply interested in Georges Dumézil's work on comparative mythology. Dumézil's risky but provocative theory stated that all Indo-European peoples, from India and Persia to the Celtic and Germanic world, were united by a common ideology based on a tripartite conception of the world.[19] "I am convinced," says Paz, "that something similar occurs with peoples of the Mongoloid zone, both Asian and American. This world awaits another Dumézil to demonstrate its profound unity."[20] Elsewhere he adds:

> From the perspective discovered by Dumézil perhaps someone someday will dare to study East Asian civilizations and pre-Columbian America. It would not be impossible for such a study to verify what many of us suspect: that the tendency of both civilizations to think in quadripartite terms is more than mere coincidence. . . . I believe that India is the opposite pole of Western civilization, the other version of the Indo-European world. The relation of both with the Far East is the relation between two different systems. . . . What is the other pole of the world of China and Japan? Perhaps it is pre-Columbian America.[21]

Pedro Henríquez Ureña, the great Dominican philologist exiled in Mexico, where he influenced Paz, insisted on this brilliant observation: that the Spanish Conquest "decapitated" Native American culture by severing its higher cultural forms, without which its civilization crumbled. These higher forms of Amerindian culture were the *system of thought*, including their cosmology, philosophy, and religion; and the pictographic *system of writing*, which preserved and embodied their system of thought. As a result, centuries later Latin Americans still search for their own form of expression.[22] "The life and history of our people," says Paz, "present themselves to us as a will, intent on creating the Form with which to express it and, without betraying it, to transcend it" (*El laberinto* 148).

But could these higher forms of autochthonous culture be poetically reconstructed from the standpoint of Eastern thought and writing systems? Is this what Tablada meant when he said, "Of Mexico and Asia is my soul a hieroglyphic"? It seems certain that this was Paz's most ambitious poetic and cultural project: to construct modern Mexican sensibility as that "other pole" of the Eastern world. This could not be done naïvely and lightheartedly, like Tablada, but critically and selectively, like Villaurrutia, and yet without the latter's gravity and existential angst. In contrast, Paz's poetry is not intimate and personal but detached and philosophical. He is aware of embarking on something larger than himself: "Over 2,000 years apart, Western poetry discovers what constitutes the central teaching of Buddhism: the self is an illusion, a collection of sensations, thoughts, and desires" (Conjunciones 142). Art, he maintains, is a higher form of knowledge.

The poem "Custodia" (Monstrance), referring to the transparent or glass-faced shrine in which the consecrated host is presented for adoration in the Catholic Church, illustrates Paz's syncretic handling of both

CUSTODIA

El nombre
Sus sombras
El hombre La hembra

El mazo	El gong
La i	La o
La torre	El aljibe
El índice	La hora
El hueso	La rosa
El rocío	La huesa
El venero	La llama
El tizón	La noche
El río	La ciudad
La quilla	El ancla

El hembro La hombra
El hombre
Su cuerpo de nombres
Tu nombre en mi nombre En tu nombre mi nombre
Uno frente al otro uno contra el otro uno en torno al otro
El uno en el otro
Sin nombres

Fig. 8.4 MONSTRANCE The name Its shadows The man The woman The mallet The gong The i The o The tower The well The index The hour The bone The rose The dew The grave The spring The flame The firebrand The night The river The city The keel The anchor The shemale The hegirl The man His body of names Your name in my name In your name my name One before the other one against the other one around the other The one in the other Without names

thought and writing systems. Let us not forget that the Greek etymology of *hieroglyph* is "sacred inscription." Here a series of dualities circulate in opposition: name and man, male and female, tower and well, and so on. The poem begins with "the name and its shadows," moving down to "man and his body of names," and ending in the conjunction of opposites: "the one in the other, nameless."[23] At the transparent center, beyond language, lies the sacred abyss, the unnamable space of illumination common to both Eastern thought and Western mysticism. Language cannot address it directly; it can only talk around it in a series of false opposites.

As a Latin American, Paz is aware of his own Western legacy, and for this reason his system of thought as a Mexican must itself be a conjunction of opposites, East and West. He had always pursued a confluence between his main Eastern influences (Lao Tzu, Chuang Tzu, Nagarjuna), on the one hand, and Western mysticism, poetry, and philosophy, on the other. But in the 1960s and 1970s he also became interested in structuralism, from Saussure to Lévi-Strauss.[24] Saussurean linguistics taught him that language was a communal system of signs adopted by social convention. Moreover it confirmed his belief that the relation between language and reality, between the word and the thing it names, is wholly arbitrary. Thus in the following verses Paz combines Eastern and Saussurean conceptions of language: "the world we invent among all of us / a city of signs / and at its center / the solitary *Perpetual incarnate*." Paz also realizes that language and thought, the two higher aspects of culture, are inextricably related. In the same stanza, he says, "Word of all with which we speak alone" (*Poemas* 410). Then Paz relates Saussure with Lao Tzu's principle of the contemplation of nature, which we already encountered in Tablada's haikai. Nature is contemplated in order to intuit, to apprehend by illumination, the generative principle *behind* nature: Tao, the Way. As a result, Paz begins to conceive of nature itself as a language, as another system of signs whose relation to ultimate reality is also arbitrary, precisely because it is perceived by the human senses and organized into dualities by the human intellect. That is, he conceives thought in three parallel spheres: the sphere of language; the phenomenological sphere of nature (that is, the empirical world of the senses as primary datum of "ideas" in Husserlian phenomenology); and at the still center of the vortex, the sacred sphere of ultimate reality, Tao, the Whole, the Godhead—the indivisible, the only One that is not made up of signs (and is therefore unnamable), that is, the Perpetual incarnate.

A peacock's tail the entire universe
myriads of eyes
in other eyes reflected

modulations reverberations of one single eye
one solitary sun
hidden
behind its mantle of transparencies. (*Poemas* 423)

Lévi-Strauss's structural anthropology, in turn, shows Paz that cultures too are systems of signs, that mythologies *are* languages. Thus Paz begins to see cultures as translatable, social signs as reversible or interchangeable, and history as a succession of epochs with alternating preferences for a sign or its opposite. A revolution, for instance, is just a rotation of a set of false opposites, a shift in polarity between certain positive and negative values, while the true core of social life remains unchanged. Cultural history is for Paz a "tradition of rupture" with tradition. His essays during this time will carry titles like *Alternating Current* and *Rotating Signs*. This image of rotating signs refers to the process of poetry, to the basic procedure Paz uses for showing the fallacy of opposites and suggesting the nameless, nondual Absolute: "The spirit is an invention of the body / the body is an invention of the world / the world is an invention of the spirit" (*Poemas* 496).

Consistent with his view of Art as a higher form of knowledge, Paz conceives poetry as a method of thought and constructs it as an alternative to logic. He particularly attacks the "law of the excluded middle" in logic, which states that if $A \neq B$, then C may be equal to either A *or* B, but not both. Paz would reply that opposites are a false representation of an unnamable unity. He would often say, "It is not this *or* that, but this *and* that." In his book-length essay, *Conjunctions and Disjunctions* (a title that refers to the signs for *and* [&] and *or* [∧] in logical notation), he examines the alternating epochs of celebration and negation of the body in the history of Western culture, what he calls the rotations of "body" and "nonbody." The last poem I will consider here illustrates this notion of the rotation of signs as an alternative method to Western logic.

The poem "Reversible" has been misinterpreted as meaning that it can be read backward or forward, or from the left or right column. But the meaning of its reversibility is quite different. In my translation, I have inserted punctuation in order to isolate its logical propositions.

In conclusion, modern Western Orientalism has two historical moments: the first one originates in France toward the end of the nineteenth century and is mainly aesthetic in nature; the second one originates in the United States some time after World War II and is rather spiritual in nature, partly as a reaction to existentialism's over-preoccupation with the

REVERSIBLE

En el espacio
                estoy
dentro de mí
                el espacio
fuera de mí
                el espacio
en ningún lado
                estoy
fuera de mí
                en el espacio
dentro
        está el espacio
fuera de sí
            en ningún lado
estoy
        en el espacio
etcétera

REVERSIBLE

In space
                I am;
within me,
                space;
outside of me,
                space; [A]
nowhere
        am I
outside myself
                in space; [B]
within,
        space is
outside itself; [C]
                nowhere
am I
        in space; [D]
et cetera [E]

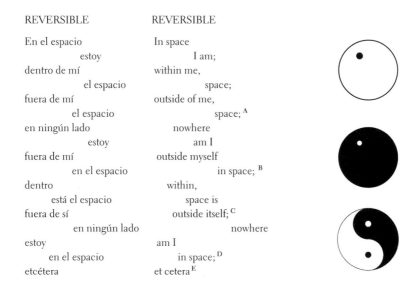

[A] Thus far, this relation can be represented logically as a Venn diagram. The white circle is space (or non-body), and the black dot is the Self (or body).

[B] Now comes the inversion:

[C] That is, from the point of view of space, space is body (the black circle) and the self is non-body (the white dot).

[D] Here, the existence of the Self is reduced to the absurd, using Nagarjuna's Middle Doctrine dialectics. [25]

[E] The "etcetera" implies the repetition and alternation of the above propositions. In Chuang Tzu's Taoism, the One originates from non-being and appears as *Yin* and *Yang*. The Self, by becoming empty, or vacuous, can reunite with the One.

Fig. 8.5 Reversible

Self. Both have influenced Latin American poetry, resulting in a deepening Orientalism, which goes from mere decor to theme, to form, to thought. But is there truly a difference between these pairs, or is it just the same old binary battle between content and form, word and idea? As Paz would say, "Thought takes the form of the vessel into which it is poured, and which it ends up corroding."[26]

His search for the East, however, is not merely aesthetic, or even philosophical. It is a matter of identity, a search for Self that is more cultural than personal. For Paz, Eastern and Amerindian cultures have a common ancestor; they are "independent germinations of a single seed" ("Asia y América" 141). His poetry is a journey back to that archetypal seed. It is, to be sure, an essentialist quest that produces one of the core master narratives of Latin American modernity: the myth of a universal culture (to supersede Vasconcelos's ethically flawed concept of a "cosmic race").

Like other master narratives of modernity, Paz's essentialist project would be both admired and subverted by the relativist skepticism of a newer postmodern generation. Wringing the swan's neck this time is José Emilio Pacheco (b. 1939), an heir to the Orientalist tradition in Mexican poetry initiated by Tablada and a winner of both the Xavier Villaurrutia and Octavio Paz awards. Marveling at the first poem he ever composed on a computer, Pacheco appears to pay tribute and, at the same time, to subvert the tradition established by Tablada's calligraphy, Villaurrutia's silent mirrors, and Paz's incarnate signs. The links between Mexico and Asia, system of writing and system of thought, being and nonbeing, are resolved in the virtual irony of Pacheco's "Haikú de la IBM" (1984):[27]

HAIKÚ DE LA IBM

Letras de luz
trazando en la pantalla
el poema que no existía.

THE IBM HAIKU

Letters of light
tracing on the screen
the poem that had not existed.

With humorous superficiality that corrodes the virtual vessel into which it is poured, Pacheco taps into the deep structure of Mexican Orientalist poetics, deconstructs its ever elusive Will to Form, and, without betraying it, transcends it. The poets come and go, but the Tao of Mexican poetry carries on.

Notes

1. Ivan A. Schulman and Manuel Pedro González, *Martí, Darío y el modernismo* (Madrid: Gredos, 1969); Julio Ramos, *Divergent Modernities: Culture and Politics in Nineteenth-Century Latin America* (Durham, N.C.: Duke University Press, 2001); Araceli Tinajero, *Orientalismo en el modernismo hispanoamericano* (West Lafayette, Ind.: Purdue University Press, 2003); Ricardo Llopesa, "Orientalismo y modernismo," *Anales de Literatura Hispanoamericana* 25 (Madrid, 1996): 171–79.

2. Rubén Darío's short story "The Death of the Empress of China," *Selected Writings of Ruben Dario* (New York: Penguin, 2005), 302–9, is a case in point. Darío's Orientalist short stories include "El rey burgués," "El humo de la pipa," "La muerte de la emperatriz de China," and "La muerte de Salomé."

3. "González Martínez . . . urges us to wring the neck of the swan, the symbolic bird of Symbolism, the indifferent, decorative, foreign swan. . . . Mexican poetry is not prone to decoration. *Modernismo*, which was exceedingly decorative, left no monsters of decoration in Mexico. Hence González Martínez's famous sonnet: *Tuércele el cuello al cisne de engañoso plumaje*." Xavier Villaurrutia, "Introducción a la poesía mexicana," *Antología: Prólogo y selección de Octavio Paz* (Mexico City: FCE, 1980), 115. Written in 1911, this landmark sonnet ("Wring the neck of the swan with the deceitful plumage") proclaims the end of *modernismo* and the beginning of the avant-garde in Latin American poetry.

4. Cathy L. Jrade, *Rubén Darío and the Romantic Search for Unity: The Modernist Recourse to Esoteric Tradition* (Austin: University of Texas Press, 1983) and *Modernismo, Modernity and the Development of Spanish American Literature* (Austin: University of Texas Press, 1998).

5. In this regard, it is fruitful to compare Tablada to his compatriot, the Orientalist *modernista* Efrén Rebolledo (1877–1929), who published his *Rimas japonesas* (1915) after serving as a Mexican diplomat in Japan. Unlike Tablada, Rebolledo remained firmly rooted in traditional *modernista* aesthetics. His *Poemas escogidos* (Selected Poems) (Mexico City: Editorial Cultura, 1939) were published posthumously with a prologue by Villaurrutia, who considers Rebolledo's overwrought verses "eternally out of vogue" and salvages but a handful of poems, particularly those written after his trip to Japan, for their more enduring "erotic passion" (12–15). "Tablada began like Rebolledo but soon discovered certain elements in Japanese poetry—verbal economy, humor, colloquial language, a love for the exact yet surprising image—which propelled him to abandon *modernismo* and seek a new style." Octavio Paz, "La tradición del haikú," *El signo y el garabato* (Mexico City: Joaquín Mortiz, 1973), 122.

6. See Rodolfo Mata, ed., *José Juan Tablada: Letra e imagen (poesía, prosa, obra gráfica y varia documental)*, CD-Rom (Mexico City: UNAM, 2008); Octavio Paz, "Estela de José Juan Tablada," *Las peras del olmo* (Mexico City: UNAM, 1968), 80–89; Adriana García de Aldrige, "Las fuentes chinas de José Juan Tablada," *Bulletin of Hispanic Studies* 60 (1963): 109–19; Guillermo Carnero, "El tránsito del modernismo a la vanguardia en José Juan Tablada: Del Japón exótico al haiku," *Las armas abisinias: Ensayos sobre literatura y arte del siglo XX* (Barcelona: Anthropos, 1989), 64–83.

7. Published in *El florilegio* (1898). As in subsequent citations, the page numbers and the division of Tablada's poetry into three periods follow José Juan Tablada, *Los mejores poemas* (Mexico City: UNAM, 1971). All translations are mine.

Amo tu extraña mitología,
los raros monstruos, las claras flores
que hay en tus biombos de seda umbría
y en el esmalte de tus tibores.
¡Japón! Tus ritos me han exaltado
y amo ferviente tus glorias todas;

¡yo soy el ciervo de tu Mikado!
¡Yo soy el bonzo de tus pagodas! (17–19)

8. Published in *Al sol y bajo la luna* (1918):

Es de México y Asia mi alma un jeroglífico.
¡Quizás mi madre cuando me llevó en sus entrañas
miró mucho los Budas, los lotos, el magnífico
arte nipón y todo cuanto las naos extrañas
volcaron en las playas natales del Pacífico!
Por eso amo los jades . . . por su doble misterio
pues ornó a los monarcas de Anáhuac y de China
y sólo nace en México y en el Celeste Imperio.
. . . exornado de jades, mi numen es de América,
y en el vaso de ónix que es mi corazón,
infundiendo a mi sangre su virtud esotérica,
¡florece un milagroso
cerezo del Japón! (45)

9. Atsuko Tanabe, *El japonismo de José Juan Tablada* (Mexico City: UNAM, 1997); Seiko Ota, "José Juan Tablada: La influencia del haikú japonés en *Un día . . . ,*" *Literatura Mexicana* 16.1 (2005): 133–44; Ricardo de la Fuente Ballesteros, "En torno al orientalismo de Tablada: El *haiku,*" *Literatura Mexicana* 20.1 (2009): 57–77; Lily Litvak, "El haikai mexicano," *Comparative Literature* 18.4 (1966): 300–311; Mark Cramer, "José Juan Tablada and the Haiku Tradition," *Romance Notes* 16.2 (1975): 530–35.

10. Published in 1918, Guillaume Apollinaire's *Caligrammes* (Paris: Gallimard, 1995) were certainly an important influence, but Tablada's fusion of Japanese pictorial aesthetics takes him beyond the French avant-garde. See also Klaus Meyer-Minnemann, "Formas de escritura ideográfica en *Li-po y otros poemas* de José Juan Tablada," *Nueva Revista de Filología Hispánica* 1 (1988): 433–53.

11. Ramón López Velarde (1888–1921), a *posmodernista*, was considered the intellectual father of the Contemporáneos generation, which included Villaurrutia's peers Jaime Torres Bodet (1902–74), Salvador Novo (1904–74), Jorge Cuesta (1903–42), Gilberto Owen (1904–52), José Gorostiza (1901–73), and Carlos Pellicer (1897–1977). See Gloria Ceide-Echevarría, *El haikai en la lírica mexicana* (Mexico City: Ediciones de Andrea, 1967); Salvador Oropesa, *The Contemporáneos Group: Rewriting Mexico in the Thirties and Forties* (Austin: University of Texas Press, 2003).

12. See Octavio Paz, "Prólogo," in Xavier Villaurrutia, *Antología* (Mexico City: FCE, 1980), 9–62. Page numbers for Villaurrutia refer to this edition. Beside theater and critical essays, Villaurrutia published the following poetry collections: *Primeros poemas* (1923), *Reflejos* (1926), *Dos nocturnos* (1931), *Nocturnos* (1933), *Nostalgia de la muerte* (1938), *Décima muerte y otros poemas* (1941), and *Canto a la primavera y otros poemas* (1948).

13. Published in *Nostalgia de la muerte* (Nostalgia for Death) (Buenos Aires: Sur, 1938).

14. Octavio Paz, *Libertad bajo palabra, 1935–1958* (Mexico City: FCE, 1960), 70. Subsequent citations refer to this edition.

15. "Entre el silencio y la música . . . hay un hombre. Ese hombre es John Cage (committed to nothing in between)." Octavio Paz, *Ladera este, The Collected Poems of Octavio Paz 1957–1987*, ed. Eliot Weinberger (New York: New Directions, 1987). See also John Cage, *Silence: Lectures and Writings (1939–1961)* (Middletown, Conn.: Wesleyan University Press, 1961) and *A Year from Monday: New Lectures and Writings* (Middletown, Conn.: Wesleyan University Press, 1969), 119; Octavio Paz, *Reading John Cage* (Purchase, N.Y.: Center for Editions, 1989).

16. Octavio Paz, *Poemas 1935–1975* (Barcelona: Seix Barral, 1979), 481. Subsequent citations refer to this edition.

17. Edmund Husserl's *Ideas* (1913) and his disciple Martin Heidegger's *Being and Time* (1927) were both translated in Mexico by the Spanish expatriate José Gaos (Fondo de Cultura Económica, 1949 and 1951). A disciple of José Ortega y Gasset, Gaos immigrated to Mexico in 1939 after the Spanish Civil War and became a mentor to an entire generation of Mexican intellectuals, including Leopoldo Zea and Octavio Paz. Husserl and Heidegger became enormously influential in existentialism, whose over-preoccupation with the self was succeeded, after the Beat Generation in the late 1950s, by a rapprochement with Eastern thought.

18. See Miguel León-Portilla, *Aztec Thought and Culture: A Study of the Ancient Nahuatl Mind* (Norman: University of Oklahoma Press, 1963).

19. Georges Dumézil, *L'idéologie tripartie des Indo-Européens*, vol. 31 (Brussels: Collection Latomus, 1958), *Mythe et epopée I-III* (Paris: Gallimard, 1969, 1971, 1973). Also see Gerald James Larson, C. Scott Littleton, and Jaan Puhvel, eds., *Myth in Indo-European Antiquity* (Berkeley: University of California Press, 1974).

20. Octavio Paz, "Asia y América," *Puertas al campo* (Barcelona: Seix Barral, 1966), 25.

21. Octavio Paz, *Conjunciones y disyunciones* (Mexico City: Joaquín Mortiz, 1969), 47–48.

22. Pedro Henríquez Ureña, *Seis ensayos en busca de nuestra expresión* (Buenos Aires: Editorial Babel, 1928), 23; "La América Española y su originalidad" (1937), *La utopía de América* (Caracas: Ayacucho, 1978), 25; *Historia de la cultura en la América hispánica* (Mexico City: FCE, 1947). In *The Labyrinth of Solitude* (1950) Paz makes a direct reference to Henríquez Ureña's ideas when he speaks of "the destruction of their temples and their manuscripts, and the suppression of the higher forms of their culture." *El laberinto de la soledad* (Mexico City: FCE, 1982), 95.

23. Octavio Paz, "Custodia," *Ladera este* (Mexico City: Joaquín Mortiz, 1969), 127.

24. See Octavio Paz, *Claude Lévi-Strauss: An Introduction* (London: J. Cape, 1971) and "El antropólogo ante el Buda," *Los signos en rotación* (Madrid: Alianza Editorial, 1971), 224–34.

25. Nagarjuna (ca. 150–250) asserted, "'Empty' should not be said, nor should 'Nonempty,' nor 'both and neither'; but they are spoken of only for the purpose of teaching" (*Mulamadhyamakakarika*, 22:11). See Kenneth K. Inada, *Nagarjuna: A Translation of his* Mulamadhyamakakarika *with an Introductory Essay* (Tokyo: Hokuseido Press, 1970); David J. Kalupahana, *Nagarjuna: The Philosophy of the Middle Way* (Albany: State University of New York Press, 1986); Frederick Streng, *Emptiness:*

A *Study in Religious Meaning* (New York: Abingdon, 1967); Jay L. Garfield, *The Fundamental Wisdom of the Middle Way: Nagarjuna's* Mulamadhyamakakarika (New York: Oxford University Press, 1995).

26. Octavio Paz, *El laberinto de la soledad* (Mexico City: FCE, 1982), 56.

27. Anthologized in José Emilio Pacheco, *Contralelegía*, ed. Francisca Noguerol (Salamanca: Universidad, 2009). Also see his earlier "Homenaje al haiku," *Desde entonces: Poemas 1975–1978* (Mexico City: Era, 1980), 104–11.

CHAPTER NINE

The Dragon's Footprints along Cuban Narrative

Rogelio Rodríguez Coronel

In his 1967 novel *De donde son los cantantes* (Where the Singers Are From), Severo Sarduy, with the grace and subtlety of his genius, brought attention to one of the most overlooked components of Cuban culture: the Chinese imprint.[1] Literary and cultural studies in Cuba, however, while having paid increasing attention to the process of transculturation between Hispanic and African cultures since Fernando Ortiz's and Lydia Cabrera's early twentieth-century studies on Afro-Cuban ethnography and folklore, have only recently, and in a most isolated way, begun to assess the Chinese presence in the formation of certain aspects of Cuban culture. Yet it is already clear that although less visible than the African, and similarly prone to generalization, the Chinese infusion should not be underestimated.

Chinese presence in Cuba has been documented since the seventeenth century. Since 1647 a few records and writs make reference to Chinese residents or attest to the sale of Chinese slaves. Such isolated events, however, are not even a prelude to the intercultural phenomena that would develop later. It was only in the second half of the nineteenth century that Chinese immigration became a large-scale lucrative enterprise, given the need to replace the African slave trade, a practice that had become increasingly stigmatized.

On July 3, 1847, the first shipment of Chinese immigrants arrived in Havana aboard the steamship *Oquendo* from the port of Macao. Thus began the regular trafficking of the so-called coolies, who became a part of the agricultural labor force under near slave-like conditions. Between 1848 and 1874, 141,515 Chinese servants, mainly from Canton Province, left their country, and 124,937 were sold in Havana. Evidently 16,578 died en route. The death toll reached almost 20 percent during the busier years.[2] Letters to the colonial government from landowners who contracted the new immigrants typically complained about the state of their cargo: Chinese settlers ravaged by scabies and generally weak from ill treatment, disease, and poor food. According to the demographer Pérez de la Riva, their life expectancy on arrival was between eighteen and twenty years. Unlike the African diaspora, they were all adult men, from the poorest areas of Guangdong and Fujian. In theory they were free, but they were reduced to slave-like conditions similar to those suffered by the Africans and were subjected to similar forms of discrimination. Like immigrants from other migratory waves, the Chinese population concentrated in the western part of the island.

After 1860 Chinese immigrants who had established themselves in California during the Gold Rush began to arrive in Cuba. They abandoned their U.S. homes because of the racist backlash against them. Unlike those of the first wave, these immigrants had access to money and arranged for their own trips to Cuba, passing through Mexico or New Orleans. In Cuba they were called "Californians." They occupied a special place in the social pyramid. While they were also discriminated against by the white Spaniards and *criollos*, their having capital, which they quickly invested in businesses and services, entitled them to a certain lifestyle and a measure of integration into the island's colonial society. This was noted early on in the literature of that period.

The breakthrough of the "California" Chinese character in Cuban fiction came with *Carmela* (1887) by Ramón Meza, the most notable of late nineteenth-century Cuban novelists. Its plot is similar to that of *Cecilia Valdés* by Cirilo Villaverde. Both concern a Creole woman and her unfortunate love life caused by racial prejudice in colonial society. Carmela, the illegitimate daughter of a mulatto woman, Doña Justa, whom everyone, including Carmela, believes is only her godmother, falls in love with a high-society Spaniard, Joaquín, whose parents send him to the United States to prevent his marriage to Carmela, who is pregnant with his child. After giving birth, Carmela decides to accept the love of Cipriano Assam, a Chinese merchant of good financial standing, "a very fine gentleman, very dignified, pleasant, considerate," according to Miss Chucha, a friend of the family: "He was only Chinese in appearance, in all other respects he was a decent person." Meanwhile Joaquín returns to Havana to marry a wealthy cousin. Carmela goes to the wedding and tries to stop the ceremony by showing her child to Joaquín, but she does not succeed. The deceived Assam commits suicide.

Meza's realism affords a glimpse at some interesting sociological aspects of Assam's makeup as a character, with significant implications for the narrative's social structure. Next to Justa and Carmela, there is the Black man Tocineta (Bacon), whose nickname itself describes this domestic servant employed by the house governess. Tocineta is secretly in love with Carmela. This character, who at the end of the novel remains Carmela's only refuge, complements the depiction of Havana's racial and economic stratification in the second half of the nineteenth century. Hegemonic racist values remain in place: Assam is appropriate for Carmela only after it becomes obvious that marriage with Joaquín is impossible. Doña Justa resigns herself to the fact that her daughter, even though she could pass for White, cannot climb the social ladder. However, Assam and Tocineta are not seen as equals given their differing economic standings. Assam has capital and can offer Carmela and her son all kinds of comforts, but he must adopt Cuban family values manifested in religion. At a minimum, the Chinese immigrant must become Catholic, since he can never become White.

This demand from Carmela and Doña Justa reveals the process of transculturation that began with the presence of Chinese immigrants, mostly male, who could find a mate only among mulattas in the lower classes. From this union arose the Cuban Chinese mulatto and mulatta—privileged phenotypes in these interracial relationships. Examples of this mixture include the painter Wilfredo Lam, the novelist, poet, and essayist Severo Sarduy, and the poet Regino Pedroso, author of *El ciruelo de Yuan Pei Fu: Poemas chinos* (Yuan Pei Fu's Plum Tree: Chinese Poems, 1955), an excellent example of poetic interculturalism and one of the most important books in Cuban poetry.

In contrast to the African experience, Chinese immigrants were adults with an already formed consciousness. As nominally "free" men they could pay for private lodging, thus allowing for intimacy. Then the arrival of the "Californians" structured the Chinese community along economic class lines and allowed for the establishment of power relationships through the founding of different kinds of nominally secret societies—clannish, sporting, and cultural.[3] These were particularly strong at the beginning of the twentieth century, when, in addition to preserving the language and customs from the continent, members of the Chinese bourgeoisie controlled the community's business and political relations. Thus the Chinese community was much more insular than the African, and this allowed for a much faster intercultural exchange through superimpositions rather than the hidden process of transculturation. However, in the area of religious syncretism, there are some significant examples: in the Catholic Iglesia de la Caridad church in Havana's Chinatown, one can visit a Chinese image of Cuba's patron saint, the Virgen de la Caridad, decorated like Oshún for the believers in the Regla de Ocha Afro-Cuban cult, as well as an image of San Fancón, nonexistent in Catholic hagiography but linguistically Christianized and interpreted as Changó by the Santeros.[4]

Meza, given his *modernista* sensibility, could not help but notice and take advantage of the insertion of the Asiatic world into Havana's space. From the beginning of the novel, there is in Doña Justa's living room "a little Chinese basket of paper flowers"; another "Chinese basket" hung from the lamp, and Carmela uses a "Chinese fan." Later, in Assam's house, the narrator dwells on the "folding screens, lampshades, and sandalwood boxes." He even gives a detailed description of the *charada china* or Chi Fa, surely a recent import: "Behind the counter, nailed to the wall, there was a sort of map, and clumsily painted on it, Chinese-style, there was a large puppet with up to thirty-six figurines scattered like ulcers all over its body."[5]

The riddles of this lottery-like game have a dazzling metaphorical significance. Its unusual analogical leaps condense the full figurative alchemy of Chinese culture. Seemingly nothing more than a game, the Chinese charade actually holds the knowledge of transmutation, the alpha and omega of Chinese philosophy. Meza does not entertain any such considerations, nor does he offer a glimpse at the charade's meaning, and yet this is perhaps the most far-reaching and suggestive image of the profound significance the Chinese footprint has in Cuban culture.

Writing from New York during the same time frame, José Martí sent his chronicle "A Chinese Funeral" to *La Nación* in Buenos Aires. This piece is one of the finest examples of Martí's profound artistic and ethical sensibility. Its topic is the funeral of Li-In-Du, a general in the battle against French colonialism and a strong opponent of China's imperial dynasty. Martí's chronicle honors the man who fought for liberty and country and who, in the United States, "scraped a living selling trinkets from his homeland, which along with washing clothes and serving food, is all the Chinese are allowed to do here. For those who work in the mines or the railroad are hunted down like wild animals, shot out of their shacks, and burned alive." Even though he did not set out with this goal in mind, Martí subsumes the various reasons the "Californians" had to migrate to Cuba: "The Yellow man has the eyes of a hunted animal: he goes around looking back and forth, taking precautions against any offense. He goes around blaspheming under his breath, his eyes full of fire. He walks around with his head bowed, as if he needed to be pardoned for living."[6]

I do not doubt that Martí selected the subject matter of this chronicle for its expressive possibilities, above all from a pictorial point of view, but also for the opportunity for reflection it offered him. His prose exhibits a radiant chromatics, akin to the *modernista* sensibility of the times, which to a great extent he helped define. Moreover his universal humanism brings forth the spiritual sap of Chinese culture, the most enduring meaning of an ancient wisdom. Martí shows empathy for the Chinese general because the departed "does not believe in images, nor in any god beyond the pure creative Tao, which is all and one, and begot the two, and from two engendered three, and from three the world." He believed "in the aerial community, in the warrior's rest, in the eternal oneness and its transfigurations, and in a final seat, after fulfilling one's duties, on the mountain of Tao: but all of this down here, and free!"[7]

Martí's chronicle is a gateway to Cuban literary modernity, the soil from which springs, for example, José Lezama Lima's "Las eras imaginarias: La biblioteca como dragón" (Imaginary Eras: The Library as a Dragon, 1965), an essential text for understanding the poetic world of the author of *Paradiso*, a novel that crystallizes like no other Cuba's intercultural density.

The Cuban wars of independence from Spanish colonialism (1868–78, 1895–98) facilitated social integration, but it was a difficult and even tragic process: in the 1850s Cuba had the world's highest suicide rate (one in four thousand inhabitants), attributable exclusively to Chinese victims.[8] Many "coolies" and "Californians" fought against the Spanish: the former to rise above indentured servitude; the latter for the same economic reasons as the Creole bourgeoisie. Some attained a high rank in the Mambí liberation army; Captain José Tolón and Commander Bu were even granted the right to be elected president of the Republic, according to the Constitution of 1901.[9] An obelisk commemorating the fallen soldiers is inscribed, "There was no Cuban-Chinese deserter, nor was there any Cuban-Chinese traitor." This relative social integration did not mean, however, that racial prejudice had ceased. In the first decades of the Republic, the Asian (including Japanese) influx continued and was particularly large between 1920 and 1930.

This was the backdrop for one of Alfonso Hernández Catá's short stories, published in a 1923 issue of *Social*, a premiere Cuban magazine, and later collected in *Piedras preciosas* (1927). The story "Los chinos" is extremely significant from a literary-historical standpoint for marking the transition from naturalism to the new avant-garde aesthetics. Yet it is also salient as a sign of the tensions that prevailed in intercultural relations. Hernández Catá's task is to describe the slave-like exploitation of Chinese farm workers. In the process, he also depicts horizontal class-based contradictions stemming from Cuban perceptions of Asian otherness. The story revolves around a group of workers of different ethnicity: Black Jamaicans, Black Cubans, Germans, Spaniards, Creoles, Haitians, Italians, and others. Stirred by a mulatto from the western part of the island, they decide to strike for better wages. After a few days, their exploiters bring in a group of Chinese workers to replace the insubordinate. Stuporous and thirsty for revenge, the strikers, who did not believe the Chinese could handle the work, were again instigated by the mulatto leader into poisoning the Chinese workers' coffee. To the narrator's surprise, after the poisoning, an "absurdly identical" batch of Chinese laborers appears, making it seem as though the poisoned had come back to life. The social conflict is intensified aesthetically by the strangeness of the Chinese "resurrection."

Bordering on expressionism, the story's atmosphere is rarified by its time-space indeterminacy and the absence of proper names. The narrator sketches collective entities differentiated through a parallel comparison of traits. The strikers, though ethnically diverse, share similar values. The monolithic crew of Chinese workers appears strange, due to their sheer endurance. We are presented with a clash of cultures, opposites to a certain extent, and yet subjected to the same socioeconomic determinants. The Chinese are sketched from the resentful, discriminatory gaze of the other side, and not only from the narrator's. All of this contrasts with the deep structure of the text, conceived from a Chinese perspective.

In its constituent parts, narrative perspectives, and incidental allusions, the story is structured by the number three and then combined in parallel with the two sets of workers. As in Tao, it mirrors the principles of Chinese cosmology, yin and yang, and the three elements that make up the One: sky, earth, and humanity (the *xun-zi*, the universe as a triad). As we know, the *I Ching*, the classic text of Confucianism, is composed of sixty-four hexagrams, each formed by a pair of three parallel lines or trigrams. Continuous lines signify yang, the active principle; discontinuous lines represent yin, the passive principle. All that exists contains yin and yang in integrative tension, but one can be transformed into the other, according to the shifting point of view; hence the *I Ching* is known as *The Book of Changes*.

In the story, the "Westerners" (non-Chinese) initially appear as yang (strong, vigorous, active), while the Chinese are considered yin (small, pale, thin) and described as "puppets . . . yellow macaques . . . good only at selling in their little city stores . . . excellent for cooking in their cheap restaurants, or for washing and ironing with grace. . . . For women's work, great! But to sweat under the sun for eight hours, bore through iron, rip and plane tree trunks almost harder than iron, you need real men!"[10] Yet to the Westerners' amazement, the Chinese not only can do the work, but they have more resilience and accomplish anything they set out to do. They changed from yin into yang. After being rendered passive again in death through active poisoning, they return once more as yang in the final transformation: "And with the diligence of ants, before my crazed eyes, they began to work."

"Los chinos" is considered a gateway to the avant-garde in Cuban narrative for its expressionistic atmosphere, its focus on the absurd and contradictory, and its nonregionalist universality, all of which is based on an intercultural texture whose dominant principle is constituted by the signs of ancient Chinese culture. The spell this symbolic universe casts, the wisdom expressed through those adversaries that contain each other, and the signification issuing from such interplay of transmutations, all contribute to the aesthetic shift from decorative *modernismo* to the radical avant-garde.

When disparate convergences cross in the tapestry of popular transculturation, they become incentives for discursive transformation. In Cuba, and across the Caribbean, African sources were privileged for their vigorous presence, while Asian sources were absorbed in a subtler manner, around the edges, as it were. Within the literary canon, an eloquent example of syncretic assimilation of Chinese culture can be found in the works of José Lezama Lima. Lezama makes countless allusions in his works to philosophers like Lao-Tzu and Confucius, as well as poets, painters, and writers from ancient China. His admiration for Confucius, for example, is evident from the title of his collection of essays *Analecta del reloj* (Analect of the Clock, 1953), in homage to the work of the Chinese master. In his "Delphic Course" he introduced young writers to the reading of *I Ching*.[11]

The poetic, narrative, and essayistic works of Lezama, an intercultural totality par excellence, meander toward his opera magna, his great novel *Paradiso* (1966), the highest achievement in Cuban narrative, where his substantive understanding of Chinese culture seeks communicating vessels with the whole of ancient Western knowledge. His earlier stories, which he regarded as mere exercises for crafting a writing style, already evince the fundamental principles of his narrative: the concretion of imagery; his use of the enigmatic as a germinating center of parallel or diverging planes that enable his apparent self-referentiality; and his ability to reveal, through symbol or allegory, the deeper substrates of existence. They already reveal the compositional integration of dissimilar cultural symbols and the possibility of knowledge in and through the image.[12] These stories, and even those that appear paired with his poems, are simply bursts of brilliance that prepare the conquest of a much greater space, a cosmologic quantity: *Paradiso* and *Oppiano Licario*, his unfinished posthumous novel.

"Decapitation Games" (1941) was conceived as a Chinese riddle, in which magic and power, image and reality, transgression and authority, are confronted in the circularity of yin and yang, and further combined with a symbolic dimension that points to the three cards that make up the Tarot's Greatest Secret: the Wizard, the Emperor, and the Empress, along with their multiple positive and negative meanings.[13] Wizard Wang Lung is in love with Empress So Ling and covets the throne. He performs an illusion that consists in decapitating a young woman. Emperor Wen Chiu orders the trick done on the Empress, imprisons the Wizard, and urges So Ling to free him. On their journey of escape, Wang Lung abandons So Ling, who falls into the hands of the bandit El Real, an enemy of the Emperor. After a series of betrayals, imprisonments, and skirmishes, the Wizard decapitates the Empress and dies. The Emperor finds them dead, goes mad, and kills himself. El Real returns, merges his troops with the Imperial Army, finds the three bodies, and exhibits them for three days before incinerating them. The new Emperor governs for fifty years. He entreats each wizard who arrives at his court to perform the decapitation act on his head, though the ruse has become obvious. Upon his death, his corpse is laid out for three days. On the third day, he is left alone.

Two later essays, "Las eras imaginarias: Los egipcios" (1961) and "Las eras imaginarias: La biblioteca como dragón" (1965), retrospectively shed light on the story. In the former, Lezama establishes a synonymy between the Tarot and the *I Ching*, both being "conjectural formulas to rip out of the mystery *another* formula that needed to be deciphered. Tarot was the anaphora of the word *rota* [in Latin, *wheel*] with a *t* at the end, indicating that serpentine circle, which unfolds, coils, and divides infinitely to penetrate into the invisible."[14] In the second essay, the author complements the image: "One of the glories of the *I Ching* is to teach us to scrape, with a burning spike, its incoming tail, earth or yin, in order to reach its outgoing tail, sky or yang" (139). This essay is Cuban literature's most important text on Chinese cosmology. It elucidates the principles that the *Tao Te Ching* by Lao-Tzu and the *I Ching* have contributed to Lezama's poetic system, including Lezamian categories such as "Stellar Eros," "Eros of Remoteness," "Concurrent Chance," and "Oblique Experience." What excited Lezama about the *I Ching* is the protean dimension of the trigrams in the concretion of images through successive transmutations:

> *I Ching*, the book of books, *The Book of Changes*, where Chinese wisdom's most essential concepts are expressed, one of the most daring books that exist, with its formulas for penetrating death, the combinations of chance, and the unfinished counterpoint of what is to come . . . in it the Chinese specify the onset of chronology, the separation of earth and sky, the mythic and the historic, remoteness as the image of the creative source. (111)

There are many possible approaches to *Paradiso*, a text that opens many provocative roads to understanding while at the same time resisting comprehension. It is impossible to cover here all of the areas of the novel that invite analysis. I will therefore select only one central motif: the death of the protagonist's father and the recovery of his image.

Paradiso tells the story of José Cemí's journey, from his birth until he reaches his full stature as a poet, his conquest of the image. The protagonist traverses three stages: the first, which Lezama calls "placental," deals with Cemí's infancy and family history (chapter 1–7); the second, the "fall," represents his sally into the world and his learning about sexuality, the political world, and friendship (chapters 8–11); the third relates Cemí's initiation into poetic creation (chapters 12–14)—that is, paradise, fall, and redemption into another paradise recovered by the image. The central force that impels him in this trajectory is the death of his father, whose absence—emptiness—must be filled by the poetic image, victorious over time and the ephemeral. This absence/presence becomes the Tao of the creative process. In his essay on the *I Ching*, Lezama attempts to define this notion:

> While Taoism in its fullness considered Tao as the cipher for infinite transformations, for the road from non-being to being, from remoteness to image, it existed as the root of every vital principle or efficacious nameless. Efficacious for being the absence that generates presence and the presence excluded from absence, which acts as image. . . . But the Tao is not a tree, it is not the fruit, Tao is the creative space, which comprises the polarization of the embryo and the image. (113)

There is an extremely revealing passage in chapter 7 of *Paradiso*: Rialta, whose name alludes to the arched Rialto Bridge in Venice, was playing jacks with her children, sitting in a circle, engrossed, when all four gazes met in the center of the circle. "A sudden animism began transforming the tiles, as if that inorganic world were becoming transfused into the receptive cosmos of the image" (162).[15] Little by little, in snippets, the image of the late Colonel José Eugenio Cemí began to take shape. The basis for that moment of epiphany is thought of as the meeting of the stellar and the earthly in their continual mutations; the circle creates a space of enchantment where the image is revealed. It is the Tao.

The enigma of this apparition is elucidated through the hexagrams alluded to by the numbers in the passage: there are four participants (Rialta and her three children); in the progression of the game of pickup jacks, Rialta is approaching number 12, Violante had reached 7, Eloísa 3, and José 5. The most revealing hexagrams are those pertaining to Rialta and José Cemí, characters crucial to the semantic level of the novel.

The meaning of the hexagrams results from a pattern in the mother's game, which is the cause of the mutations of space and the coming forth of the image. Rialta was able to collect eleven jacks and tries to take hold of the next; that is, she is in transit between hexagrams 11 and 12, opposing hexagrams that indicate Peace (T'ai) and Stagnation (P'i).[16]

The colonel's death had deeply affected family life: harmony and security were ruptured, happy times were gone, it was the loss of a guiding center, but family values were preserved in the privacy of Doña Augusta's house. His death marks a period of stagnation in the changing fate of the family, especially the son's.

In this situation José Cemí's hexagram is clarified, 5: "The Wait (The Nourishment)" (Hsü).[17] It is not yet time to break out into his outer life, though it will not be long. It is just time for his first "nourishment," that inner strength that the search of a coded destiny requires. Only then will it be favorable to "cross the great waters" that are approaching. It is a preparatory time for the fulfillment of a purpose.

From a structural point of view, this chapter marks the end of the "placental" stage and the transition to the "fall," Cemí's sally out into the world, his descent into hell (chapter 8) in order to begin his uphill road to becoming a poet, up until the conquest of the image fixed in memory.

All references to Chinese culture in Lezama's works are part of an integrative macrocosm that finds its center of gravity in Christian asceticism: the unitive way. The oldest books of wisdom, from the Egyptian *Book of the Dead* to the *Popol Vuh* of the Mayans, and above all the Hebrew Bible, nourish his Catholic hunger for knowledge and expression, for questions and answers, harbored within the most fertile Cubanness. It is always possible to isolate one strand, as I have done, but it is undeniable that Lezama's true alchemy as a writer is to be found only in that multiplicity of cultural referents he unifies in his writing.

An heir to Lezama, though more carnivalesque, Severo Sarduy continues the exploration of cultural hybridity and its potentialities for an evolving image of Cubanness.[18] Evidence of this inheritance is found, as a tribute, in Sarduy's novel *Maitreya* (1978), whose protagonist, the mystical cook Luis Leng, was once a minor character in Lezama's *Paradiso*. Sarduy's search for cultural crossings had already attained foundational significance in *De donde son los cantantes* (1967), a novel in which caricature and parody play a central role in articulating, across the body of the text, the different layers that have come to characterize Cuban culture.[19] In his collection of essays *Escrito sobre un cuerpo* (Written on a Body, 1969), he states his objective: "A Cuban novel should bring to light all of the strata, show all of the 'archaeological' planes of superimposition—I could even classify them into narratives, for example: the Spanish, the African, and the Chinese—and arrive at the Cuban, where all of them meet, in their coexistence within the volume of the book."[20] As such, his writing promotes a disarticulated reading, distanced from the immediate social context by its appeals to ethnocultural archetypes, to a mythic, symbolic dimension that firms up its texture by means of the ludic and connotative capabilities of language. The referent for his representation of the Chinese archetype is the Shanghai Theatre in Havana's Chinatown, a unique sociocultural space in the Cuban capital throughout the first half of the twentieth century.

Havana's Chinatown began to emerge toward the end of the nineteenth century as a result of racial segregation, the need to preserve a communal identity, and the concentration of a large population on the western side of the island. Restaurants, stores, associations, bordellos, and theaters began to appear, making for a socially stable community, thanks to the relative prosperity of the "Californians." We know that by the 1870s there was already a Chinese theater.[21] Havana had two opera houses at the time, the Cantonese opera being the more popular. Theatrical production developed considerably in the Chinese community during the first three decades of the twentieth century. Several Chinese opera companies came to Cuba during this period; some of them directly from Hong Kong. The most famous theater among men up to the 1940s was the Shanghai, which featured six erotic shows per week. Sarduy could not have chosen a more emblematic setting as an opening for his novel.

De donde son los cantantes is composed of an *introito*, "Curriculum cubense," and three "pieces" that are essentially "acts" of the same "play": "Next to Rosa's River of Ashes," "Dolores Rondón," and "Christ's Entrance into Havana." Each act symbolizes the branches that merge in Cuban culture. The first one points to the Chinese, the second to the African, and the third to the Hispanic, yet not to any purity of sources but rather to the superimpositions and contaminations among them, and even with others outside their immediate realm.

In "Next to Rosa's River of Ashes," a spoof of Chinese opera, Sarduy's writing reveals the ritual of transfiguration, the transvestism of original qualities in a new world of relations. "Dolores Rondón" develops like a farce full of references to republican politics, dramatizing the adventures and misfortunes, the rise and fall of a mulatta from Camagüey, the legitimate daughter of Oshún, next to the politician Mortal Pérez. Its discursive modulations reproduce the sociolinguistic strata as well as the rhetoric of the period in a parody that borrows its topic from the country verses on the mulatta's tombstone.

More than a tragedy, "Christ's Entrance into Havana" is a sort of *Via Crucis* or *Auto Sacramental*, a satirically pious allegory about being Hispanic. The story begins in medieval Spain and continues with the pilgrimage of a Christ made of rotting wood, traveling from Santiago de Cuba to Havana amid tribulations, anachronisms, the metamorphosis of the landscape, and a rarified reality that ends with a barrage of bullets: the end of an era, the Apocalypse. The same characters run through the different stories: Mortal Pérez appears as the general in the first act, as a politician in the second, and as a young lover in the third—One and Triune, as though to string together the novel's totalizing parable. Two others, Auxilio and Socorro, are in constant transformation. At the center, Nothingness molds its kingdom, filling the void delimited by the successive masks of a Cuban *being* in need of historicity.

The peculiarity of Sarduy's narrative discourse stems from the construction of a universe in which the ritual of metamorphosis—a joyful multiplicity of superimposed masks—erases the logocentric limits of human understanding to place the reader in a new state of comprehension.

The fragmentary, discontinuous composition of the text, projected onto divergent spatial planes with differing degrees of opaqueness and transparency, finds its unity in the syncretic nature of the theatrical image. "Syncretic" is not here a mixture or fusion that leads to a paradigm of hybridity but rather the constant interrelation of the diverse; hence the successive masks, metamorphoses, transvestisms. This syncretic character gives the novel its sense of ritualizing an experience that, in principle, is historical but ultimately performs its artistic transfiguration through the recomposition of cultural signs. The purposeful deconstruction of the sequential storyline and the reordering fixed in the writing are underscored by the constant self-reflexivity of the literary discourse, the flaunting of its literariness as sacralizing verbal material. It is the linguistic sign exhibiting itself in its rituality.

Theater, ritual, transvestisms, masks, metamorphoses, and changes are visible traces of Chinese—or more extensively, Oriental—culture in the literary creation of Severo Sarduy. This begs an inquiry into the author's explicit poetics. His references in this regard are few but significant.

In *Simulación* (1982), a crucial essay for understanding his literary method, Sarduy reflects upon essential questions in art: "Who simulates (or copies), from where, why? What urge impels the sophist toward mimesis, what compulsion for disguise, for appearing-other, what will-to-representation, to launch a desire into the world of visible proportions, subverting the model's original proportions so that their imitation appears real?" He responds:

> In the West, or in that outline of its technique that is the Platonic dialogue, we find nothing on this question other than answers that are too immediate and assertive, too affirming of presence. In the East, it would be said that knowledge itself is a bodily state, that is, a compound being, a simulation of being—of being *that* knowledge—which cannot but raise the awareness that the nature of every being is simulation—by virtue of manifesting itself as *that* being. . . . Beyond the knowledge that can be possessed—in the same way that we possess languages and things—we find in the East, at the center of the great theogonies— Buddhism, Taoism—not a fullness of presence, whether god, man, or logos, but a generative vacuity whose metaphor and simulation is the visible universe, and whose true understanding is experienced as a liberation. It is vacuity, or the initial zero, which in its mimesis and simulacrum of form projects the one, whence issue all the myriad series of numbers and things, as in a primordial big bang, not of an atom of hypermatter—as present-day cosmological theories postulate—but of pure non-presence, which cross-dresses as pure energy, engendering visible reality with its simulacrum.[22]

He then supports his assertion with a footnote citing François Cheng's explanation about vacuity and yin-yang in his book *Vide et plein* (Empty and Full),[23] as well as the definition in the great Taoist books of wisdom: the *Tao Te Ching* (chapter 40) and the *Chuang-Tzu* (chapter on "Heaven-Earth"). It is significant that these citations appear at the center of the body of the essay, as though a culmination of the dragon's imprint.

In Chinese mythology, the dragon is the symbol of supreme spiritual power, of the meeting of heaven and earth, of knowledge. Also, according to popular belief, it brings rain to the harvest. No doubt: it is enough to see its imprint on five Cuban writers.

Notes

Author's Note: This essay was originally published as "La huella del dragón en la narrativa cubana," *Temas* 30 (Havana, 2002): 99–108. It has been translated here by Erik Camayd-Freixas and Lucas Katz.

1. Severo Sarduy, *De donde son los cantantes* (Mexico: Joaquín Mortiz, 1967).

2. Juan Pérez de la Riva, *Demografía de los culíes chinos en Cuba (1853–74)* (Havana: Biblioteca Nacional, 1967).

3. José Baltar Rodríguez, *Los chinos de Cuba: Apuntes etnográficos* (Havana: Fundación Fernando Ortiz, 1997).

4. The prayer to San-Fan-Con begins, "Oh, All-powerful Saint of all of China, Supreme Emperor of the Heavenly Empire, I turn to thee so that this evil that plagues me might be banished through this prayer that invokes thy name, SAN-FAN-CON. Bless me in body and soul so that I may be as generous as thou art." An offering of three sandalwood candles is recommended. About the origin of San-Fan-Con, see Baltar Rodríguez, 182–85.

5. Ramón Meza, *Carmela* (Havana: Editorial Arte y Literatura, 1978), 145.

6. *La Nación*, December 16, 1888, in José Martí, *Obras completas* (Havana: Editorial de Ciencias Sociales, 1975), 12:77–83. Also see 9:281–82 for another of Martí's texts in which he denounces the terrible situation of the Chinese in the United States.

7. Ibid.

8. See Pérez de la Riva.

9. About Chinese participation in the wars of independence, see Juan Jiménez Pastrana, *Los chinos en la historia de Cuba: 1847–1930* (Havana: Editorial de Ciencias Sociales, 1983).

10. Alfonso Hernández Catá, *Cuentos y noveletas* (Havana: Letras Cubanas, 1983), 48. For a detailed structural analysis, see Sergio Chaple, "Tradición y modernidad en la cuentística de Alfonso Hernández Catá: La estructura literaria de 'Los chinos,'" *Estudios de narrativa cubana* (Havana: Ediciones Unión, 1996), 13–45.

11. Manuel V. Pereira, "El Curso Délfico," in José Lezama Lima, *Paradiso*, critical ed. (Madrid: Archivos, 1988), 598.

12. Cintio Vitier, "Introducción del coordinador," *Paradiso*, xxi; Rogelio Rodríguez Coronel, "Los cotos narrativos de Lezama Lima," *Crítica al paso* (Havana: Ediciones Unión, 1998).

13. José Lezama Lima, "Juego de las decapitaciones," trans. Suzanne Jill Levine and Rachel Philips, *Fictions* 6.2 (1981).

14. José Lezama Lima, In *La cantidad hechizada* (Havana: UNEAC, 1970), 102–3. Page numbers refer to this edition.

15. José Lezama Lima, *Paradiso* (Madrid: Archivos, 1988). Page numbers refer to this edition.

16. For the interpretation of the hexagrams, I am using D. J. Vogelmann's Spanish translation of Richard Wilhelm's German edition, *I Ching: El libro de las mutaciones*, 5th ed. (Madrid: EDHASA, 1976). The *Fortune* for Peace states, "Peace. The small takes leave, the great arrives. Good fortune! Success!" The *Image* is "Heaven and Earth come together: The image of Peace. The sovereign so divides and completes the cycle of Heaven and Earth. He fosters and orders the gifts of Heaven and Earth, and in so doing he helps his people." The *Fortune* for Stagnation states, "Stagnation. Evil men

favor not the noble man's perseverance. The great takes leave, the small arrives." The *Image* is "Heaven and Earth do not come together: The image of Stagnation. Thus the noble man withdraws and takes refuge in his inner worth, hoping to evade difficulties. He does not allow others to honor him with money."

17. The *Fortune* of this hexagram states, "The Wait. If you are true, you will have light and success. Perseverance brings about good fortune. It is favorable to cross the great waters." The *Image* is "Clouds rise to the sky: The image of Waiting. This is how the noble man eats and drinks, and stays calm and good-humored."

18. See Severo Sarduy, "Un heredero," *Paradiso*, 590.

19. I reiterate here various ideas I developed earlier in "De donde es Severo Sarduy," *Casa de las Américas* 34.192 (1993).

20. Severo Sarduy, *Escrito sobre un cuerpo* (Buenos Aires: Sudamericana, 1969), 69.

21. Antonio Chuffat Latour, *Apuntes históricos de los chinos en Cuba* (Havana: Molina, 1927).

22. Severo Sarduy, *La simulación* (Caracas: Monte Ávila Editores, 1982), 19–20.

23. François Cheng, *Vide et plein* (Paris: Seuil, 1979).

CHAPTER TEN

Renace el sueño

Remaking Havana's Barrio Chino

Kathleen López

In 2002 Felipe Luis, a ninety-eight-year-old Chinese former bodega owner, had not left his second-story Havana apartment in five years. Yet he was fully aware of the changes occurring in his neighborhood, the *barrio chino*, or Chinatown. News of the construction of a Chinese government–funded portico and of the annual festival of overseas Chinese had reached him, despite his inability to roam the streets as in former days. Like Luis, many members of the aging community of native Chinese in Cuba are often mere observers of the government-sponsored "revitalization" of Havana's Chinatown, spearheaded by "mixed" descendants of Chinese. After providing historical context to Chinese migration to Cuba and the formation of the *barrio chino*, this essay considers the formation of a Chinese Cuban identity and the contradictions inherent in the revitalization project during its first decade. The aspirations of the community of aging native Chinese and the goals of the state-sponsored Havana Chinatown Promotion Group have resulted in a complex set of interactions. Compounding the picture is the involvement of multiracial descendants of Chinese who maintain varying notions of a Chinese identity.

Chinese Migration and the Formation of the *Barrio chino*

The first major migration of Chinese to Cuba began in 1847 with a massive scheme to import low-cost workers for sugar plantations leading to the gradual abolition of slavery. Approximately 142,000 men, mostly from Guangdong Province, left for Cuba between 1847 and 1874. Roughly 17,000 died on the journey due to sickness, violence, and suicide.[1] The "coolie trade" ended after a Chinese imperial commission investigated abuses in the system in 1874.[2] Thereafter the population of Chinese in Cuba declined due to secondary migration to the United States and other parts of Latin America and the Caribbean, a relatively small return migration to China, and deaths.[3] Those who remained continued working as day laborers in plantations, construction, and shipyard docks. By 1858 former coolies had laid the foundations for Havana's *barrio chino*. Buoyed by the arrival of Cantonese immigrants from California and directly from China, Chinese settlements began to take shape in towns throughout Cuba during the latter half of the nineteenth century.[4]

Restricted during the U.S. occupation from 1899 to 1902 and the early years of the Cuban Republic, Chinese labor immigration was reinitiated in response to a demand for agricultural workers to boost sugar production during World War I. By the early twentieth century, Chinese had formed bustling communities across the island. Havana's Chinatown was lined with small commercial establishments such as restaurants, bodegas, laundries, shoe and watch repair shops, bakeries, photography studios, and pharmacies. In addition to district, clan, occupational, and political associations, there were also theaters, four newspapers, a cemetery, two bilingual schools (one Catholic and one Presbyterian), a hospital, and a residence for the elderly. Unlike coolies from the previous century, the newer migrants were better able to maintain political, economic, social, and cultural links with their hometowns in China.

Chinese migration to Cuba dropped significantly during the Depression and after World War II, when the United States eased restrictions on Chinese entry and sugar prices dropped. After 1949 Chinese fleeing political upheaval in the aftermath of China's Communist Revolution produced a brief resurgence in migration. In the years following the Cuban Revolution of 1959, which nationalized Chinese-owned businesses, a significant secondary migration of Chinese Cubans to Miami, New York, and Toronto was part of the larger exodus. Today the remaining Chinese are mostly elderly men who came to Cuba in the 1950s. With little new immigration since 1959 and the loss of private businesses, the *barrio chino* fell into decline.[5]

The Revitalization of the *Barrio chino* and Ethnic Identity

Today the Chinese Cuban community is composed of two major groups: the *chinos naturales*, or native Chinese, mostly men who came before 1959, and the *descendientes*, or children, grandchildren, and great-grandchildren, most of whom are descendants of Chinese men and Cuban women. In addition to the few hundred elderly native Chinese who remain, it is these mixed descendants who form contemporary Chinese Cuba.[6] Cubans, both in Cuba and the United States, continually join the Chinese Cuban community after learning they have a Chinese grandfather or great-grandfather.[7]

With the end of subsidies from the former Soviet Union, a severe economic crisis in the early 1990s forced Cuba into reforms, resulting in a mixed socialist economy and the legalization of the U.S. dollar. The ongoing revitalization project in Havana's Chinatown coincides with the Cuban government's efforts to develop tourism as a solution to its economic problems and to attract foreign investment. The priority of the Grupo Promotor del Barrio Chino de la Habana has been to transform the historic *barrio chino* into a tourist attraction. For five days every spring, the Festival de Chinos de Ultramar commemorates the arrival of the first ship of Chinese coolies in Havana on June 3, 1847, with Cuban and international scholars, businesspeople, and community members participating. The theme of the Fifth Festival of Overseas Chinese, held in Havana in May 2002, was "Chinatowns of the World as Zones of Tourist Attraction."

In addition to promoting tourism, this government organization was formed in 1993 to "recover" Chinese culture, customs, and traditions for the Cuban community. Its projects include a center for Chinese arts and traditions, an evening language school with native Mandarin speakers, a martial arts club, a clinic for traditional Chinese medicine, celebrations of festivals, food stands and Chinese restaurants on the pedestrian walkway (Calle Cuchillo), and a magazine.[8] The Promotion Group sponsored a residence for elderly Chinese who do not have family to assist them. The residence also arranges excursions and provides medicine and food. Promotion Group Director Neil Vega Paneque emphasized that the entire community living in Havana's Chinatown benefits from the organization's work, which includes street repairs and building renovations.[9]

The Promotion Group's goal to strengthen political and economic ties with the People's Republic of China and "improve relations between the Chinese people and the Cuban people" gelled with that of the Cuban government. Official relations between Havana and Beijing have warmed, especially after Fidel Castro's visit to China in 1995. China has become a major exporter of food products and manufactured goods to Cuba. In a symbolic display of *amistad*, China funded the construction of a traditional-style portico on Calle Dragones at the entrance of the original *barrio chino*. The Chinese Embassy provided supplies to the Promotion Group and to the Chinese-language school and was instrumental in the restoration and reopening of the famous Cantonese restaurant El Pacífico.[10] The Promotion Group also focused efforts on renewing commercial exchanges with diasporic Chinese, especially in the Americas. Some restaurants on Calle Cuchillo are backed by Chinese Canadians. (Americans are banned by the U.S. embargo from investing in Cuba.) The Promotion Group director visited Cuban exchange students in China and toured Vancouver's Chinatown to promote business ties. Luciano Wong, president of the Minzhidang (a Chinese fraternal association dating back to 1887) in Cárdenas, exemplifies the diasporic ties of Chinese in the Americas. He is a Cuban citizen, and his two brothers are citizens of Canada and the People's Republic of China, respectively.

The Promotion Group supported the preservation of Cuba's only remaining Chinese newspaper, an important component in community building. In 2003 *Kwong Wah Po* had a biweekly circulation of about six hundred.[11] It contains articles mostly on Cuba and China and has a section in Spanish for descendants who are unable to read Chinese. Using thousands of metal Chinese characters that must be typeset by hand on a vintage printing press, the newspaper, with its delayed news of China extracted from a Hong Kong newspaper, remains an important link to the homeland. For instance, in March 1999 Ricardo Chao, who came to Cuba in the early twentieth century, enthusiastically told me about the latest developments in the transition of Hong Kong and Macao back to China, events he had read about in the Chinese newspaper.

Facing dwindling membership and funds, the remaining Chinese clan and regional associations have opened their doors to mixed descendants. Descendants of Chinese may apply for a permit to open a small business, such as a food stand or shop. The associations have also received permission to open restaurants in former meeting rooms. One of the best-known restaurants in the *barrio chino* is Los Tres Chinitos. Although originally a Chinese association, it is the restaurant's pizza that draws long lines of Cubans. Profits from these restaurants have enabled some Chinese to visit their home villages in China. The Zhongshan Regional Society (Sociedad Regionalista Chung Shan) operates the restaurant and bar Los

Dos Dragones, offering original Chinese food. Francisco Lee, the association's secretary and restaurant proprietor, has recently made four trips to China. Although he has family in China, Lee has decided not to return permanently because, he says, "I am accustomed to Cuba."[12]

Despite criticism of the government's revitalization, many feel that it has benefited descendants of Chinese in Cuba, especially economically. One descendant, Juan Seuc, now living in Miami, had received a permit to open a food stand in Havana. He explained, "The old Chinese were living in poor conditions. There was no special attention given them. I think it's a good idea. For the young people it's an opportunity to make some money." He continued, "You have the interests of the Chinese people and their descendants on the one side and the interests of the government on the other. It is difficult to balance the two." Although he feels there is room for improvement, Seuc says, "I noticed a change since the Grupo Promotor started working, and it's a change for the better."

Chinos naturales

Tensions are inherent in a project that, on the one hand, claims to promote the interests of the Chinese community and an authentic Chinese culture and, on the other hand, actively promotes Havana's Chinatown as a tourist attraction to boost the Cuban economy. Efforts from above to impose homogenizing coherence on the Chinese Cuban "community" can be both exclusionary and artificially inclusive. Ironically, those excluded are often the native Chinese themselves, mostly retired men who spend their days sitting in the meeting rooms of the associations. During the 2003 Festival of Chinese Overseas, the original community members were present at the opening ceremony but absent during the debates over the incorporation of the *barrio chino* into Cuba's tourist industry. Yet these same Chinese are being commodified as part of the tourist circuit, with visits to the associations included in the official festival schedule.

The native Chinese are receiving some material benefits from the Chinese Embassy and the Promotion Group. But some Chinese Cubans (both ethnic Chinese and descendants) expressed concern that the group's ends are more economic than cultural. One native Chinese who is active in the community is doubtful that the Chinese residents will benefit from the tourist impetus. "The old Chinese men are living in poor conditions," he said. "Overseas Chinese should come to help us revive the Chinese community rather than participate in a festival."

These tensions have not gone unnoticed by the Promotion Group. The director declared, "The biggest challenge we have encountered is to make it understood—above all by the native Chinese—that the Promotion Group's project is not economic but cultural, and to achieve unity of action to perfect the work." When further questioned about the push for tourism, he responded, "The project is not *essentially* economic," but he admitted that it recognized the tourism impetus. As the project approached its first decade, the director's goal was to build a coalition between the elderly native Chinese, younger descendants, and the Promotion Group. He spoke of a good relationship marked by "cooperation and respect" between the Promotion Group and the thirteen associations.

Rather than festivals, for an "authentic" revival to reach these elderly native Chinese it may take a return to some form of entrepreneurial autonomy. Retired Chinese lament the devastating impact of losing their businesses (and livelihood). Both Santiago and Felipe Luis are former bodega owners who vividly recalled the *barrio chino* of the old days: ice cream made with fresh fruit, a plethora of Chinese food and products, and Sunday cockfights after the shops had closed. Today, like many other Cubans, elderly Chinese survive on government-issued ration cards and a monthly pension paid in pesos. Chinese tea and medicine are sold in the *barrio chino*, but only for *pesos convertibles*, which are difficult to come by. The wooden drawers of the traditional Chinese pharmacy are usually empty. Instead Santiago depends on medicine mailed from friends in Hong Kong. Cuisine has also suffered a major impact. Santiago prepares Chinese-style dishes with the food and condiments available, carefully slicing one piece of bok choy to make it last over several meals.

Descendientes

As the Promotion Group seeks to encompass native Chinese and mixed descendants within the rubric "Chinese Cuban," some members of this group question how they can identify themselves as Chinese. One descendant in Havana describes his "mixed" father as follows: "He was not raised by his [Chinese] father. People call him 'chino' because of his last name, but he's a Cuban. I know how to use chopsticks better than him. I look more Chinese than him."

In her discussion of Asian American identity, Lisa Lowe analyzes a short story in which two Asian American women explore their guilt at not being "authentically" Chinese enough. Lowe writes:

The story suggests that the making of Chinese American culture—the ways in which it is imagined, practiced, and continued—is worked out as much "horizontally" among communities as it is transmitted "vertically" in unchanging forms from one generation to the next. Rather than considering "Asian American identity" as a fixed, established "given," perhaps we can consider instead "Asian American cultural practices" that produce identity; the processes that produce such identity are never complete and are always constituted in relation to historical and material differences.[13]

Today a Chinese Cuban identity based on ancestry and incorporating Blacks, Whites, and mulattos (in addition to native Chinese) has been created. Many descendants subscribe to markers of Chinese culture, religion, and language, even without the ethnic gestures promoted by an official organization. They cook Chinese food in the home, know a few words of Cantonese, have a statue of San Fan Con, or participate in painting and calligraphy or martial arts classes.[14] For example, Maria Isabel León, the granddaughter of the former president of the Chinese Association of Lajas, recalled that her Cuban mother "learned to cook Chinese food." She proceeded to relate the recipe for a marinated "100-year-old egg."

Beneath this outer surface is another layer of Chinese identity, marked by childhood memories and attachments to the homeland (although most of the descendants have never been to China). Even third-generation descendants of Chinese in Cuba have created imaginative ties to an ancestral homeland. Blas and Santiago Pelayo Díaz are descendants of a Chinese indentured laborer who shared their family history with me. In 1859, at age fifteen, their grandfather Tung Kun Sen (Pastor Pelayo) arrived in Cuba from Guangdong to work on a sugar plantation. Pastor Pelayo eventually became a contractor of Chinese laborers in Cienfuegos and purchased freedom for his wife.[15] Blas and Santiago pointed out the building of the former Chinese association La Gran China, of which Pastor Pelayo was president in 1884, and its patio where a theater company rehearsed in the evenings.[16] The dilapidated skeletons of Chinese shops and associations highlight the stark contrast between the tourist-oriented revitalization of the barrio chino in Havana and the reality of the former Chinese communities in smaller Cuban towns. We proceeded to La Reina Cemetery, where Pastor Pelayo was buried in 1913, now overgrown with weeds and inundated with water from the adjacent bay. Blas has raised money "little by little" from family members to refurbish his grandfather's grave and erect a memorial plaque. Although he maintains good relations with the Promotion

Group, Blas had developed an interest in his Chinese ancestry (and his African ancestry) long before the revitalization project. Extremely proud of his Chinese heritage, he has researched his family tree, learned elementary Cantonese (as opposed to the Mandarin that is emphasized in the *barrio chino*), and is writing a novel based on his grandfather's life.

Given the economic and cultural incentives, it is not surprising that descendants of Chinese are finding their way to the *barrio chino*. The pull of the revitalization project has even reached those who previously had little knowledge of their Chinese heritage. However, this does not mean that expressions of Chinese ethnicity are a fabrication. As Lynn Pan writes in her history of the Chinese diaspora, "Clearly the Chinese, like any ethnic minority, lead lives that are balanced on an invisible see-saw between two or more identities. Circumstances, the nature of their audience, and calculations of risk and benefit dictate whether their 'backstage' or 'frontstage' identity is to the fore in any particular situation."[17]

Within the broad, supposedly inclusive category of Chinese Cuban, subtle racialized distinctions are nonetheless maintained. While native Chinese are still viewed as in a sense foreign, Cuban-born descendants fall into the full spectrum of racial categories that exist in Cuba. Whiteness and Blackness thus figure into the formulation of a Chinese Cuban identity. Although a Black Cuban may be just as Chinese as a White Cuban and equally attracted by the economic and cultural pull factors of the revitalization project, the difference is often implicitly or explicitly noted. Several of the Afro-Cuban youths who participate in the martial arts and language classes were pointed out to me as *negrito*, a racialization of difference that emphasizes their Blackness over Chinese ancestry and ability to speak Chinese.

Although the 1959 Cuban Revolution embraced the notion of *cubanidad* and declared an end to institutionalized racial discrimination, it failed to achieve a color-blind society.[18] Since the Revolution, the question of race has been subsumed under a nationalist and socialist (often imagined as raceless and classless) umbrella.[19] As Cuba enters an undetermined future with the reforms of the past two decades, the unresolved question of race and *cubanidad* resurfaces. Within the hegemonic Cuban social formation, individuals incorporated into the ethnic formation "Chinese Cuban" continually change as negotiations between state interests and those supposedly included are played out. The multiracial nature of societies in Latin America and the Caribbean, coupled with the fact that the revitalization of the *barrio chino* in Havana is government-sponsored, allows for a project that is more inclusive, drawing in White, Black, and mulatto descendants who have made varying claims on their own Chineseness.

Conclusions

The Promotion Group brings together native Chinese and descendants, providing organization, public space, and, in a restricted society, an outlet for personal expression. However, alongside its project, there exists another phenomenon, marked by a lack of neat categories. The restoration, if there is such a thing, is *around* rather than *on* Calle Cuchillo, and even beyond Havana, in other provinces. What transpires in private interactions and within individuals is a matter often outside of the hegemonic construction of a Chinese Cuban identity.

Alongside the government-sponsored revival, the University of Havana has established a chair of Studies on Chinese Migration in Cuba. Recent work by Cuban scholars has reached beyond the traditional scholarship on Chinese coolies in Cuba, utilizing oral interviews and archival documents for investigations in history, anthropology, literature, and linguistics.[20] These publications have stimulated new interest in the Chinese in Cuba, as well as in China itself. Two great-grandchildren of a Chinese from Cienfuegos can be found reading a book on Chinese legends written by the wife of the former Cuban ambassador to China.[21] Books published in Cuba remain one of the few remaining products that are affordable to Cubans who earn only pesos. Cuba maintains a high literacy rate, and with the lack of varied programming, many Cubans are avid readers and flood local book fairs.

The remaining native Chinese in Cienfuegos are discussing the possibility of reviving Chinese associational life. However, they face a challenge: according to Cuban law, no new associations may be formed; only branches of existing associations may be established. Besides Havana, associations remain in Cárdenas, Santa Clara, and Santiago de Cuba. These regional associations never lost their original, though dilapidated, buildings.

Without significant new immigration, the future of Havana's Chinatown remains uncertain. Jorge Alay, in his presentation on the history of the *barrio chino* at the 2003 Festival of Overseas Chinese, described it as a "Chinatown without Chinese." However, the possibility exists of a new trickle of Chinese immigration, as relations between the Cuban and Chinese governments are solidified and niches open up for Chinese entrepreneurs. The Alay brothers are three relatively young ethnic Chinese who live in Havana. Their parents, who came to Cuba in 1949 for business, stressed the importance of learning Mandarin (mainland China's official language). Now, Jorge proclaims, not only can he communicate with Chinese in China, but he can teach Mandarin to descendants of Chinese in the *barrio chino*. His brother Ernesto, who is in the tourist industry, recommended the establishment of a Chinese museum that would fulfill both tourist and community needs.

Rather than being restored to an approximation of what it once was, Chinatown is being remade into something new, out of both demographic and economic necessity. During the course of this government-sponsored project, second-, third-, and fourth-generation descendants of Chinese, by taking advantage of special economic opportunities and participating in Chinese traditions, are claiming an ethnic and cultural identity and redefining themselves. In the process, they are ultimately forging new spaces along the margins, where the expression of identity and the satisfaction of intellectual curiosity may develop.[22]

An unchanging *barrio chino* in Havana is unrealistic. In a different political and economic context, Chinese migration to Cuba would likely reflect the types of changes that have occurred elsewhere in the diaspora. As Lowe writes, "Rather than representing a fixed, discrete culture, 'Chinatown' is itself the very emblem of shifting demographics, languages, and populations."[23] In the 1950s the composition of the *barrio chino* was similar to that of other "bachelor society" Chinatowns in cities such as San Francisco and New York. These Chinatowns have since been transformed due to a continual flow of immigration from mainland China, Hong Kong, and Taiwan, as well as movement to the suburbs.[24]

The revival of Havana's Chinatown has largely left behind the native Chinese, providing them only incidental economic benefit. While it has not attracted new Chinese immigrants, the revival has created economic and cultural pull factors to draw descendants who may have had little prior Chinese identity. It has also enabled connections between native Chinese and descendants.

Mitzi Espinosa Luis is the granddaughter of a Chinese merchant, Lü Fan (Francisco Luis), who came to Cuba in 1918. Through remittances and return trips, Francisco Luis also maintained a family in China. He actively promoted communication between his Cuban daughters and his Chinese daughters, shaping their conceptions of family and identity. When Francisco Luis died in 1975, their correspondence ceased. I located and met the elderly Chinese daughters in 2001. They still lived in Lü Village and maintained the house that their father built upon his first return trip from Cuba. Since then, communication with their Cuban relatives has resumed. Lü Fan's Cuban daughter Violeta Luis and granddaughter Mitzi Espinosa Luis have been integral to this renewal of family ties.[25]

Matthew Frye Jacobson suggests that a diasporic imagination and attachments to the homeland are linked by a "cultural thread" to descendants of early twentieth-century Irish, Polish, and Jewish immigrants in the United States.[26] Like the Pelayo brothers, some Chinese Cubans possess such an imagination and hope to visit China, though political and economic restraints in Cuba remain a barrier.

An essay Blas Pelayo wrote for the Chinese Cuban community, chronicling the visit of China's president Jiang Zemin in 1993, depicts the layered connections with native Chinese in Havana's *barrio chino*. Pelayo compares the official visit to the imperial commission that came to Cuba over a hundred years earlier to investigate the abuses in the coolie trade. The significance of the president's visit varied for different segments of the population: for Cubans, it held the promise of improved diplomatic relations and material goods in a time of scarcity; for Chinese in Cuba, it reestablished a connection with a homeland that had been severed for nearly half a century; and for descendants of Chinese, it may have been a "cultural thread" linking their past with the present. Pelayo writes, "The moment is significantly emotional: the native at my side yells immediately in Cantonese 'Forever China!' Even though I do not know that language, perhaps out of ethnic instinct and solidarity, I repeat it in Spanish. . . . In another very old native, I was surprised to see his tired eyes filled with tears of emotion and joy, so rarely expressed among the Chinese."[27]

Notes

Author's Note: Portions of this essay appeared in "The Revitalization of Havana's Chinatown: Invoking Chinese Cuban History," *Journal of Chinese Overseas* 5.1 (2009): 177–200. It was first presented at the international symposium Cuba Today: Continuity and Change since the "Periodo Especial," Bildner Center for Western Hemisphere Studies, City University of New York, October 4–5, 2004. I thank Mauricio Font for initiating the symposium and the participants for their valuable feedback.

1. Juan Pérez de la Riva, *Los culíes chinos en Cuba (1847–1880): Contribución al estudio de la inmigración contratada en el Caribe* (Havana: Editorial de Ciencias Sociales, 2000), 179.

2. From 1849 to 1874 about 100,000 Chinese also signed contracts to work in Peru. See China, Zongli geguo shiwu yamen, *Chinese Emigration: Report of the Commission Sent by China to Ascertain the Condition of Chinese Coolies in Cuba, 1874* (1876; Taipei: Ch'eng Wen Publishing Company, 1970). See also the reissue of this document, *The Cuba Commission Report: A Hidden History of the Chinese in Cuba*, introduction by Denise Helly (Baltimore: Johns Hopkins University Press, 1993).

3. Between 1865 and 1874 only two thousand Chinese returned to China (Helly 25). By 1899 official census data reported 8,035 Chinese laborers in Cuba (8,033 males and 2 females). U.S. War Department, *Report on the Census of Cuba 1899* (Washington, D. C.: Government Printing Office, 1900), 472–75.

4. According to Pérez de la Riva (178–83), approximately five thousand "Californians" went to Cuba between 1860 and 1875 for business opportunities.

5. See Antonio Chuffat Latour, *Apunte histórico de los chinos en Cuba* (Havana: Molina, 1927); Duvon C. Corbitt, *A Study of the Chinese in Cuba, 1847–1947* (Wilmore, Ky.: Asbury College, 1971); Denise Helly, *Idéologie et ethnicité: Les chinois Macao à Cuba 1847–1886* (Montreal: Les Presses de l'Université de Montréal, 1979); Juan Jiménez Pastrana, *Los chinos en la historia de Cuba: 1847–1930* (Havana: Editorial de Ciencias Sociales, 1983); Evelyn Hu-DeHart, "Chinese Coolie Labour in Cuba in the Nineteenth Century: Free Labour or Neo-slavery?," *Slavery and Abolition* 14.1 (1993): 67–86; Baldomero Álvarez Ríos, *La inmigración china en la Cuba colonial: El Barrio Chino de la Habana* (Havana: Publicigraf, 1995); José Baltar Rodríguez, *Los chinos de Cuba: Apuntes etnográficos* (Havana: Fundación Fernando Ortiz, 1997); Napoleón Seuc, *La Colonia China de Cuba (1930–1960): Antecedentes, memorias y vivencias* (Miami: Ahora Printing, 1998); Miriam Herrera Jerez and Mario Castillo Santana, *De la memoria a la vida pública: Identidades, espacios y jerarquías de los chinos en La Habana republicana (1902–1968)* (Havana: Centro de Investigación y Desarrollo de la Cultura Cubana Juan Marinello, 2003); Kathleen López, "'One Brings Another': The Formation of Early-Twentieth-Century Chinese Migrant Communities in Cuba," *The Chinese in the Caribbean*, ed. Andrew R. Wilson (Princeton, N.J.: Markus Wiener, 2004), 93–127; Ignacio López-Calvo, *Imaging the Chinese in Cuban Literature and Culture* (Gainesville: University of Florida Press, 2008); Lisa Yun, *The Coolie Speaks: Chinese Indentured Laborers and African Slaves in Cuba* (Philadelphia: Temple University Press, 2008); Mauro García Triana and Pedro Eng Herrera, *The Chinese in Cuba, 1847–Now*, ed. and trans. Gregor Benton (Lanham, Md.: Lexington Books, 2009).

6. In 2002 the president of the Casino Chung Wah Alfonso Chao Chiu reported that 314 native Chinese were registered with the association.

7. A similar phenomenon exists among Jewish Cubans. See Ruth Behar's documentary on the search for identity and memory among Sephardic Jews with Cuban roots, *Adio Kerida*, VHS, 82 min., Women Make Movies, New York, 2002.

8. *Presencia China en Cuba*, map and pamphlet (Havana: Fundación Fernando Ortiz, Grupo Promotor del Barrio Chino, Ediciones GEO, 1999); Álvarez 49–54; Isabelle Lausent-Herrera, "El renacimiento de la comunidad china en Cuba," *Oriental*, December 1998. The inaugural issue of *Fraternidad 2* was published in May 2002. The magazine *Fraternidad* was originally founded in 1934 as the official organ of the Unión de Detallistas del Comercio de la Colonia China en Cuba (Union of Commercial Retailers of the Chinese Colony in Cuba). In 2006 the Office of the Historian of the City of Havana took over the restoration of Havana's Chinatown.

9. Testimonials are owed to onsite interviews conducted by the author between 1999 and 2003 with (in order of appearance) Neil Vega Paneque, Luciano Wong, Ricardo Chao, Francisco Lee, Juan Seuc, Abel Fung, Santiago and Felipe Luis, Julio Tang Zambrana, Maria Isabel León, Blas and Santiago Pelayo Díaz, Jorge and Ernesto Alay.

10. Zhao Tiesheng, consul, Embassy of the People's Republic of China, interview by author, March 2002, Havana; Álvarez, 51–55.

11. Before the revolution *Kwong Wah Po* was published daily and had a circulation of 1,500. In addition, there were three other Chinese-language newspapers in Havana.

12. For an interview with Felipe Luis before he died in September 2003, see Mitzi Espinosa Luis, "*Si tú pleguntá, a mi gusta hacé cuento.* 'If you ask, I'll be happy to tell you': Felipe Luis Narrates His Story," trans. Kathleen López, in Wilson 129–42.

13. Lisa Lowe, *Immigrant Acts: On Asian American Cultural Politics* (Durham, N.C.: Duke University Press, 1996), 64.

14. In the nineteenth century a syncretic religious tradition known as San Fan Con developed, mixing elements of Afro-Cuban *santería* with the cult of Guan Gong, who was transformed into a protector of Chinese immigrants in Cuba. San Fan Con was a development particular to Cuba, and from May to September related festivals took place throughout the provinces. For an analysis of how San Fan Con became monotheistic and Confucian in its Cuban setting, see Frank F. Scherer, "Sanfancón: Orientalism, Self-Orientalism, and 'Chinese Religion' in Cuba," *Nation Dance: Religion, Identity, and Cultural Difference in the Caribbean*, ed. Patrick Taylor (Bloomington: Indiana University Press, 2001), 153–70. According to Ernesto Alay, born in Cuba to two Chinese parents, San Fan Con today is practiced in the home by burning incense and does not necessarily involve public display.

15. Parroquia "La Purisima Concepción" S.I. Catedral de Cienfuegos, Libro de Bautismos, tomo 15, folio 242, número 698.

16. Enrique Edo y Llop, *Memoria histórica de Cienfuegos y su jurisdicción*, 3rd ed. (Havana: Úcar, García, 1943), 626–27.

17. Lynn Pan, *Sons of the Yellow Emperor: A History of the Chinese Diaspora* (New York: Kodansha International, 1990), 247.

18. Pedro Pérez Sarduy and Jean Stubbs, eds., *Afrocuba: An Anthology of Cuban Writing on Race, Politics and Culture* (New York: Ocean Press, 1993), 7.

19. Alejandro de la Fuente, *A Nation for All: Race, Inequality, and Politics in Twentieth-Century Cuba* (Chapel Hill: University of North Carolina Press, 2001), 322–29; Pérez and Stubbs, 9.

20. Examples of this research are a special issue of the Fundación Fernando Ortiz's journal *Catauro* dedicated to the Chinese presence in Cuba, *Catauro* 2:2 (2000), and, most recently, Herrera and Castillo.

21. Mercedes Crespo, *Leyendas Chinas* (Havana: Editorial SI-Mar, 2001). Crespo spent a decade in China accompanying her husband, the former Cuban ambassador.

22. However, Scherer states:

> The recent revival of "Chinese" ethnicity in Cuba is based both on a number of Euro-American Orientalist assumptions of a distinctive and essential Chineseness, and on the "Oriental" use of Orientalist discourse, which perfectly illustrates the "indigenous" employment of what I call *strategic* Orientalism. While the former is being promoted, somewhat ambiguously, by the Cuban state and its intelligentsia, the latter is articulated by first- and second-generation Chinese Cubans. In this way, the very process of reintegrating, re-creating, and re-ethnicizing the Chinese Cuban "community" is marked by the peculiar practice of self-Orientalization. . . . This complex discursive practice, complete with Confucian ideas and certain capitalist aspirations, facilitates the articulation of difference conceived in ethnic and cultural terms by first- and second-generation Chinese Cubans and allows—at least in Cuba—for the opening of alternative spaces, where the construction of identities other than those prescribed by the Cuban state can take place. (153–54)

23. Lowe, 65.

24. Peter Kwong, *Chinatown, N.Y.: Labor and Politics, 1930–1950* (New York: Monthly Review Press, 1979); Timothy Fong, *The First Suburban Chinatown: The Remaking of Monterey Park, CA* (Philadelphia: Temple University Press, 1994).

25. I extend my deepest appreciation to Chen Liyuan and to the Daze Overseas Chinese Affairs Office for their role in reuniting the two sides of the Lü family. In 2009 Mitzi Espinosa Luis realized her lifelong dream of meeting her relatives in China.

26. Matthew Frye Jacobson, *Special Sorrows: The Diasporic Imagination of Irish, Polish, and Jewish Immigrants in the United States* (Cambridge, Mass.: Harvard University Press, 1995), 5.

27. Blas Pelayo, "Breve crónica sobre la visita del presidente de La República Popular de China, Jieng Ze Ming a La Habana, del 21/11/93 al 22/11/93, ambos inclusive" (Short Chronicle of the Visit of the President of the People's Republic of China, Jiang Zemin, to Havana, from November 21, 1993 to November 22, 1993), my translation.

CHAPTER ELEVEN

Of Chinese Dragons and Canaries on the Isthmus of Panama

Margarita Vásquez

Above the meeting hall door, a little dirty devil mask with a dragon's face jumps out to accost me.[1] The painting of a similar mask beside it repeats the gesture. Through its big open mouth protrudes the minute head of another of those mysterious animals; yet another one leans out over the top. I had seen similar masks on many walls as decorations, but this one conveys a particularly rich meaning due to its context: the Panamanian-Chinese School in Panama City. I know the mask is originally from Panama's Azuero Peninsula, but I am not sure whether the painting depicts Oriental motifs. I then realize that the mask's Panamanian folk roots clouded my perception of the similarities and that the small Chinese heads in the painting appear to be added elements, arbitrarily reproduced.

The spectacle surprises me, because in Panamanian culture these little dirty devils reveal formal elements issuing from a cultural heritage that is at once Spanish (guitar and castanets), Amerindian (natural dyes and macaw feathers), and African (a cowskin percussion bladder), but I had never detected a Chinese presence in the folklore of the Azuero region. This dragon, which I discern as active within a markedly Hispanic cultural region, was to become the starting point for my cautious, identity-bound search for elements of the Far East in Panamanian literature.

Such a task is not free from difficulties. Orientalist and postcolonial theories ought to be cautiously applied to the case of the Chinese in Panama, because here we are not dealing with the typical colonization of one people by another in an "invaded" geographical space, not even with silenced groups, but rather with the immigration of human beings who spoke another tongue and who were deceived when they accepted their work contracts and paid for their resident visas.[2]

The incorporation of the Chinese element in twentieth-century Panamanian literature came as quietly as the reception of Chinese immigrants by Panamanian society starting in 1854. Between 800 and 1,040 arrived that year, according to sources. Henceforth immigration grew due to the building of the interoceanic railroad. In all, some 535,000 Chinese workers came to the Americas between 1840 and 1872. These men arrived in the Antilles, the Guyanas, Peru, Mexico, the United States, Panama, and elsewhere to engage in "free" contractual labor (or so they thought). They came as settlers, even though they could not bring their women. After their long, perilous journey the promised living conditions turned out to be deplorable, and they suffered a disillusionment of "a different American dream," as Juan David Morgan calls it in his 2005 novel.[3]

Panamanian literature has been nourished by the accounts of those first arrivals. Willis J. Abbot, among others, writes in 1913 about the railroad company's experience with the Chinese workers: eight hundred landed, sixteen died en route, thirty-two fell ill on arrival, and within a week another eighty had fallen ill as well. Panamanians had little knowledge of this tragedy, thanks to agreements among the government, the Panama Railroad Company, and the middlemen who guaranteed the deal in Hong Kong.[4] The interpreters who accompanied the immigrants declared that their affliction was due to the lack of opium, to which they were accustomed; so for a while the company supplied it, but later discontinued it, citing the need to "humanely" rescue them from vice "for their own good."[5] Perhaps, as Abbot suggests, the cost of opium—fifteen cents per worker per day—influenced the fatal decision. Then again, what occurred could have been the result of what Frantz Fanon calls "existential marginalization."[6] The sources indicate that, deathly ill, these Chinese workers made no effort to cling to a life that sunk its teeth in them, such that suicide came to channel their despair. It would seem that the name Matachín, a small town on the railroad line, is the only surviving reminder of those events.

A century later, an alternate literary space began to emerge in Panama, configured in a language that was neither that of the nineteenth-century Asians nor that of the owners of the railroad company; it was the Spanish of Panamanians who were moved to revisit the events from a different perspective. The plight of the Chinese newcomers reappeared in novels like *Los Capelli* (1967) by Yolanda Camarano de Sucre, José Franco's *Las luciérnagas de la muerte* (Fireflies of Death, 1995), Luis Pulido Ritter's

Sueño americano (American Dream, 1999), and Juan David Morgan's *El caballo de oro: La gran aventura de la construcción del ferrocarril de Panamá* (The Golden Horse: The Great Adventure of the Building of the Panama Railroad, 2005), as well as numerous short stories.

One of these short stories, Rosa María Britton's "El jardín de Fuyang" (Fuyang's Garden), dealt directly with the Chinese suicides.[7] Its structure is quite remarkable. For most of the story the narrator hides the true point of view from the reader: the idealized vision of an Imperial China, where the action had been taking place, turns out to be nothing more than a pipe dream. The reader's imagination is led abruptly from a poetically idealized realm of princesses, porcelain, gold, and silk to a dimension characterized by brutality, pain, and insult. Lin Wan, the devoted caretaker of Mr. Fuyang's garden, will not receive another dose of opium, and neither will the coolies who work on the railroad. Tragedy then strikes: the Chinese hang themselves with their own braids, impale themselves with machetes and stakes, or drown themselves in the river, while their horrified employers are left to stare at the face of death. The point of view returns to Lin Wan's conscience at the moment of his suicide; to the reader's amazement, his inner perception of death is once again an Oriental paradise—in Rubén Darío's *modernista* style—where peacocks reign over the garden and a smile lights up the princess's face.

Lin Wan, despite his oppression, remains a dreamer capable of love even in a caste society, a man devoted to a garden with an artist's passion, respectful of family, who must imagine such goodness as a refuge from the degraded condition in which he lives. The story's two worlds, the vision of Imperial China and the harsh work on the railroad, meet at a place where death has two faces, two vantage points, internal and external: those of the dying man and of the man who watches him die, worker and boss in a master-slave relationship, the gaze of the white man and that of the yellow. A layered irony results from the fact that the internal viewpoint of the dying Chinese worker is defined as a hallucination, pure fantasy, a fool's paradise, which nevertheless is the only view that will set him free. Meanwhile the external viewpoint of the onlookers, the white bosses, spectators of death, claims to be representation, testimony, truth, but it is only the copy of another matrix: that of the master, the all-powerful gringo with his scornful gesture under his black umbrella, chaining the worker to an inferno that takes shape at daybreak. With this interplay of matrices, the story reinterprets historiography and subverts the workings of colonial ideology.

Enrique Jaramillo Levi's story "El agua" (Water) presents a variation on the theme of suicide among the Chinese.[8] Edwin Pan-Kai II, a descendant of coolies who dug the French canal, relives the plight of his forebears (hence the ordinal II after his name). From them he inherited not only his thin body and his shyness (he suffers from psychological marginalization) but also his ability at juggling. He worked hard to have his own circus, but while crossing the Darien jungle, yellow fever decimates his troupe, "as though the dark times of the French canal had returned, leaving behind its trail of helpless victims." Abandoned by Fanny, the girl he kidnapped to be his wife; hired to act for a faceless audience in someone else's theater; and facing for the third time, from his fifth-floor window, a daunting scene that becomes clear only at the end of the story, he joyfully jumps to his death. The workers he saw pitching a circus tent across the street were his old troupe members who had died of yellow fever. They now line up under the rain to see the result of his suicide.

At the time Jaramillo Levi published this story in 1985, waves of Chinese and other immigrants were arriving in Panama under the military government. Many were made to pay large sums of money to be registered illegally as Panamanian citizens or were defrauded with lengthy promises to legalize their immigration status.[9] Not knowing Spanish, the newcomers were unable to establish links in Panamanian society, which began to see them as a threat. They hid behind storefronts, while the newspapers reported, "These Chinese do not integrate into our nation. They are racists. They avoid, or preach against, any union or marriage with Panamanians. They expect to live in neighborhoods all to themselves."[10] These views were shared by many citizens, without much critical consideration of circumstances, such as the fact that the contracting agents this time around were probably Panamanian officers, underscoring the marginality of this new group of Chinese outsiders.

Although Edwin Pan-Kai II does not belong to this later wave of migrants, he shares with them his lack of assimilation into the system of ideas accepted as normal by the local milieu. He is in this sense a dissident, a self-marginalized figure. He breaks the social mold in his relationship with Fanny and in his way of earning a living. He is a circus magician, a spectacle for curious onlookers, as were those first Chinese who landed in Panama on March 30, 1854, forming a long line, like the ghostly images of Pan-Kai's circus troupe. "Even their silence is impressive," states a historical source. "The Chinese march without a word, their heads lowered, their delicate hands hidden between flowing sleeves."[11] We can imagine their anguished puzzlement; no matter how hard they tried, they could not figure out instructions, social relations, duties, manners, and ceremonies taking place around them. Words were not accessible to them. They could only perceive images and gestures, as in a silent film. With what voice could such subalterns speak?

Jaramillo Levi's story confronts the reader with the possibility that those ghostly figures who arrived at the Isthmus in the nineteenth century could have repeated, years later, the same fatal attempt to set up camp in our midst. His troubling vision of historiography's disconnectedness goes on to question the relationship between textuality and reference. In this sense, Pan-Kai's suicide is part of his speech (a discourse of gestures), which points to the need for a line of communication with the citizenry in order to articulate the possibility of insertion and belongingness.

Among Orientalist stories by the foremost Panamanian contemporary writers, Rogelio Sinán's "Sin novedad en Shanghai" (All Is Quiet in Shanghai) and "Hechizo" (Witchcraft) are set in China rather than Panama.[12] However, a closer reading of "Hechizo" takes the reader to a transculturated space that alludes to the Caribbean. This story in five parts is interesting for its narrative viewpoint: that of a Caucasian photographer and rabbit hunter in the suburbs of Hong Kong. He sees a house in the distance. As he approaches, he is enthralled by a charming Chinese girl in a red bandanna who offers him a glass of water. Later, while she farms, he tries to win her love. Offered lodging for the night, he slips into the girl's bed, despite there being other men in the house. The girl warns him of death threats by those men. Even though fear races through his body, he satisfies his appetite and, feeling bad, leaves the place at dawn. He then falls gravely ill and becomes delirious. Only the exorcism and concoctions of a sorcerer save him. In the ceremony, torches are placed to remove evil spirits. The sorcerer ties a bundle of the photographer's clothing to one end of a bamboo stick and drives the stick into the ground in the middle of the backyard. There are murmured prayers and rites in a strange tongue, and he receives blows with the body of a decapitated rooster that was left hanging from the bamboo stick. The ritual ends at the sound of a gong with a big blow to the photographer's stomach. Chinese people, a voice said, have unshakable faith in these things, so they expect a miracle. Indeed at dawn the photographer's health improves. His strength gradually returns, until he feels a great sexual attraction for the Malaysian adolescent who accompanied him on his daily walk. Afraid of falling again under a curse, he retreats because the youth is a virgin. But the sorcerer gives him comforting news: he is cured, and the curse will not return.

On the one hand, the deeds that bring the narrator to this crisis are predatory in nature. First, he hunts rabbits for pleasure; later he seeks out a charming Chinese girl, a "helpless little creature with large, dark frightened eyes," who wears a red bandanna (a warning sign), "runs like a rabbit" from the barking dogs, and is assaulted in the night by this man who needs to impose his manliness. The narrator's actions break the social norms, and for his intrusion in a foreign culture he receives a punishment: the curse. He sinks "into a night of death," but after falling, he begins to hear voices, to crawl, to return, like Orpheus, from the other world.

Curiously, he can be saved only by a Chinese "sorcerer," who rather resembles an Afro-Caribbean Yoruba priest. Clearly, he could recover normalcy only through the host culture. By the same token, at the end, the sorcerer is also the one who gives him his blessing to pursue another maiden, the Malaysian girl—both girls being exotic virgins. Yet we must not forget that the narrator is a photographer and that photography has the ability to freeze the existing space in time. His gaze, however, is not that of a conventional photographer. What he captures is not only the representation one would expect of a Chinese landscape. Somehow the image that is gradually developed corresponds also to an ordinary Caribbean space. It has captured an interstitial space between both cultures. Only in this way can the sorcerer of slanted eyes and African rituals give the photographer his space back in life. At the same time this scene captures the sense of mysterious power and knowledge that the average Panamanian accords to the proverbial Chinese doctor, whose occult practices may involve the blood of stray dogs and cats, foxes or monkeys (but never roosters, as in Afro-Caribbean rites). In this refractive manner, Rogelio Sinán artfully registers the Chinese presence in Panama's Caribbean culture.

Rosa María Britton's *El ataúd de uso* (The Used Casket, 1982) deals with another aspect of the Chinese insertion in Panama. This novel presents the very familiar image of a free merchant, Ah Singh, a Chinese storekeeper like many who can be seen every day in the city or in remote towns since olden days. As the novel shows, the Chinese reached the farthest corners of the country, participating in the daily life of the towns, which received them without much problem. They would marry local working-class women and form peaceful families. They would start a small store even if they spoke little Spanish, living frugally during the first few years in a simple storeroom upstairs or in back. They were reputed to be always honest, such being the view of the average Panamanian, which the novel faithfully transcribes. But Ah Singh would not achieve such a simple, happy life. He sends for a Chinese woman to marry. She arrives in the tropics, delicate and pale, bleeds to death during labor, and the child dies with her. Ah Singh withdraws into his inner self. Shortly afterward, Bernabela, a happy and energetic Black woman, comes to the store, learns the business, and makes it thrive. The new couple has a daughter, but when Bernabela has an affair, Ah Singh will not forgive her. He sails back to China with his daughter and dies en route. Bernabela would never again see her child, the symbolic union of races and cultures. This Chinese merchant had established a relationship with the townsfolk apparently based on fruitful dialogue. Yet without any drama or vengeance, he simply grows silent until his departure. He no longer wants the voice he had earned. Perhaps the townsfolk misjudged Ah Singh. He had other values, different from theirs.

Beside the mainstream Panamanian authors who delve into the Chinese experience, there are many noteworthy writers of Chinese ancestry, among them Raúl Wong (1916–46), whose literary criticism is dispersed throughout the periodicals of his time; the poets Carlos Francisco Changmarín (b. 1922) and Antonio Wong (b. 1933); Eustorgio Chong Ruiz (b. 1934), an essayist, playwright, and short-story writer; César Young Núñez (b. 1934), a poet, essayist, journalist; Enrique Chuez (b. 1937), a poet and novelist; and the poets Carlos Wong, Luis Wong Vega (b. 1958), and Gloria Young (b. 1952).

Among Chinese Panamanian authors, I would like to focus on the essayist Eustorgio Chong Ruiz and the poet César Young Núñez because their sharp contrast illustrates the broad range of modes of insertion and the different degrees of creolization of the Chinese in Panamanian culture.

In Chong Ruiz's essay *Los chinos en la sociedad panameña* (1993) the historical memory and the coming together of the Chinese in Panama are finally expressed in accordance with the interests of their own community. Chong Ruiz's discourse validates the impression that the nationalist tradition that promoted Panamanian culture throughout the twentieth century and served as a barrier to further colonization was suspended as a result of compliance with the Canal treaties. His essay appears in the wake of the events of June 18, 1990, in which, according to his book, both Panamanian and ethnic Chinese were publicly demeaned without distinction under the pretext of investigating a crime. Chong Ruiz states that during the last five years of the military dictatorship 20,537 Asians entered Panama illegally. This corrupt human trafficking produced close to 200 million dollars in bribes for military and civilian government officials. In 1989, with a new government installed, the human trafficking exposed, and some of the culprits behind bars, an unprecedented crackdown against illegal immigrants began. Like cornered dogs, the writer tells us, these men of the yellow race, denied permanent residence, unable to return to their distant land, and in fear of reprisals, went into hiding, living clandestinely behind small shops, storerooms, and mezzanines or crowding into "unimaginably wretched hovels" in the city or in rural areas.

Shortly before this, when the admission of Chinese immigrants into Panama had been relaxed and the Tiananmen Square massacre of June 1989 led to humanitarian grants of permanent residence, Panama was still billed as "a country of warm climate, low cost of living, and easy access to the U.S." (Chong Ruiz 80). Then, one fine day, the aliens found themselves subjected to regulations interpreted in accordance with the mood of the times. The date June 18, 1990, will remain imprinted in the hearts and minds of many Panamanians who protested through the news media. Milson Cornejo painted a vivid picture in *La Prensa*:

> The moving cry of children clinging to the skirts of their mothers and grandmothers, the look of horror on the faces of men and women, the terrified parents hugging their infant children, the pleas of those who could hardly express themselves in Spanish, the mute terror of the newly arrived unable to utter anything except in their own tongue, the cries of the old who will never learn to speak another language and will die speaking only their melodious dialect brought from the distant Orient. (In Chong Ruiz, 82)

The wave of protests in the news media and the national essay prize awarded to Chong's book in 1992 were a call to fairness for the Chinese who lived in Panama during those critical years. The essay led the readers to imagine how the Chinese faced the harsh circumstances of their lives, and how they looked at world affairs from the perspective of the oppressed and not as mere spectators. This means looking at the Oriental not as an "Other" but as an "I" (who can *then* become a role model for the national "self"). It means looking at things from the vantage point of an individual member of the group, or what in Panama is called a *paisano*.[13]

The first of the book's two-part structure is titled "From the Yangtze Kiang to the Chagres," in reference to Chinese migration and the great rivers of China and Panama, the Chagres being a tributary of the Panama Canal. This first part is in turn subdivided into nine narratives linked by the voice of an authorial narrator and interwoven with quotes from journalists, historians, philosophers, and poets. A controlled orchestration of voices is thus arranged into a layered discourse in which events take shape not only in the narrator's present but also from what the old writings of Oriental sages and poets, keepers of the ancestral memory, tell about events of the past. In these nine subchapters, the events selected to characterize key historical moments are woven sequentially: 1854, marking the arrival of the first group of Chinese who came to build the railroad and whose numbers ironically increased despite the mass suicides; 1941, when the Constitution sponsored by Arnulfo Arias included an article on nationality and immigration that was full of racial prejudice and provided for the exclusion of persons of specific ethnic origins, resulting in abuses against Asians and their labor; and 1990, when the persecution of the Chinese who arrived during the military dictatorship was unleashed.

These three moments mark the violence against the Chinese in Panama under the authority wielded by men who, according to the narrator, were protecting their economic interests or playing upon populist chauvinism and xenophobia. Yet the Chinese decide to stay and integrate productively into society, as though following Shiteh's advice: "Hanshan asked Shiteh: And if someone slanders, insults me, mocks me, holds contempt for me, wounds me, hates and deceives me, what should I do? And Shiteh answered: The only thing you must do is to bear it, surrender to it, shun it, let it be, respect and ignore it. And in a few years, only look at it."[14] Opposites follow each other, says the *Tao Te Ching*; so do not act, but let things run their natural course.

The book's second part, titled "Historia de los chinos en Panamá," includes six chapters that describe "the interaction of values and attitudes" within the Chinese community (93). It covers organizations and publications, medicine, production, agriculture and husbandry, ecology, architecture, recreation, holidays, social groups, food, funerals, the cemetery, and Chinatown—a sampler of Chinese contributions to Panamanian culture. The text makes it evident that conditions in Panama have changed. The Chinese, as well as the Isthmians, have changed. Panamanians perceive a fusion of cultures, particularly in their literature. At the same time, cultural interactions and mutual readings are increasingly free from misinterpretations because they take place within the same cultural framework.

Nonetheless a satirical structure hides in a text that emphasizes the repetition of similar issues at different historical moments (1854, 1941, 1990, and what next?), starting with a great irony: the decision of the Chinese to remain in Panama is juxtaposed to the mass suicide of the coolies. An image of dead bodies stretched out side by side, like the ties under the railroad tracks, is alluded to by the title of one of the chapters, "Entre rieles y durmientes." And it was indeed from "among rails and ties" that the prospering Chinese settlement that became Salsipuedes, Panama's Chinatown, eventually rose to life. Remembering the tribulations of the *durmientes* (the departed), the narrator says that, for the Chinese, "a man living between heaven and earth is the swift passing of a stallion seen through a crack: a mere instant that cannot be ignored" (29). Later a poet adds that we must "allow the living to live as well as they can, since there is no return for the departed" (112).

The streets of Salsipuedes, the narrator tells us, are home to a multitude of people representing all the races of the earth, a place that shelters all newcomers: "Those who live there, live as best they can." Its images in motion, the sounds, fragrances, tastes, and colors of the East, evoke for Panamanians myriad emotions, perceptions, dreams, desires, pastimes, places, and people that ceased being alien long ago. There are nostalgic laments throughout Chong Ruiz's book. A century and a half after the diaspora, an immigrant resident of Salsipuedes echoes the poet Wang Ji, saying that when he comes in contact with someone from the homeland, perhaps that person cannot perceive all that is going through his soul (148).

The Chinese Panamanian poet César Young Núñez offers a different perspective in an interview for the book *Ser escritor en Panamá*: "To be a writer in Panama is like walking in the opposite direction of the rest of the people who make up our society. It could be compared to those creatures mentioned by Umberto Eco in *The Name of the Rose*, whose feet aim backward, so that whoever follows their footprints always ends up at the point of departure and never where he intends to go."[15] For that reason, Young Núñez explains, he declared himself a "leap-year" poet, meaning one who writes "occasionally," as in once every four years. In a 1986 lecture titled "Confessions of a Leap-Year Poet," he spoke about the "influences" in his poetry with these opening words: "There are situations in life that have an amusing background. And when I speak about poetry, for me in particular, I have to refer to this experience, either because I have been involved many times in situations of this nature, or because humor is a unique ornament of Chinese civilization that I have inherited from my father, whose great and wonderful sense of humor, incidentally, sprung from the fact that most of the time he was in a bad mood."[16] It is noteworthy that Young Núñez points to a close link among different situations in life, in which he looks for the pleasant and the poetic. He thus alludes to two central characteristics of Asian culture, according to Lin Yutang (1895–1976): poetic sensibility and good mood.[17]

Thus he starts by taking us, his audience, almost inadvertently to the roots of his poetry, which for him is nothing more than a means for capturing the world with irony, amusingly, smilingly. Full of mirth, he makes us smile at the humor he inherited from his father, who was always in a bad mood. This irony of opposites allows him to recognize and savor humor in contrast to and as an antidote for lamentation and misfortune, as though through alternation and complementary, Yin and Yang.

In one of his poems he chooses to locate himself in between both phases and, perhaps, both cultures:

FILOSOFÍA ANTIGUA

Entre el Ser y el No Ser
Escojo
la
Y griega.

ANCIENT PHILOSOPHY

Between Being and Non-
Being
I choose
the
and.[18]

His concept of beauty, as in Taoism, is opposed to falsehood. Only the authentic is beautiful, the agreement between words, ideas, and things. To attain beauty, he places himself between being and nonbeing, in that empty space where meanings engender each other. His poetry is often succinct and synthetic, easy and difficult; it deals with the high and the low. As in Taoism, sound and voice harmonize in order to signify.

Another poem makes intertextual and intercultural allusions:

NO ME REGAÑES MAMA

Pasarás por mi vida
sin saber que pasaste
                    —José Ángel Buesa
          Buesa
     Tal vez lo pongas en duda
     Tal vez no lo tomes en serio
     Tal vez lo tomes en duda
     Tal vez lo pongas en serio
     Yo únicamente quería saber
               Mamá
               De dónde son los cantantes.

DON'T SCOLD ME MAMA

> *You shall pass through my life*
> *without ever realizing it*
>   —José Ángel Buesa
> Maybe you cast it in doubt
> Maybe you don't take it seriously
> Maybe you take it in doubt
> Maybe you cast it seriously
> I only wanted to know
>   Mama
>   Where the singers are from.[19]

At first sight these verses do not say much; they seem to be just words, pure signifiers, empty (like Tao's abode). Yet there is an interplay of cultural allusions. The last verse readily points to Severo Sarduy (1937–93, also of Chinese ancestry), who sought to unveil the Chinese imprint on Cuban culture, alongside the African and the Spanish, with his novel *De donde son los cantantes*.[20] Both Sarduy's title and Young Núñez's verse refer to an old Cuban *son* from Oriente Province that was equally popular in Panama, "Son de la Loma": "Mamá, yo quiero saber / de dónde son los cantantes" (Mama, I want to know / where the singers are from).[21] In Young Núñez's ironic title, the poetic voice begs the proverbial Mama not to scold him for prying into his doubtful ethnicity (he was only singing a popular song). Not only is the title encrypted, but the epigraph too refers to one of the most popular verses of the radio era by another (possibly Chinese) Cuban poet, José Angel Buesa (1910–82): "You shall pass through my life without ever realizing it."[22] In sum, the Chinese imprints in the poem, as in Panamanian culture, are often recognized by their absence rather than their presence. They are not in the words, but in their silent, ironic allusions. Between seriousness and jest (like the "little dirty devil"), Young Núñez points to a layered ethnocultural synthesis, implicit in the creolization of several Chinese generations across Panamanian history.

This overview of the Chinese presence, both thematic and authorial, in Panamanian literature, historiography, and popular culture shows a constant reflection about the often difficult, yet at times harmonious integration of Oriental and Caribbean cultures. It is a process marked by the struggle to preserve a painful collective memory and, at the same time, negotiate new unfolding identities. As a result, it is safe to say that the diverse contributions of the Chinese immigrants, their descendants, and community now constitute a firmly rooted tradition that has profoundly changed and enriched Panamanian society, opening unsuspected possibilities in a globalized future.

Notes

Editor's Note: This essay was translated by Humberto Leignadier and Lucas Katz.

1. The "little dirty devil" is a folkloric character from the Azuero Peninsula in Panama, whose origins are lost in the sixteenth century. It once had religious significance, but nowadays he comes out dancing to the guitar and castanets at carnivals and patron saint celebrations. A key element of his costume is a mask of an animal or devil that covers the dancer's face.

2. See Aims McGuinness in Alfredo Castillero Calvo, ed., *Historia general de Panamá* (Panama City: Digital Designs Group, 2004), 2:145.

3. Juan David Morgan, *El caballo de oro: La gran aventura de la construcción del ferrocarril de Panamá* (Barcelona: Ediciones B., 2005).

4. Willis J. Abbot, *Panama and the Canal in Picture and Prose* (London: Syndicate Publishing, 1913). Also see Otis Fessenden Nott, *Illustrated History of the Panama Railroad* (New York: Harpers, 1861).

5. Albert Memmi, *Portrait du colonisé / Portrait du colonisateur* (1957; Paris: Payot, 1973), 112.

6. Fanon theorizes in *The Wretched of the Earth* that colonization produces psychological and existential alienation and marginalization on the colonized in a system where the closed colonizer-colonized relationship generates the entire set of binary constructs on which colonial ideology rests.

7. Rosa María Britton, *La muerte tiene dos caras* (San Jose: Editorial Costa Rica, 1987).

8. Enrique Jaramillo Levi, *Ahora que soy él* (San Jose, Costa Rica: Imprenta Nacional, 1985), 29–54.

9. Eustorgio Chong Ruiz, *Los chinos en la sociedad panameña* (Panama City: INAC, 1993), 71.

10. "El negociado chinero y sus peligros" (The Chinese Business and Its Dangers), editorial, *El Panameño*, November 21, 1988.

11. Joseph Schott, *Rails across Panama: The Story of the Building of the Panama Railroad, 1849–1855* (New York: Bobbs-Merrill, 1967), 177.

12. Rogelio Sinán, *Cuentos de Rogelio Sinán* (San Jose, Costa Rica: EDUCA, 1971).

13. Country folk in Panama call the Chinese population *paisanos* (fellow countrymen), denoting their condition as sharing the same country.

14. Cited by Lin Yutang, *Mi patria y mi pueblo*, in Chong Ruiz, 78.

15. César Young Núñez in Enrique Jaramillo Levi, ed., *Ser escritor en Panamá* (Panama City: Fundación Cultural Signos, 1999), 394. This book is a compilation of interviews with twenty-nine Panamanian writers at the end of the twentieth century.

16. César Young Núñez, *Lectura para lectores* (Panama City: Ediciones Formato Diesiséis, 1987), 65.

17. Lin Yutang, *La importancia de vivir*, trans. Román A. Jiménez, 33rd ed. (Buenos Aires: Editorial Sudamericana, 1977); Lin Yutang, *The Importance of Living* (New York: Reynal & Hitchcock, 1937).

18. César Young Núñez, *Poemas de rutina* (Panama City: Escritores Asociados, 1967), 55.

19. César Young Núñez, *Carta a Blancanieves* (Panama City: INAC, 1976), 18.

20. Severo Sarduy, *De donde son los cantantes* (Mexico City: Joaquín Mortiz, 1967).

21. *Editor's Note:* "Mamá, son de la Loma" (1922), by the Cuban music icon Miguel Matamoros, was first performed in Panama by his trio in 1933. The idea for the song originated when Matamoros overheard a girl in Santiago ask her mother where such new-sounding singers were from: "Are they from Havana?" The mother replied, "No, they're from the Hill," meaning they are local country boys. The chorus repeats, "They're from the hill (Oriente) and sing on the plain (Havana)." Sarduy plays on Matamoros's "hidden" Chinese ancestry, hinted at by his facial features and his compositions "La conga de los chinos buenos" (1939) and "La corneta china," as well as his album *La China en la rumba: 1928–1951*. Thus, presumed to be of Spanish and African origin, the quintessential Cuban *son*, a centerpiece of Caribbean musical and cultural identity, ironically bears a hidden Chinese imprint.

22. César Young Núñez recognizes his share of Creole sentimentalism and his weakness for romantic Latin American songbooks with their *boleros* and *corridos*, which make up a souvenir album of his poetic vision. See "Confesiones," *Lectura para lectores*, 81.

CHAPTER TWELVE

Siu Kam Wen and the Subjectification of Chinese Peruvians in "El tramo final"

Debra Lee-DiStefano

The concept of an Asian Latin American identity is an elusive creature in Latin American literary and cultural studies. The Orientalist approach, which still permeates Latin Americanist discourse, is to deny the ethnic classification of Latin Americans of Asian ancestry, such as Japanese Peruvians or Chinese Cubans, as representative of what a Latin American is. When history books talk of the composite of Latin American ethnicity, the trinity of Indian, European, and Black still stands as the marker. However, the ethnic and cultural mixture of hundreds of thousands of Asian immigrants, from the Far East, Southeast, and South, Middle, and Near East, over the past two centuries adds new branches to the model.[1] The contributions that Latin Americans of Asian descent have made are not minuscule. They are simply often excluded when placed alongside the history of the dominant culture.

The field of literature is no exception. As Ma Sheng-Mei states in *Immigrant Subjectivities* regarding literary studies, "The emphasis has been largely on Francophone and Anglophone literatures of Africa, Australia, the Caribbean, and the Indian sub-continent with scant scrutiny of the Pacific Rim or its continuum in immigrant enclaves in the West."[2] Coincidentally, although few works attempt to treat the many facets of Asian Latin Americanness, two anthologies do serve as justification for the feasibility of the study of Asian Latin American literary and cultural impacts: *Encounters: People of Asian Descent in the Americas* by Roshni Rustomji-Kerns, Rajini Srikanth, and Leny Mendoza Strobel and *Asians in Latin America* by Jane Cho.[3] Moreover researchers such as Jeffrey Lesser, Clara Chu, and

Russell Leong, to name a few, have strived to achieve an integration of the experiences and cultural production of Asians south of the border into codified fields of academic study in the United States.[4] Such research suggests that Asian immigrants to Latin America and their experiences often replicate the transnational experience of other diasporic groups. The issues of language, culture, place, and Otherness resound just as strongly in the Asian Latin American experience as they do in those of the Asian American, African American, and Indigenous groups.

In this essay I discuss the difficulty of legitimizing the claim that Asian Latin Americans and their accomplishments, as academic notions, merit inclusion in the definitions of national identity in their respective nations of origin or residency. I present the case of Chinese Peruvians as an example of the legal and social milieu into which Asian Latin Americans have been catapulted and how they in turn have responded to questions regarding their national identity. I review the case not only as history but also in terms of the literary response to the Chinese Peruvian situation as presented by Siu Kam Wen.

The works of Siu Kam Wen are hidden treasures within Peruvian literature. They portray a vision of Peru that could never be expressed in a Mario Vargas Llosa novel. His characters are Chinese Peruvians; some are immigrants, some second or third generation, but all depict to some degree the dilemma of the Peruvian of Asian descent. This centralization of Chinese Peruvians as protagonists and subjects permits the reader to enter into a subculture whose history is as pertinent to the history of Peru as that of the Chinese in the United States, but likewise just as forgotten.

The academic approach to the concept of Asian Latin Americanness has expanded throughout the past decade as the limits of long-established categories of identity have come under question. Globalization and the postmodern fragmentation of established social structures have brought to light the erroneous vision of homogeneous groups whose borders were at one time unpassable. For example, the fields of Afro-Romance studies and Pacific Rim studies defy the traditional positions of where Blacks and Asians legitimately belong. The recognition of the heterogeneity of a nation's ethnic composite obliges academia to question the definition upon which national identities are established. In 1989 Shirley Hune stated, "There is a need to develop a theoretical explanation of the contemporary Asian Diaspora in the post-colonial period."[5] The exclusion of non-U.S. Asian populations in Asian American studies and the same exclusion of Asian populations in Latin American studies prompted the current research into these forgotten groups.

Lane Ryo Hirabayashi addresses this polemic by posing the two main questions that complicate the issue: "Does the study of Asians in the Americas fall readily within the domain of traditional Latin American/Area studies? Or should Asians in the Americas be studied as an integral part of Asian American Studies?"[6] I would argue that the answer to both questions is an emphatic "Yes." By definition the very term Asian Latin American implies an explicit relationship to both fields of study. Asian diaspora studies would find interest in the successes and obstacles experienced by Asians in Latin America. Their identification and self-realization as Latin American succeeds over all other concepts of what Latin American studies considers authentic. And the very term *American* denotes a questionable realm of signification, having been usurped by the United States while realistically applying to all of the Americas. I would also contend that the need to go beyond mere historical circumstances and concentrate on the integrative elements (philosophy, art, social institutions) of Latin Americans of Asian descent in their respective countries is still prominent.

To be sure, the field of Asian Latin American studies is traversing the same path as did African American, Asian American, and Afro-Hispanic studies. The history of academic exclusion in the United States of minority literature, as it was once called, also extends to Latin America, due partially to the fact that academic discourse in the Americas has often stemmed from the research and foci of U.S. academics.[7] Various scholars have attempted to initiate closer inspection of the Asian Latin American situation. Starting in the 1999–2000 academic year, Stanford University and the Center for Latin American Studies sponsored courses that promoted the study of Asian immigration to Latin America and the cultural impact it had on both the immigrants and the various receiving countries, a significant step toward codifying the field as a legitimate academic and humanistic topic. That same year, funded by the U.S. Department of Education, Florida International University launched its Asian Globalization and Latin America Project, which joined its Asian Studies Program, Modern Languages Department, and Latin American and Caribbean Center in ongoing research, curriculum development, conference series, and publications, culminating in this book, which explores the many facets of Hispanic Orientalism and whose apropos nature supports the necessity for the inclusion of this topic into the academic arena.

Recently various Latin American countries have initiated their own versions of the Second Harlem Renaissance in the United States by encouraging the promotion of their ethnic minority groups. In reference to Asian groups, in both Cuba and Peru organizations have been established to encourage inquiry into their histories and impact on society. In Cuba the Grupo Promotor del Barrio Chino (inaugurated in 1996) holds annual conferences on issues that affect Chinese Cubans. In 1999 they partnered with the International Society for the Study of Chinese Overseas and the University of Havana to hold a conference on the status of Chinese abroad and throughout Latin America. In Peru the relationship established with Japan under Alberto Fujimori's presidency prompted the construction of the Japan Culture Center, which explores the history of Japanese Peruvians and encourages a reconnection to the language and culture that were prohibited during World War II. Notwithstanding these efforts, the lack of examination regarding how these citizens engage their own positions within their countries is still prevalent.

Bearing all this in mind, this study attempts to steer clear of relegating the Asian Latin American to a fixed position. My goal is rather to explore one of the many Asian Latin American voices and determine how that voice demonstrates its position, cognizant of its individual situation while at the same time expressing a viewpoint that reflects aspects of what could be said to be the Asian Latin American experience.[8] I focus on an example of literary self-expression: a short story that depicts the lives of members of the Chinese *barrio*. My analysis begins with a brief recounting of the initial history of Chinese Peruvians, followed by an introduction to the literature of Siu Kam Wen and an examination of his story "El tramo final" (The Final Stretch), which serves as an example of the integration of Chinese in Peruvian society from a Chinese perspective.

Consistent Chinese immigration to Peru has its starting point in the Law of November 17, 1849. Like other countries whose agricultural economies had been dependent on slave labor, Peru encountered a labor shortage after Independence, with the abolition of slavery, and had to look for other means of acquiring workers. The Law of November 17 legalized the entry of Chinese immigrants, promising exclusive importation rights to Domingo Elías and Juan Rodríguez for four years. The law also stipulated that those who contracted the laborers would receive thirty pesos per individual who arrived in groups of fifty or more. The law exonerated the Chinese immigrants from military service. Essentially the Chinese would be contracted for a certain period of time, paid an agreed-upon salary, and allowed to return to China at the end of the contract or else recontract themselves.[9]

The first seventy-five Chinese arrived aboard the Danish boat *Frederic Wilhelm* on October 15, 1849, one month before the law officially went into effect. The trip from Chinese ports such as Amoy, Wampoa, and Swataw, known as the Camino de China, was almost double the length of the

Middle Passage in the Atlantic slave trade. While contracts were supposed to guarantee fair and humane treatment, the manner in which Chinese "coolies" were contracted was often suspect. Kidnapping and false pretenses served as the impetus for many of those who immigrated. By 1853 problems were plaguing the system to the point that the government revoked the Law of 1849. It was apparent that Peruvian nationals were not prepared for the introduction of another racial element into their already stratified system. Subsequent legislation proved the discriminatory turn that the government had taken toward the Chinese. In 1856 contract labor was banned in a law stating that "the introduction of Asian settlers, in addition to not bettering the country because they are a degraded race, is degenerating into a sort of black slavery" (70). As the trade continued, ignoring the ban, it was stipulated that individual contractors could bring imported laborers but that "they should not be weak, sick, degenerated, and corrupted men as are the Asians" (70). The insistence that Chinese not become an integral part of Peruvian society is witnessed in the Supreme Decree of June 5, 1869, which ordered that Chinese whose contracts had expired had thirty days to find a job or they would be considered vagrants. By 1872 Asian immigration was considered "a formal cancer" and "a social problem that our public officials are painfully faced with" (71). In 1873 the Registro de Inmigrantes Asiáticos was created to oversee all immigrants from Asia who entered the country.

Notwithstanding Peruvian sentiment, the contract labor system was about to meet its demise. International incidents such as the *María Luz* affair, which pertained to the mutiny of Chinese coolies bound for Peru, brought the first direct contact between the Chinese and Peruvian governments. China had ignored the abuse sustained by its subjects in the Americas; however, the involvement of the Japanese, Russian, and U.S. governments, coupled with complaints from Chinese citizens, convinced the emperor to investigate the conditions of Chinese contract laborers. The governor of Macao ended the coolie trade in March 1874. An agreement between Peru and China known as the Tratado García y García–Lu Hun Chang assured that all Chinese whose contracts had expired would receive passage back to China if they so desired. A free trade and immigration agreement was also signed (71).

Friendly and open ties between both countries were never established. In 1908 a rumor that over fifty thousand Chinese were about to immigrate to Peru led to attacks on Chinese immigrants and their businesses. In May 1909 a decree banning all Asian immigration was enacted. This was rescinded in August with the Porras–Wu Tang Fang agreement that set immigration restrictions on both sides. Other agreements followed, but the dislike of Asian immigrants culminated in the Resolución Suprema No. 737 of November 30, 1939, which suspended immigration yet again. The severity of the law was offset slightly by the Solf y Muro–Li Tchuin Act of 1941, which provided that only Chinese who had lived in Peru prior to January 1, 1940, and their wives and children under the age of ten could immigrate (71). Xenophobic attitudes and legislation against Chinese immigrants also extended to the Japanese, who began to arrive in 1899. In 1918 a letter to the president on behalf of Peruvian workers stated that the Chinese and Japanese "are impoverishing our homes and degenerating our race" (71). By this time, Chinese presence in Peru had lasted almost seventy years, enough for third and fourth generations to be born. But their experiences were foreign still.

To be sure, Siu Kam Wen is well aware of the skepticism regarding integrating the Asian Latin American into a definition of national identity.[10] In an interview, he stated that he experienced Peruvian racism on many occasions. He arrived in Peru in 1959 with his mother, traveling from China to Hong Kong before heading for Peru. They were joining his father, who had immigrated to Peru in the 1930s, returning briefly to China once to get married. Siu spoke only Hakka and Cantonese. For three years he studied in the Sam Men, or Chinese school, until circumstances forced him to attend a state high school. He completed his studies in literature at the University of San Marcos. Siu confesses that his lack of knowledge of Spanish hindered his integration into Peruvian society. Later the fact that he was an immigrant would preclude him from working in places where there was a mandatory quota of native Peruvian workers, as well as from receiving scholarships reserved for Peruvian nationals. He also discovered that the publishing world did not approve of the characters in his stories, as he was told that they were not representative of Peru or Peruvians. In an effort to change his life, Siu moved to Hawaii, where he resides today and works for the Foundation of Art and Culture.

Siu's stories began garnering academic attention only in the late 1990s.[11] The French academic Béatrice Cáceres, who has studied how Siu discursively deals with his transnational status as well as how his works fit into the scope of Peruvian literature, observes, "Siu Kam Wen offered Peruvians, on one hand, a new appraisal of today's Chinese community, its culture, and literature, and on the other hand, he methodically and meticulously studied the Spanish language in order to transform it and to integrate in it Chinese aesthetics. . . . He remains today the most prolific writer in Chinese-Peruvian literature."[12] Siu's stories are prime representations of the Chinese Peruvian neighborhoods.

His short story "El tramo final" is a marvelous example of the situation in which transnationals like Siu often find themselves. The story is about a second-generation Chinese Peruvian named Lou Chen, who has achieved a great deal of success. He is married to a Peruvian *chola* (mestiza). They have two sons and live in a grand mansion with servants in Monterrico, a wealthy *colonia* of Lima. Chen's mother, Ah Po, who had immigrated to Peru after the Japanese occupation of China, is the antagonist in his new life. She still wears the old style of dress, regardless of what her son is able to buy her. At a crucial point in the story, she decides to return to their old neighborhood to live with her other son, Ah Seng, who is not a success. She reunites with old friends of the family with whom she is happy to speak, because they speak Cantonese and she speaks no Spanish. The figure of Ah Po, and a comparison between Lou Chen's and Victor Choy's families, will serve as the focal points for the discussion of transnational identity and integration into mainstream society.

The first discussion revolves around the two families and a comparison of their situations, particularly the family units and how the family members interact with one another. Lou Chen and Victor Choy portray very different fathers. Chen, who had once owned a store, made his fortune off the poor: "The Choys [are] tenants of Lou Chen's to whom he had sold the sundry shop, the same shop where he had worked for more than a decade before discovering that the business of microbuses—and later usury—was much more profitable" (25). His unethical approach to success and the great wealth he accumulated have affected his wife and children, who are spoiled and preoccupied with spending money. Mercedes, his wife, is always getting her hair done and having new dresses made. She is "of irritable temperament" and "tended to make life difficult for her husband" (21). His sons, Juan Carlos and Francisco José, always sport the newest fashions and are constantly changing girlfriends. The children cannot even communicate with their grandmother, who speaks no Spanish. To fit the part of his new luxurious surroundings, Chen even takes to dying his hair. In his home, assimilation to Peruvian society is complete. All vestiges of Chinese culture have been erased: "In a word, all the occupants of the new and elegant mansion were as if they were made to live there, or at least they made a fervent effort to that effect" (22).

The Choy family is different. Victor Choy has not achieved the economic success of Chen, although he would like to. In fact the family used to live in the back of the store before the Chen family vacated the apartment to move to the mansion. Choy's family, however, observes the customs of their Chinese heritage. Victor reads the Chinese newspaper, his daughters all attend Sam Men, the Chinese school, and they all speak Cantonese. The oldest daughter, Teresa, speaks with an ease that is almost instinctual. Her use of the language is remarkably beautiful given that the narrator says that "nobody, not even Don Victor, had taught her to speak Cantonese that way" (28). Their father's rigidity at prohibiting Spanish at home assured that the family's Chinese ties would prevail. Mrs. Choy, unlike Chen's wife, is Chinese and shares a common background with Ah Po. They reminisce together about life in China before and after the Japanese occupation. Ah Po prefers to spend every day in the Choy family store rather than in the company of her older son and his family.

Chen's economic success and new lifestyle convince Ah Po that she needs to return to the old neighborhood to live with her younger son. She refuses to assimilate to the new life. She is "the only sour note. . . . [She] didn't realize that there existed a certain moral obligation . . . that the owners or occupants of a new house . . . all fit the mold"—a refusal comparable to "una profanación" (22).

Ah Po, the character around whom all the action is set, appears to be a person trapped in time. She cannot live in the new house with Chen. She wears the same clothes that women of Hakka origin wear, clothes that she makes. Chen is embarrassed to be seen with his mother because her simple style of dress, in contrast with his and his family's, "had the deplorable effect of reminding Lou Chen, and proclaiming to the rest of the world, his parvenu origin" (23). Ah Po speaks no Spanish. Her first twenty years in Lima were spent in the Barrio Chino, where she spoke with no one who wasn't Chinese. Her husband, who had worked as a cook in a *chifa* when he first arrived in Peru, became the typesetter for the Chinese newspaper *La Voz de la Colonia China*. He never had his own business or achieved the success of his son. After his death, Ah Po went to live with Lou Chen. Her life outside the Barrio Chino cut her off from all social interaction; she couldn't, and wouldn't, make the effort to learn Spanish, and her son's family never attempted to learn Hakka or Cantonese. She would speak only to her sons and any other Chinese she might be lucky enough to meet. Her inability to interact makes her an island in a sea of strangers.

Her decision to live with Ah Seng allows her to walk to the Choys' store to see them, to speak, to be the person she knows how to be. The comfort of the store is her only real joy in life: "Seated on the stool or in the company of the girls, Ah Po was immensely happy. . . . Ah Po had only needed to spend four months in Monterrico to understand that the simple act of sitting on those hard wooden stools or listening to the sing-song voices of Don Victor's daughters could bring her such comfort" (28). She is saddened to learn that the Choys are leaving the country for El Salvador because of fears of a communist takeover. The new proprietors, although Chinese, are two single men who are engrossed in the nocturnal activities of Callao and have little time for a lonely old woman.

The departure of the Choy family marks the point of Ah Po's eventual demise. Her sense of belonging that the Choys and their store gave her is gone. Her ministrations to Ah Seng are trying on her health, although they are the only incidents in her life that allow her to feel useful. Lou Chen, alarmed by her state of decline, asks her again to come live with him, but she declines. It is Ah Po's death that marks the end and climax of the story. She does not wither away from depression but is killed when a drunk driver hits her. She realizes she is dying and welcomes the moment: "Ah Po understood that she was dying and although she couldn't move a single muscle, she mentally extended her arms towards the angels that were descending from heaven in a sign of welcome and gratitude" (31). Death is a welcome moment for Ah Po. Since she speaks no Spanish and does not mix with Limeña society, it is highly unlikely that this is a Christian welcoming. In fact it is a historical marker, describing the gates of a cemetery in Lima. Ah Po is happy to leave a world in which she has no voice or place.

The focus on the contrast between the Chen and Choy families as well as on the figure of Ah Po demonstrates the polarized positions in which the transnational often finds himself. Ah Po and Victor Choy depict rigid adherence to the previous culture. Ah Po does not assimilate to the new culture but allows her children to do so. Choy does not assimilate, nor does he permit his daughters to do so in his presence. Chen completely assimilates, to the point that he is embarrassed by reminders of his past. His progeny do not understand their father's ancestry. There is no middle ground; this story shows no character who has mediated successfully between both worlds, that of Lima and the Peruvian community and that of the Chinese neighborhoods.

The transnational must decide between one venue and the other. His economic success is dependent on his assimilation to the new country's values, language, and practices. His original cultural integrity remains intact if he isolates himself from the new culture. It is this polarized, paradoxical situation that is witnessed in "El tramo final." The figures of Lou Chen and Ah Po embody opposite sides of the transnational experience. The family unit disintegrates from pressures coming from both the outside and the inside. As Ma writes, "The process of searching for identity goes beyond mere individual efforts, but it derives from, as well as contributes to, a larger cultural ethos" (2). The choices of the transnational in the new society are manifested in these two characters. Chen depicts the assimilated immigrant. He directs his life in a way that would erase his past. His marriage to a Peruvian *chola* permits the erasure of Chinese practices within the family, including both language and tradition. His economic success allows him to live among the elite of Lima. His clothes, cars, and appearance all form a comfortable façade within which he can hide his past. His only reminder of his roots is a mother who refuses to change. Ah Po, the other side of the coin, is obstinately against change. Her sense of self is derived from being Chinese and all that it entails. While she never attempts to integrate, the loss of her cultural outlet (the Choy family) deprives her of a sense of community.

Moreover, in its depiction of this polemic of transnational identity, this story achieves what few Latin American stories with Asian characters have: it places the Chinese Peruvian at the center and tells his story through psychological descriptions of difference rather than physical markers of difference. The characters are Chinese; their experiences are told through their eyes, as they would see their society. The evidence of their situation is not expressed as an opposition to Limeña society; rather Limeña society revolves around them and the issues that they face. There are few physical descriptions. The author uses cultural markers such as language and style of dress to show the "Chineseness" of his characters. This non-Orientalist approach to the material demonstrates the naturalness and, dare I say, authenticity of the characters and their situations. Siu displaces the focus away from the dominant culture, objectifying it, while subjectifying the characters. That is not to say that the dominance of Limeña society is nonexistent. On the contrary, Siu's characters are all affected by it. The effect is so ingrained that there is no need to describe it.

What Siu manages to accomplish in this story, and others, is to rewrite the Peruvian experience. His characters are Peruvian; they just happen to represent another part of Peruvian society. His stories, when compared to those of other Asian Hispanic writers, such as José Watanabe or Pedro Shimose, actually bring to light in an open yet subtle manner what the Asian Latin American experiences. Siu's stories are examples of what Rustomji-Kerns describes as "works of literature and art as creations of the writer's or artist's personal, unique vision, rather than as 'factual' social documentaries for entire communities" (6). Through individual characters and their personal experiences, he is able to depict what the Asian Peruvian community faces in regard to cultural inclusion and its effects on their sense of identity.

The vision of the transnational's experience that permeates the works of Siu Kam Wen is but one of the many facets of what can be called the Asian Latin American experience. Not all authors, painters, journalists, or politicians hold the same viewpoints as Siu. However, it is this variegation of thoughts and ideas that makes this field of study so fascinating. Further inspection of its varying histories and cultural significances can only serve to enrich academic inquiry.

Notes

1. Studies show that 2 percent of the population in the Americas is of Asian ancestry, a figure that approaches 15 million people. See Tony Affigne and Pei-te Lien, "People of Asian Descent in the Americas: Theoretical Implications of Race and Politics," *Amerasia Journal* 28.2 (2002): 4.

2. Sheng-mei Ma, *Immigrant Subjectivities in Asian American and Asian Diaspora Literatures* (Albany: State University of New York Press, 1998), 1.

3. Roshni Rustomji-Kerns, Rajini Srikanth, and Leny Mendoza Strobel, eds., *Encounters* (Lanham, Md.: Rowan and Littlefield, 1999) contains literary accounts written by Asian Latin Americans as testaments to their experiences. They engage many key topics in postcolonial studies: place, language, home, and marginalization. Jane Cho's *Asians in Latin America* (San Francisco: Bolerium Books, 1999) provides an extensive bibliography on Asian Latin American life and history.

4. See Russell Leong, ed., "One Decade Later: Asians in the Americas," *Amerasia Journal* 28.2 (2002): v–viii. Clara Chu, a professor of information studies at UCLA, spearheaded a website on the Chinese Diaspora (http://www.gseis.ucla.edu/faculty/chu/chinos/). Jeff Lesser researches Japanese communities in Brazil; see his *Negotiating National Identity: Immigrants, Minorities and the Struggle for Ethnicity in Brazil* (Durham, N.C.: Duke University Press, 1999). Other prominent critics include Evelyn Hu-DeHart, Lisa Hun, and Karen Tei-Yamashita.

5. Shirley Hune, "Expanding the International Dimensions of Asian American Studies," *Amerasia Journal* 15.2 (1989): xxii.

6. Lane Ryo Hirabayashi, "Reconsidering Transculturation and Power," *Amerasia Journal* 28.2 (2002): xi. Hirabayashi utilizes the concept of transculturation as defined by Fernando Ortiz in *Cuban Counterpoint: Tobacco and Sugar* (Durham, N.C.: Duke University Press, 1995) to demonstrate the confusion and limitations of prevailing notions of diaspora and transculturation.

7. The strides made by critics such as Renato Rosaldo, Gloria Anzaldúa, Debra Castillo, and Walter Mignolo to develop theoretical approaches from within the Latino and Chicano communities instead of using U.S. or European models serve as hope for the possibility of developing a theory, as mentioned by Shirley Hune.

8. This point, that it is an individual voice that may or may not reflect on the whole group, is essential because some Asian Latin Americans do not necessarily recognize any effect that their *mestizaje* may have had on their self-identification nor on how they are perceived by their communities. See Debbie Lee, "Entrevista con Pedro Shimose," *PALARA* (Fall 2000): 84–89.

9. Abraham Padilla Bendezú, "Inmigración china," *Boletín de Lima: Peruvian Scientific Cultural Review* 20.114 (1998): 69. Subsequent page numbers cite this article. All translations are mine unless otherwise noted.

10. Kam Wen Siu, "El tramo final" in *El tramo final* (Lima: Lluvia Editores, 1985).

11. Maan Lin, "Writers of the Chinese Diaspora: Siu Kam Wen in Peru," PhD diss., Columbia University, 1997; Roy Kerr, "Lost in Lima: The Asian-Hispanic Fiction of Siu Kam Wen," *Chasqui* 28.1 (1999): 54–65; Huei Lan (Lourdes) Yen, "Identity, Culture, and Resistance in Two Stories of Siu Kam Wen," *Alternative Orientalisms in Latin America and Beyond*, ed. Ignacio López-Calvo (Newcastle, U.K.: Cambridge Scholars Publishing, 2007), 146–55; Ignacio López-Calvo, "Sino-Peruvian Identity and Community as Prison: Siu Kam Wen's Rendering of Self-Exploitation and Other Survival Strategies," *Afro-Hispanic Review* 27.1 (2008): 73–90; Debra Lee-DiStefano, "Identity Confusion in Siu Kam Wen's 'La conversión de Uei Kong,'" *One World Periphery Reads the Other: Knowing the "Oriental" in the Americas and the Iberian Peninsula*, ed. Ignacio López-Calvo (Newcastle, U.K.: Cambridge Scholars Publishing, 2010), 102–13.

12. Béatrice Cáceres, "De Zulen à Siu Kam Wen: Cent ans de littérature sino-péruvienne," *Exils et Créations Littéraires* (Angers: L'Harmattan, 2001), 155. Also see her "Siu Kam Wen entre la Chine et l'Occident," *Cosmopolitisme ou Ethnicite* (Angers: L'Harmattan, 2002).

CHAPTER THIRTEEN

Zen in Brazil

Cannibalizing Orientalist Flows

Cristina Rocha

The head of Sôtô Zen or any Japanese Buddhist school is like a prince, a Japanese prince. I experienced this when I was lecturing at the university in Londrina.[1] When the head of the Higashi Hongwanji *came from Japan, they invited me for the ceremony since they knew I was connected to Buddhism and was a lecturer at the university. It was a fantastic experience! The way "the prince" behaved was so different! The way he conducted the ceremony, the way he looked at me, his elegant movements. . . . He was incredibly aristocratic! So unlike the Brazilian-Japanese here!*

In considering the Japanese Diaspora in Brazil, I will examine how European ideas of Orientalism mediated the Brazilian cultural elite's perceptions of Japan, Buddhism in general, and Zen. Rather than viewing Japanese immigrant communities in Brazil as a source of the "exotic East," Brazilian artists and intellectuals—and eventually the general public—were inspired either indirectly by ideas of Orientalism originating from cultural centers in the West such as France, England, and the United States, or directly through assumptions about the "authenticity" of Japan itself.[2] As a result, Zen was never confined to the narrow boundaries of the temples established by Sôtô Zenshû (the only Japanese Zen school in Brazil),[3] but has been disseminated in elite culture.

In this light, I start by examining the history and predicament of the reception of foreign products and ideas in Brazil. I contend that such a situation derives from what Edward Said has referred to as the discourse of "Romantic Orientalism" (a nostalgic yearning for a pure and pristine past) as well as from a deeply rooted set of class distinctions in Brazilian society. While the Brazilian cultural elite were drawn toward fantasies of lost wisdom in ancient Japanese classical ages long past, they did not view Japanese immigrants in Brazil as legitimate carriers of this heritage. These immigrants were either seen as inhabitants of a "modern" and degraded Japan and hence lacking in "authenticity" or lacking in artistic and cultural refinement by virtue of their status as peasants at the time of their arrival in Brazil. For the same reasons, non-Japanese Brazilians very seldom turned to Japanese Brazilian religious practices and beliefs, and did so only if they matched their own *imaginaire* of Zen.

Misplaced Ideas: Fascination, Copy, and Struggle for Authenticity

We Brazilians and other Latin Americans constantly experience the artificial, inauthentic, and imitative nature of our cultural life. An essential element in our critical thought since Independence, it has been variously interpreted from romantic, naturalist, modernist, right-wing, left-wing, cosmopolitan, and nationalist points of view, so we may suppose that the problem is enduring and deeply rooted.

The Brazilian literary critic Roberto Schwarz identifies this predicament of inauthenticity in Brazil's 1822 Declaration of Independence, when the newly created empire adopted the British parliamentary system, along with republican ideas of the French Revolution, but kept the colonial system of slavery. In this context, equality, civil liberties, and the separation between public and private were juxtaposed with the slave trade, clientelism, and large agricultural states. This explicit "contradiction between the 'real' Brazil and the ideological prestige of the countries used as models" has since been at the core of discussions of national identity and culture (such as those between nationalists and internationalists) and has adopted different forms.[4]

According to Schwarz, in the nineteenth century the discussion ranged from those who thought the colonial system should be supplanted by new foreign ideas, to those who identified the colonial system with the "real" or "original/authentic/genuine" Brazil that should be protected against the uncritical imitation of foreign models. Although slavery was abolished in 1888 and Brazil became a republic the following year, harsh inequalities persisted, and questions regarding which foreign ideas had a real place in Brazil and which were just imitative or mimicry were constantly on the agenda. In the 1920s the modernist movement tackled these questions in a different way. Instead of regarding this disjuncture between rural patriarchy and bourgeois ideology as problematic, the modernist Oswald de Andrade (1890–1954) published his *Manifesto Antropófago* in 1928, in which he offered a response to the perceived problem of Brazilian cultural dependency by celebrating creolization's ability for absorbing or "cannibalizing" European metropolitan culture and thus giving it a local flavor. The outcome of these "digested" foreign influences was seen as something new and unique. Andrade's witty pun in his manifesto was the perfect metaphor for such cultural cannibalism: "Tupi or not Tupi, that is the question!"— Tupí being one of the main indigenous peoples of Brazil.

In subsequent decades, the dominant nationalism of the Vargas regime (1932–45 and 1950–54) and the ideology of industrial development in the 1950s kept the question of national identity vis-à-vis foreign culture alive. In the 1960s the rise of the mass media, the internationalization of capital, and the associated commodification of social relations further exposed the country to foreign influences. The United States took over from Europe as the primary source of culture, models of behavior, and worldviews.[5] Schwarz shows that such "hankering for the latest products of advanced countries" has been disseminated throughout the whole of society, be it in the form of popular culture and its products or academia's new doctrines and theories (2). It was not only literary critics and philosophers who were concerned about the autochthonous viability and valence of Brazilian culture. As we shall see, writers and poets also agonized about the originality of their own work and ideas.

Schwarz, however, has identified a viable and interesting way out of this national preoccupation with originality. He concludes his article by saying that copying is a false problem if one realizes that the original and the copy, that is, the foreign and the national, are not real oppositions but are deeply interconnected. Imitation entails translation and the consequent generation of "misplaced ideas," which are distinctively Brazilian.[6] Of course, the process of copying "foreign" repertoires of cultural codes, imagery, and ideas is always framed by historically specific relations of hierarchy and asymmetry.[7] As Schwarz notes, "creation *ex nihilo*" is a myth: ideas evolve from ideas, which are meshed in power relations (17). In a globalized world, the flows and patterns of cultural influence and absorption are inevitably enmeshed in what Doreen Massey calls a "power-geometry" that produces uneven effects on the local spaces over which they traverse.[8]

The complex and dynamic relationship between original and copy, global and local, foreign and national offers a useful framework for understanding how and why ideas about Buddhism, Japan, and Zen that emerged in Europe and the United States made their way into Brazilian culture, initially in the academic and intellectual setting and subsequently in 1990s popular culture. In this context, I will address the historical literary production dealing with the Orient, Japan, Japanese poetic forms, Buddhism, and Zen.[9]

Brazilian Orientalism: The "Exotic East" in Brazilian Letters

As early as the nineteenth century, writers such as Fagundes Varela (1841–75), Machado de Assis (1839–1908), and Raimundo Correia (1860–1911) were drawn to European ideas of Orientalism as a source of images of exoticism, wisdom, sensuality, and serenity. This was in spite of the fact that they themselves inhabited a land constructed as exotic in the European imagination. In his poem "Oriental" Fagundes Varela urges his beloved to flee with him "to the delicious Ganges plains," while in "Ideal" he sets his beloved in "the land of the Chinese Empire, in a palace of red porcelain, on a Japanese blue throne."[10]

In 1914 the Brazilian philosopher R. de Farias Brito addressed Buddhism in his *O Mundo Interior: Ensaio sobre os dados geraes da philosophia do espírito* (The Inner World: Essay on General Facts of Spiritual Philosophy). In this book, Christianity and Buddhism were presented as the two most important world religions and the basis for the greatest civilizations: the West and the Orient. Farias Brito thought his era was marked by religious crisis and loss of faith as a result of the discoveries of science. Nevertheless, by advocating the notion that religion, as the moral basis of society, was "philosophy in practice," he argued that it should still be the most important concern of the human spirit: "The religious problem may only be solved by a new religion that can satisfy the present aspirations of the human spirit. [This new doctrine] shall be the outcome of a fusion between East and West, purifying the best from each civilization into a universal synthesis that will establish the spiritual unity of humankind. It will be a battle between Christianity and Buddhism, resulting in something completely new."[11]

The word *purifying* is crucial here. For this philosopher, the new doctrine should expurgate "false dogmas and interpretations" that were imposed throughout time and thus be in accord with the new discoveries of science. Christianity and Buddhism, being religions founded by human beings, were apt for such a task. Farias Brito was clearly influenced by nineteenth-century European Buddhist scholars who, in seeking an alternative to Christianity, constructed Buddhism as "an agnostic, rationalist, ethical movement, [which could become] a foundation for morality in everyday life."[12] In this context, Buddhism could be regarded as scientific and in accord with modern times, since ritualistic and devotional practices and beliefs were thought of as superimposed cultural accretions that corrupted Buddhism over time. Because these European scholars privileged texts over actual practices, they also considered Buddhism a philosophy and not a religion per se. Farias Brito affirms instead that Buddhism is neither materialistic nor nihilistic but "an idealistic religion, derived from a deep and elevated philosophy of the spirit" (112).

The Construction of Japan in the Brazilian *Imaginaire*

In the early twentieth century, Brazilians could gain familiarity with Japan through newspaper articles and books written by the Portuguese writer Wenceslau de Moraes (1854–1929). In contrast to authors who never traveled to the East, Moraes lived in and wrote extensively about the Orient in Portuguese. After living in Macao, on which he wrote many articles for Portuguese newspapers, he moved to Japan in 1898, where he became the Portuguese consul at Kobe. Like the works of Lafcadio Hearn (1850–1904), who nevertheless wrote for an English-speaking audience, Moraes's writings depict Japanese daily life and his love for the country. His works include *Dai-Nippon* (1897), *O Culto do Chá* (The Cult of Tea, 1905), *Bon-Odori* (1916), *Oyoné e Ko-Haru* (1923), *Relance da Alma Japonesa* (Grasping the Japanese Soul, 1926), and *Cartas do Japão* (Letters from Japan, 1927).

Although this material was available in Portuguese, France remained the main source of ideas on Japan. The Brazilian elite in the nineteenth century and the first half of the twentieth century were heavily influenced by French culture through education, fashion, and travel. Pierre Loti (1850–1923), a novelist of exotica and the author of *Madame Chrysanthème* (1887), together with Anatole France and J. K. Huysmans, were widely read by this sector of Brazilian society.[13] In 1908 films featuring the Japanese dancer and actress Sadayakko, famous in Europe and North America at the turn of the century, were well received in Rio de Janeiro. In 1920 an exhibition of Japanese art held in São Paulo clearly echoed the Parisian "Japan boom."[14] In analyzing the reception of three Japanese opera singers who performed *Madame Butterfly* in Brazil (1921, 1924, 1936, and 1940), Shuhei Hosokawa has rightly observed, "No doubt Parisian interest in Japan made a stronger impact on opera-goers than the presence of a small Japanese community in the city."[15] Hosokawa notes that Brazilian journalists were more concerned with the physical appearance of Japanese opera singers than with their artistic talent, focusing at length in their reviews on their petiteness and charm. Due to these singers' ethnic origin, journalists readily identified them with the traits of the characters they played, as if they were incarnated Madame Butterflies. Moreover, heavily influenced by French Japonaiserie, reviewers employed French terms such as *petite femme*, *mignon*, and *poupée* to describe these female artists, not unlike in Loti's *Madame Chrysanthème*. Repeatedly regarding the Japanese singers as miniatures, Hosokawa argues, made them manageable, not threatening to the Western observer, "imbued with intimacy, passion and desirability. . . . Miniature is associated with nostalgia and evokes a pristine past, lost objects, and an irretrievable land" (256).

Hosokawa's analysis sheds light on how French Orientalism profoundly shaped the way many non-Japanese Brazilians regarded Japan in the first quarter of the twentieth century. The fact that Japanese immigration to Brazil had started in 1908, numbering close to sixty thousand immigrants by 1930, and that, moreover, Brazil was soon to become the largest Japanese expatriate community in the world, did not challenge the European mediation of Brazilian perceptions of Japan. This situation is due to two main reasons: first, France was perceived as the center of highbrow culture by Brazilians and the world at large and thus enjoyed a cultural authority that Japan lacked;[16] second, the Japanese in Brazil were of peasant origin and lived mostly in rural areas. The few who lived in the cities worked as small shopkeepers, laundrymen, food vendors, and so on. Because of the deep-rooted presence of slavery in Brazilian history, manual labor of any sort has been traditionally associated with African Brazilians and disenfranchised classes. Only those who have had formal education and use their acquired knowledge in their work are to be considered middle or upper class. Even if the Japanese owned property in urban and rural areas, they still did not enjoy social status and prestige in Brazilian society, since their work remained strongly associated with manual labor.[17] Therefore, in the eyes of Brazilians, they too lacked the necessary cultural capital to be regarded as a source of knowledge on Japan.

Haiku and Zen

A good illustration of European mediation in the flow of ideas from and about Japan, as well as its consequent Orientalist tendency and eventual association with Zen, is haiku, the Japanese seventeen-syllable poem (three lines of five, seven, and five syllables). Haiku has evolved throughout the twentieth century into a popular form of poetry in Brazil. According to the Brazilian literary critic Paulo Franchetti, the interest in haiku has been matched only by the interest in martial arts as a source of knowledge about Japanese culture.[18] Haiku arrived in Brazil, first in French and subsequently English translations, in the diaries of European travelers. These short poems were then regarded as exotic curiosities akin to the elaborate Japanese etiquette, the diminutive sake cups, and the communal bath. Julien Vocance's *Art Poétique* (1921) and Paul-Louis Couchoud's *Sages et Poetes d'Asie* (1923) were the main sources of knowledge on haiku in Brazil during the early twentieth century. The Portuguese writer Wenceslau de Moraes was the first to translate haikus to his mother tongue, albeit in a loose format more akin to Portuguese poetry. However, Brazilian poets took little notice of Moraes's haikus, favoring French translations instead.

Afrânio Peixoto (1876–1947) was one of the first Brazilian poets to attempt to compose haikus, which he learned from reading Couchoud's translations. However, haikus would become a renowned form of poetry in Brazil only in the 1930s through the work of the poet laureate Guilherme de Almeida (1890–1969). Like his predecessors, Almeida first learned about haiku in French translations. Yet he later became engaged with the Japanese Brazilian community as well, after meeting a group of haiku practitioners in São Paulo. He even helped establish and presided over the Aliança Cultural Brasil-Japão, a cultural center for the Japanese Brazilian community.

In the 1950s and 1960s there was a second wave of interest in haiku, which, like the earlier wave, did not draw its understanding of this poetic form from the Japanese Brazilian community. Instead, the translations and writings of Ernest Fenollosa (1853–1908), especially *The Chinese Written Character*, posthumously published in 1919 by the American poet Ezra Pound, were very influential among Brazilian poets from 1955 onward. Fenollosa's and Pound's notion that the ideogram was the core of Chinese and Japanese understanding of the world (since it constructed meaning through juxtaposition and montage) informed the newly founded Brazilian avant-garde Concretist movement established by Augusto and Haroldo de Campos and Décio Pignatari.

Whereas this avant-garde movement associated haiku with the "exotic" Chinese character (*kanji*), the next generation of poets, from the early 1970s through the late twentieth century, identified it strongly with Zen, a connection imported from the works of Reginald Blyth, Alan Watts, D. T. Suzuki, and Jack Kerouac. Suzuki devoted a chapter of his *Zen and Japanese Culture* (1959) to the relationship between Zen and haiku. Paulo Leminski, the harbinger of this Brazilian Zen haiku, would praise its paradoxical, non-Cartesian understanding of the world. In the 1980s and 1990s, through his talks, books, and poems turned into popular songs, Leminski became a highly influential source of ideas about Zen for the intellectual upper middle class of Brazil. In attempting to explain the Brazilian fascination with the haiku, Franchetti has pointed to "a search for an imaginary Japan filled with Zen, feudal ethics, and old contemplative wisdom. In other words, the Japan that exists in Brazilian contemporary imagination seems to be laden with nostalgia, idealization of a pre-industrial world, and life under the Tokugawa regime. In sum, there is still as much exoticism as always" (198).

Indeed haiku is a good example of how global cultural flows from Europe and North America shaped non-Japanese Brazilian perception of Japan and Zen. However, haiku may also be used to unveil how the two groups, Japanese and non-Japanese Brazilians, have related to each other. The strong visibility (in books, newspapers, and lectures) of non-Japanese Brazilians writing haikus obscures the fact that Japanese immigrants, albeit of peasant origin, had been composing haikus since their arrival in Brazil. Masuda Goga, a Japanese Brazilian poet, has argued that the first such haiku was composed onboard the *Kasato-maru* itself, the first ship of immigrants to arrive in Brazil in 1908.[19] Since then haiku clubs and regional and national contests have evolved.[20] Migrant newspapers published in Brazil such as the *Shûkan Nambei* (South American Weekly) and *Brasil Jihô* (Brazil Review), established in 1916 and 1924, respectively, often devoted the same number of pages to poetry as to news stories (Lesser 92). Thus Japanese immigrants and their descendants could have been a more direct source of knowledge on haiku for non-Japanese Brazilians, had they sought them.

It is also worth noting that non-Japanese Brazilians introduced new rhythms into the haiku, and some even added a previously nonexistent title while striving to preserve the connection among haiku, Zen, and Tokugawa Japan. Meanwhile Japanese Brazilians maintained the haiku's traditional format but, curiously, introduced Brazilian *kigo*, seasonal words corresponding to the fauna and flora of their new adoptive land. Thus, since the arrival of haiku in Brazil, the former group has sought to retain Japan as an essentialized, unchanging, and exotic source of Zen and lost wisdom, while the latter has sought to adapt what they understood as the core of the poem, its seasonal feeling, to the Brazilian environment. Indeed Franchetti has remarked that Japanese Brazilians have constantly been amused and baffled to find the ubiquitous presence of Zen and the overemphasis on the Chinese ideogram in the haikus of non-Japanese Brazilians.

To be sure, there are fewer Japanese Brazilians who compose haikus than non-Japanese Brazilians, but the little integration between both groups reflects two circumstances. First is the fact that their sources of understanding about Japan, haiku, and Zen were different. Whereas non-Japanese Brazilians absorbed the flows of ideas and images of Japan from Western metropolitan centers of culture, Japanese Brazilians embodied or inherited them. Second, the system of class distinction in Brazil prevented both the Japanese and the Japanese Brazilians from being seen as bearers of highbrow culture. Both these factors are paramount if one is to understand the gap and struggle between both groups concerning the authenticity of Japanese culture and, as discussed below, their religious practices and beliefs. So let us now turn our attention to how Zen was imported and has been practiced by non-Japanese Brazilian intellectuals since the late 1950s.

Intellectuals as Cosmopolitans: Accumulating Cultural Capital Overseas

Global flows have always influenced and, in turn, been localized in Brazilian society, yet the origins of these flows, rather than fixed essences, are other flows, perhaps older and regional (not global) but nevertheless themselves impure. The same principle and pattern of influence and exchange applies to Zen in Brazil. That is, the need for translation into Portuguese and into Brazilian culture guaranteed that Zen would be creolized locally, in very particular ways. Furthermore, like those who had emulated European Orientalism, later elite intellectuals did not see their knowledge of Zen as a mode of appropriation geared toward cultural resistance but as a tool for a two-pronged complementary assertion: first, of their unique role as translators and interpreters of overseas currents; second, of their prestigious position as a cosmopolitan group. As a result, both these assertions afforded them the cultural capital necessary to reinforce and maintain their own class status in their country.

Here I would like to shed light on how this process of imbuing Zen with prestige and cultural capital was initiated in the late 1950s by a small group of intellectuals, who deployed their knowledge of Zen as a marker of social distinction. While in the 1990s the dynamics of popularization within consumer culture allowed the media to play a powerful role in interpreting Buddhism and Zen for a wider audience, in the late 1950s non-Japanese Brazilian cosmopolitan intellectuals were the sole exponents of how Zen and Buddhism should be represented and understood.[21]

Pierre Bourdieu has shown that social identity is asserted and maintained through difference, which in turn is visible in people's *habitus*.[22] According to Bourdieu, *habitus* is both the system of classification (the structuring structure) and the principle with which objectively classifiable judgments are made (the structured structure). In this way, social classes would be defined by their *habitus*, that is, by their internalized unconscious dispositions as well as their relational position in a structure of taste. In other words, a social group would be identifiable by having similar choices in taste derived from a particular *habitus* situated in this system of correlation and distinction. Importantly, this system is eminently hierarchical, so the tastes of the upper classes carry prestige while those of the lower, disenfranchised classes are regarded as vulgar. Because tastes do not have an intrinsic value, the dominant classes who hold economic and/or cultural capital need to make them rare and unreachable (for either economic or cultural reasons) so that they may successfully imbue them with prestige. Conversely the tastes of the poorest sectors of society are regarded as common and identified with vulgarity precisely because they are easily accessible. This entails a constant effort by the upper classes to maintain social distance by always creating new, rarer tastes and imposing an artificial scarcity of the (cultural and physical) products they consume.

In such a structured and structuring system, Bourdieu places intellectuals as part of the dominated faction of the dominant class, for they possess a high volume of cultural capital but do not readily possess economic capital. Their cultural capital is valuable because it is ultimately converted into symbolic capital, and in so doing it accords them prestige and recognition that in turn gives them social power. By striving to retain a monopoly of the production, judgment, and hierarchy of symbolic capital, intellectuals attempt to secure their dominant position within the structure of society. By the same token, I contend that when Brazilian intellectuals translated books and wrote articles about Zen and Buddhism, when they traveled overseas to visit Buddhist places and meet either Western Zen scholars or Japanese Zen masters, they were creating new, rare, and exotic tastes, which would consolidate their role as bearers of symbolic capital. By translating this knowledge into Portuguese, these intellectuals acquired social and even "mystical" power in Brazil, for their knowledge dealt with matters of sacred and lost wisdom from the Orient. When some of these non-Japanese Brazilian intellectuals were ordained as Zen monks or nuns or became missionaries, the symbiotic relation was complete: they had not only the intellectual and thus Western knowledge of Zen but also the esoteric and practical knowledge of the Eastern masters themselves. Both kinds of cultural capital legitimized their writings and their status in a field where scarcity and monopoly of knowledge prevailed.

"Situatedness" is particularly important in view of the fact that the members of the Brazilian intellectual elite who travel overseas do not do so indiscriminately. Instead they travel to specific places at different historical moments because these offer the highest return in terms of that much sought-after cultural capital. France was the main producer and disseminator of meaning for Brazilian society up until the Second World War; thereafter the United States took its place. It is not a coincidence that intellectuals and the economic elite would learn French and later English and would emulate and travel to these geographically and historically situated cultures.

This phenomenon is not particular to Brazil, of course, as it is part and parcel of the complex relations of power among countries that seek to appropriate the culture of the metropolitan centers. It is noteworthy, however, that centers and peripheries are relational locations; that is, depending on the cultures to which they are relating, centers may become peripheries and vice versa. For instance, given that from the 1960s to the mid-1990s Brazil was not a primary producer and disseminator of meaning about Buddhism, intellectuals had to travel and read in foreign languages to be able to acquire this knowledge. However, this picture changed considerably in the 1990s, when Buddhism experienced a boom and the country, while still maintaining its peripheral location, became a center for the production and dissemination of meaning about Zen for Latin America, Portugal, and even traditional centers such as France and the United States.

In conclusion, the inequalities of wealth and power that divide the world, assigning different locations for the acquisition of cultural capital, have to be taken into account if one is to understand why elite Brazilians travel to specific places at different historical moments. Accordingly, travel destinations for cosmopolitan Brazilians may differ greatly from those of their counterparts in the developed world, since the cultural capital to be gained is differently situated and constructed in each case.

Non-Japanese Brazilian Intellectuals: Bridging the Local and the Global

Before D. T. Suzuki's *Introduction to Zen Buddhism* was translated into Portuguese in 1961, non-Japanese Brazilian intellectuals could learn about Zen from articles and translations (from English and French) published by the journalist Nelson Coelho in *Jornal do Brasil*, a leading newspaper from Rio de Janeiro.[23] According to Coelho, his weekly column (1957–61) sparked an intense wave of interest in Zen Buddhism among non-Japanese Brazilian intellectuals. The enthusiasm for Zen was such that although the newspaper owner was a devout Catholic, she was excited by the novelty and the artistic side of Zen and thus allowed the weekly translations of Zen texts, koans, and commentaries. Zen would not pose a threat to her religious conviction because it was portrayed as a philosophical path to self-knowledge.

Another intellectual who was instrumental to the spread of Zen Buddhist ideas in Brazil was Murillo Nunes de Azevedo.[24] Azevedo was deeply influenced by the ideas of the Theosophical Society, whose Brazilian chapter he chaired for nine years. In 1955 he reestablished the Sociedade Budista do Brasil, originally founded in 1923 by Theosophists in Rio de Janeiro, but which soon dissolved. As a professor at the Pontifical Catholic University in Rio de Janeiro, Azevedo taught Eastern philosophy and published articles on Theosophy and Theravada, Tibetan, and Zen Buddhism for *Correio da Manhã*, a newspaper based in Rio de Janeiro. He wrote books on Buddhism and edited a twenty-book collection of translations called *Luz da Ásia* (Light of Asia) for the Civilização Brasileira publishing house, including his 1961 translation of Suzuki's *Introduction to Zen Buddhism*, still a frequently cited and highly regarded source among Zen practitioners I interviewed in the late 1990s.

In 1966 Azevedo traveled extensively in India (where he visited the Dalai Lama), Thailand (for the World Buddhist Conference, where he met Christmas Humphreys), and Japan, all the while writing articles for *Correio da Manhã*. In Tokyo Azevedo met with Takashina Rosen Zenji, abbot of Eiheiji and Sojiji, the head temples of Sôtôshû. Takashina Zenji had been to Brazil in 1955 to survey the country for the possibility of sending a Sôtôshû mission, and again in 1964 for the commemorations of the first decade of Sôtôshû activities. At the end of the meeting, Azevedo was officially declared a monk and Sôtôshû missionary for Brazil, receiving the Buddhist name Reirin Jôdo. By also being a writer and translator, he was able to occupy a strategic position in the spread of Zen in the country.

Both Coelho and Azevedo followed a path similar to that of other intellectuals. Their initial encounter with Buddhism and Zen was through imported literature, which then led them to seek a place of practice. They found it in Busshinji, the Sôtô Zenshû temple in São Paulo. In 1961, in order to cater to non-Japanese Brazilians, Ryôhan Shingû, the *sôkan* (superintendent general for South America), created a Zen meditation group (*zazenkai*) that met each Saturday. His interpreter was Ricardo Gonçalves, then a history student who would become a professor of Eastern religions at the University of São Paulo. Unlike other intellectuals, Gonçalves had been interested in Japan from an early age, due to his contact with Japanese Brazilian children at school. He was fluent in Japanese by the time he enrolled in the university. His role as translator was paramount for the spread of Zen among non-Japanese Brazilians as well as second- and third-generation (*nisei* and *sansei*) Japanese Brazilians, as many did not understand Japanese. Gonçalves preached and celebrated funerary and memorial rites at the temple and homes of the Japanese Brazilian community and acted as an interpreter at lectures by the *rôshi* and whenever a high official from Sôtôshû arrived in Brazil. This was at a time when his university colleagues and other intellectuals frequented the temple.[25] In 1967 he published *Textos Budistas e Zen Budistas*, a seminal book in which he translated Mahâyâna and Zen Buddhist texts. This book is still cited by many Brazilian students of Zen and is suggested reading in Buddhist blogs.

In making Zen accessible to Brazilians, Gonçalves helped break down the language barrier that had been the main obstacle to the proselytizing of Buddhism in Brazil. Until very recently, when Brazilians of non-Japanese descent sought other Japanese Buddhist schools, they were redirected to Busshinji because "they speak Portuguese there, and it is the place for non-Japanese Brazilians," as some adherents told me. Nowadays Japanese Pure Land Buddhist schools (Jôdo Shinshû and Jôdo Shû) already have Japanese Brazilian monks who speak Portuguese and even some non-Japanese Brazilian monks ordained in the tradition.

Teaching Buddhism to a New Generation

An important point in the trajectories of both Gonçalves and Azevedo is their role as teachers of a second generation of Buddhists and thus as constructors of a particular representation of Buddhism in Brazil. Azevedo, like many other non-Japanese Brazilians I interviewed in the late 1990s, said he was attracted to Buddhism because of the Buddha's recommendation that one should follow one's reason and discernment, not faith, in order to decide whether to accept the Buddha's teachings. This teaching has often been cited as evidence of Buddhism's accord with science and reason. Azevedo's association of rational thought to Buddhism and his deep involvement with the Theosophical Society shaped a particular universalistic and ecumenical approach to Buddhism, which is revealed in his several published books and which he used while lecturing at the Pontifical Catholic University of Rio de Janeiro.

Some of his students at the university went on to become priests themselves, of whom the best known is Gustavo Côrrea Pinto. Pinto has been an active member of the International Association of Shin Buddhist Studies as well as a missionary for the Higashi Hongwanji temple in São Paulo. In 2002 he was frequently in the media because of his project of erecting, in an ecological reserve in central Brazil, the Bamiyan Buddhist statues destroyed in Afghanistan. In early 2002 Pinto made a fundraising trip to Japan and also to Dharamshala, India (to meet the Dalai Lama). His is an ambitious project, involving the carving of a Buddha 108 meters high on the side of a mountain (this is double the original size of the Afghan statues) and the construction of Japanese, Chinese, Korean, and Tibetan Buddhist temples, a center for interreligious dialogue, a Buddhist university, and biology laboratories to study the area's ecosystem. The project reflects the ecumenical and universalistic trend preached by his teacher at the university, Azevedo.

Gonçalves, in turn, worked as a catalyst to spread the interest in Buddhism among his colleagues at the University of São Paulo and other intellectuals. Eduardo Bastos, who like Gonçalves would also become a professor of the history of religion and an ordained Zen monk, was the first colleague to start frequenting Busshinji at Gonçalves's invitation. Bastos and other intellectuals, such as Cecília Meireles, Pedro Xisto, and Orides Fontela (all of them well-known Brazilian poets), Nelson Coelho, Gehrard Kahner (a German immigrant who worked in China and became a translator), Lourenço Borges (a lawyer and founder of the Theosophical Society), and later Heródoto Barbeiro (journalist), would meet every Saturday evening for a sitting session (*zazen*). According to Bastos, in order to sit *zazen* they had to remove the wooden pews used by the Japanese congregation during memorial and funeral rituals at the Buddha hall. This rearranging of furniture suggests that the Japanese Brazilian and the non-Japanese Brazilian congregations used the temple in different ways. This difference in practice is due to the non-Japanese Brazilians receiving Orientalist flows of ideas and images of Zen, which place *zazen* at the core of

Zen practice, while for Japanese Brazilians, devotion to ancestors would come first.

To be sure, the presence of second-, third-, and fourth-generation immigrants complicates this picture, since most of them had converted to Catholicism, and when interested in Buddhism, many tended to adopt the non-Japanese Brazilian construct of Zen. This Western construct of Zen and Buddhism in general, which is strongly inflected by Orientalism, is so pervasive in the West that conflicts have sprung up in many Western countries between immigrants and converts on the issue of what constitutes authentic Buddhist practice.[26]

Notes

Author's Note: This essay was adapted from Cristina Rocha, *Zen in Brazil: The Quest for Cosmopolitan Modernity* (Honolulu: University of Hawaii Press, 2006). The epigraph is an excerpt from an interview with a non-Japanese Brazilian university lecturer who was ordained a Zen monk at Busshinji temple in São Paulo in the early 1970s.

1. Londrina is a city in the Brazilian state of Paraná, inhabited mainly by Japanese descendants.

2. Many scholars have criticized Said's work by rightly pointing out that Orientalism is not monolithic, that different Western cultures have different understandings of and uses for it. See, for instance, Lisa Lowe, *Critical Terrains: French and British Orientalisms* (Ithaca, N.Y.: Cornell University Press, 1991).

3. For an account of how Sôtôshû arrived and spread Zen in Brazil, see Cristina Rocha, "Zen Buddhism in Brazil: Japanese or Brazilian?," *Journal of Global Buddhism* 1 (2000): 31–55.

4. Roberto Schwarz, *Misplaced Ideas: Essays on Brazilian Culture* (London: Verso, 1992), 1–2. Schwarz points out that copying did not start with Independence, but it was not a predicament until then. During the colonial period (1500–1822) it was considered natural for the colony to copy the metropolis—even more so after 1807, when King João VI and the Portuguese court fled to Brazil, fearing an invasion by Napoleon. For fifteen years Brazil became the center of the Portuguese Empire. Strong ties with the court continued after Independence, as Pedro I, independent Brazil's first emperor, was the son of the Portuguese king.

5. On this shift from Europe to the United States as meaning-producing center, see Serge Guilbaut, *How New York Stole the Idea of Modern Art: Abstract Expressionism, Freedom, and the Cold War* (Chicago: University of Chicago Press, 1983).

6. See the theoretical background for this argument in Walter Benjamin, *Illuminations* (London: Fontana Press, 1970) and Jacques Derrida, "Des Tours De Babel," *Difference in Translation*, ed. J. F. Graham (Ithaca, N.Y.: Cornell University Press, 1985), 188.

7. Gayatri Spivak, *Outside the Teaching Machine* (London: Routledge, 1993).

8. Doreen Massey, *Space, Place and Gender* (Cambridge, U.K.: Polity Press, 1994), 149.

9. For Orientalist fantasies of the Middle Eastern and Syrian Lebanese immigration in Brazil, see Jeffrey Lesser, *Negotiating National Identity: Immigrants, Minorities, and the Struggle for Ethnicity in Brazil* (Durham, N.C.: Duke University Press, 1999), 41–79.

10. My free translation of "Lá nas terras do império chinês, / Num palácio de louça vermelha / Sobre um trono de azul japonês" in "Orientalismo na Literatura Brasileira," *Dicionário de Literatura* (Porto: N.p., 1981), 772.

11. R. Farias Brito, *O Mundo Interior: Ensaio sobre os dados geraes da philosophia do espírito* (Rio de Janeiro: Revista dos Tribunais, 1914), 105, my translation.

12. Charles Hallisey, "Roads Taken and Not Taken in the Study of Theravâda Buddhism," *Curators of the Buddha: The Study of Buddhism under Colonialism*, ed. Donald Lopez Jr. (Chicago: University of Chicago Press, 1995), 45.

13. On the influence of French culture in Brazil, see Jeffrey D. Needell, *A Tropical Belle Epoque: Elite, Culture, and Society in Turn-of-the-Century Rio de Janeiro* (Cambridge, U.K.: Cambridge University Press, 1987).

14. Nineteenth-century Europe, particularly France, underwent a fad known as Japonaiserie or Japonisme. In the 1850s French artists discovered Japanese woodblock prints (*ukiyo-ê*), which would arrive by way of wrapping paper for imported porcelain pieces. By the 1860s most French Impressionists were collecting Japanese prints. Japonaiserie also involved literature (*Madame Chrysanthème*), music (*Madame Butterfly*), jewelry, and *objects d'art* (lacquer, metal work).

15. Shuhei Hosokawa, "Nationalizing Chô-Chô-San: The Signification of 'Butterfly Singers' in a Japanese-Brazilian Community," *Japanese Studies* 19.3 (1999): 256.

16. See, for instance, Walter Benjamin, "Paris, Capital of the Nineteenth Century," *Reflections: Essays, Aphorisms, Autobiographical Writings* (New York: Schocken, 1978).

17. Takashi Maeyama, "Religion, Kinship, and the Middle Classes of the Japanese in Urban Brazil," *Latin American Studies* 5 (1983): 57–82.

18. Paulo Franchetti, "Notas Sobre a História do Haikai no Brasil," *Revista de Letras* (São Paulo) 34 (1994): 197–213.

19. Masuda Goga, *O Haicai no Brasil* (São Paulo: Oriento, 1988).

20. Tsuguo Koyama, "Japoneses na Amazônia: Alguns Aspectos do Processo de Sua Integração Sócio-Cultural," *A Presença Japonesa No Brasil*, ed. Hiroshi Saito (São Paulo: Edusp/T. A. Queiroz, 1980), 17.

21. For an account of Zen Buddhism and media and popular culture in 1990s Brazil, see Cristina Rocha, "The Brazilian *Imaginaire* on Zen: Global Influences, Rhizomatic Forms," *Japanese Religions in and beyond the Japanese Diaspora*, ed. Ronan Pereira and Hideo Matsuoka (Berkeley: Institute for East Asian Studies, University of California, 2007).

22. Pierre Bourdieu, *Distinction: A Social Critique of the Judgment of Taste* (Cambridge, Mass.: Harvard University Press, 1984).

23. Nelson Coelho, *Zen: Experiência Direta da Libertação* (Belo Horizonte: Itatiaia, 1978).

24. Murilo Nunes Azevedo, *O Caminho de Cada Um: O Budismo da Terra Pura* (Rio de Janeiro: Bertrand Brasil, 1996).

25. Ricardo Mário Gonçalves, "A Trajetória de Um Budista Brasileiro," *O Budismo no Brasil,* ed. Frank Usarski (São Paulo: Lorosae, 2002), 171–92.

26. See Martin Baumann, "Global Buddhism: Developmental Periods, Regional Histories, and a New Analytical Perspective," *Journal of Global Buddhism* 2 (2001) 1–43; Charles Prebish and Kenneth Tanaka, eds., *The Faces of Buddhism in America* (Berkeley: University of California Press, 1998).

CHAPTER FOURTEEN

Writing and Memory

Images of the Japanese Diaspora in Brazil

Karen Tei Yamashita

In 1975 I traveled to Brazil as a Thomas J. Watson Fellow to research the history and anthropology of the Japanese Brazilian community. At least, that is what I proposed to do. I was a young sansei from California just graduated from Carleton College, traveling to South America for the first time, heading out with a crash course in Portuguese, conversational Japanese, and the hubris of youth. I knew about my own Japanese American community in Los Angeles; I knew something about my ancestry in Japan; and I knew from spending a year in Japan that I was not really Japanese. I did not know what it meant to research history or anthropology; my knowledge was bookish and intuitive. Somewhere in that year, I came upon the stories that I believed could be woven into a historical novel, and I turned from history and anthropology to a project that was fiction. Again, I did not know what would be involved in researching a historical novel or even what would make it fiction, or a novel. In the next three years I researched and interviewed my subjects relentlessly, and for the decade after that I wrote and rewrote and wrote again and again until I found the threads and the voices that would complete a novel. The resulting book, published finally in 1992 by Coffee House Press, *Brazil-Maru*, represents a long journey to my future in a process I could only know by doing, and a wandering through a puzzle of questions that I did not know would still remain questions.

The story of *Brazil-Maru* is based on the lives of a small population of Japanese immigrant settlers arriving in the 1920s. Japanese immigration to Brazil has followed patterns of their exclusion from the United States. In 1908, when the Gentleman's Agreement was signed to limit Japanese immigration to the United States, the first shipload of some eight hundred Japanese arrived at the port of Santos in the state of São Paulo. In the 1920s, when Exclusion Acts were passed by the U.S. government, Japanese migrated to Brazil by the thousands to work as contract labor on coffee plantations. By 1940 more than 190,000 Japanese had passed through the city of Santos, disembarking from any one of thirty-two Japanese steamships that crossed the ocean in over three hundred trips. By the time I arrived in Brazil to begin my fellowship, there were perhaps 1.5 million Japanese and their descendents living in Brazil—the largest population of Japanese outside of Japan, far larger than the combined immigrant communities in the United States today of about 850,000. The existence of the Japanese in Brazil was not only a surprise to me; it was a history largely unknown to my own Japanese American community. For three years, beginning in 1975, I traveled across the states of São Paulo and Paraná to interview several hundred persons involved in a complicated story focused on a communal settlement carved out of the virgin forest in the northwest of São Paulo. I chose this particular history because of its ties to the larger history of Japanese immigration to Brazil, allowing me to research Japanese involvement in agriculture, cooperativism, banking, politics, land use, leisure and sports, language, education, religious and political beliefs, and relationships over time to Japan and the Brazilian nation. I also chose this history because I thought I might uncover the truth of events told to me as rumor and story and because it was a great romance and a story of dreaming, conquest, hubris, and civilization.

I have sometimes said that I learned to write by rewriting *Brazil-Maru*. Part of this process was to create five separate narrators. This rewriting was perhaps the beginning of my interest in narrative voice and its complicated possibilities for storytelling, but perhaps I was not so successful in this first novel. Some American critics complained that they could not hear the differences in the voices of the narrators, even though I knew them to be distinct. Ha! I thought, of course they can't distinguish the voices; all of the narrators, except for the last speaker, are speaking in Japanese. It takes a subtler mind! Well, it's a subtle task: how to make English look Japanese on the page. Of course I am being facetious, but I could not, as in American narratives, coax slang, dialect, or even literary artifice to craft differences. Grammar and rhythm could be employed to show crudity in language and miseducation, but how to distinguish practicality, arrogance, or belief? For two of the characters, I depended at times on the memory of my own paternal grandmother, a Meiji Japanese and proud Edokko, both domineering and practical, who came to Oakland, California, at the turn of the century. It's possible that the characters in *Brazil-Maru* who are presumably Taisho immigrants to Brazil are endowed with the characteristics of a Meiji immigrant to the United States as remembered by an American sansei who went to Brazil and interviewed dozens of immigrants in broken Japanese and Portuguese and created the final product in English. I suppose you could say my version is really a bad translation. I smile to think that now the novel will be translated into Japanese. What a relief that some may finally be able to read the real Japanese translation.

Fiction itself, I have discovered, is also a kind of translation, in this case a translation of history and factual events. But fiction is not the same as history. It has to be possible to say that certain events happened, that history really happened, and this is because we must be held accountable. Fiction, on the other hand, holds an idea and an imagination about history, about time and place and memories, and as such, it is a way to travel into and away from possibility. My mother made the comment recently that she found *Brazil-Maru* a rather "depressing" book; I wondered about this because she's a good reader but also because for me the book represents an awakening, a process of knowing. I suppose it's hardly fair to think my mother should read the book and know my process as a writer or my need to find a balance between personal desire and the greater good of a community and its individual members. The characters in this story who I love best are those who suffer the greatest consequences of their tremendous egos, who pursue life with indulgence and exuberance and fail. The fiction of these lives demonstrates the treachery within us all, but it's still a fiction, with characters that cannot and do not live outside the book itself.

Now, almost another decade and a half since its publication and more than three decades since I first began my travels in Brazil, Takao Asano has made his own journey to Brazil and in the meantime has translated this book. I realize that Asano's actual traveling through Brazil to many of the same sites will make his translation very special. This is not the sort of word-for-word translation that one usually encounters. Asano's translation brings to bear knowledge of the particular pidgin, if you will, of the Japanese language mixed with Portuguese as well as knowledge of the cultural milieu—the food, the sensibility of climate, place, and time passing that cannot be exactly measured.

In this process, Asano and I find ourselves strangely linked, not only by the sharing of text transferred from one language to another or by the sharing of the solitary pursuit of writing with the solitary pursuit of translation, but also by our link to a common mentor, Walter Yukio Honma. Walter, who immigrated to Brazil around 1920 at age nine, became one of my best and dearest friends in Brazil. Although in the early years I returned constantly to his communal home in Guaraçai to coax out the stories and to interrogate every detail of his extraordinary memory, in later years we spent the greater part of our hours discussing agriculture and agronomy, Brazil's economic and political future, discussing his careful analysis of events both in his past and in the present, of civil and cultural society and the complicated array of human associations. I returned for his wisdom, his keen intelligence, his infinite kindness and belief, and I suppose Asano also knew this feeling when he met Walter in later years.

Such links between Asano and me were not planned but entirely serendipitous. We crossed paths in elevators, taxis, dinners, and road trips and over email. Indeed in this strange new world, we mourned together over email Walter's death a few years ago. It's a linking made possible by travel and technology. And yet I have come to believe that this linking is in itself a translation, a transferring of part of Walter's meaning from his conversations with me that Asano now captures in, not simply a translation, but his own rewriting of the same stories. Both of us know how indebted our final versions, however fictional, are to Walter's vision at the beginning and the close of his long and thoughtful life.

Finally, I am indebted to Ryuta Imafuku, professor, philosopher, and cultural critic, who will edit the final Japanese copy and who is also my brother traveler and diasporic. It is Ryuta who has for many years encouraged this translation to Japanese, and it is he who forced me to think about my strange and particular process as a writer and translator. In his inimitable way, he danced me around an idea to write a second epilogue for the Japanese translation that I now include here. Of course, it will be translated into and read in Japanese by a Japanese readership, but perhaps it has a curious place in this book exploring the Oriental in Latin America.

Brazil-Maru

Epilogue (2): Tamahori

I put my bags down and struggled to pull my sticky arms out from under my heavy pack. I set everything down on the brown linoleum and looked around the small entryway, brown wood paneling covering everything and sweltering in the afternoon humidity. On the counter, a buzzer button with a wire trailing off along the paneling was prominently surrounded with notices written in Japanese and Portuguese. I read the Japanese no-tice, handwritten with a marker, now faded and torn, Scotch-taped several times but still peeling up from the tepid wood. *For inquiries, please ring be-tween 9 am and 12 noon and 1 and 6 pm only.* I checked my watch and rang.

A balding man in a threadbare shirt appeared from behind a door so cleverly hidden in the paneling that his sudden appearance surprised me. He said, "Ah it's you, is it? A fellow countryman?"

"Yes, we spoke on the phone. I am Tamahori," I replied, formally intro-ducing myself, hoping to match what felt to me an archaic reference to my home prefecture.

"Furusato?" he asked.

"Matsumoto," I answered.

He chattered on about his own hometown that he'd not seen for thirty years, about the Winter Olympics that he had followed assiduously and how it gave him chills to see his homeland despite the 100-degree weather here. I followed him up the staircase and down the long corridor to my des-ignated room. He pointed out the bath and toilet, handed me my weekly set of towels, and gave me the key. "Our doors close nightly by ten o'clock. I realize this might be a problem for a young rogue like you." He laughed but left me alone in room number 22.

I threw my pack onto the springy bed and pulled a letter plastered with Brazilian stamps from a zipped pocket. I stared at the uneven handwriting surrounding one of those miniature Hello Kitty photos stuck to the center. Her tiny face was swallowed by pink kitties, impossible to see clearly. I couldn't believe this was the only photograph I had of her.

At 9 the next morning I wandered into the Japanese-Brazilian Cultural Institute. It was about five blocks from the prefectural hotel, down sooty streets with a variety of curio shops selling Japanese bric-a-brac and elec-tronics, plastic cherry tree branches hanging in muted pink over a conges-tion of cars and workers listlessly trying to get to their destination. A chubby girl at the desk sent me up to the top floor to look at the museum. "There's no one here yet to talk to you," she said. "It's like this in the sum-mer." She sighed and fanned herself. There was no air-conditioning where she sat. "You're from Japan. I can tell. It's probably snowing there. My brother's there. You know, *dekasegi*. He hates it." She paused. "I mean the weather. He sent me this." She pointed at a pink portable Sony CD player with earphones she hid under the desk. "I've got to hide it, or someone will rob me. My brother says there's no crime in Japan. Is that true?"

I wandered around the museum, in and out of the installations of thatched houses with wood-fired stoves, implements and baskets used for harvesting coffee, through the stuffed birds and animals encountered in the original forests, past painted representations of old plantation and farming life and the photographs of all the ships that carried Japanese immigrants from 1908 on. By the time I was reading the inscription beneath the Brazil-Maru, a nisei woman in a green cotton sundress bustled into the museum, empty except for its historic contents and me, disturbing the quiet dust with about five gestures and ten facial expressions too many.

"I'm sorry," she apologized. "You're early. A day early," she suggested. "Oh well," she answered herself. "What does it matter? You've come around the world." She gestured at the ships. "Have you gotten settled? I didn't expect you to be so young. A graduate student? How old are you? Twenty-five? I used to be twenty-five," she laughed. She sized up my jeans and T-shirt. I wondered if I should have dressed up, but she waved her hand. "You'll fit right in. You could be a student at USP. Anyway, we've been waiting for you. We could use your help. How's your Portuguese?"

After a long coffee break and several cigarettes at the corner bar and conversation peppered with Portuguese words I could only surmise, Celia brought me back and showed me my work space, a fairly updated computer system sitting on an old mahogany desk with one of those wood and leather chairs I'd seen maybe in a Raymond Chandler movie. She pushed the mouse around to wake up the screen, then threw up her hands. She pointed at a set of small wooden drawers lining the back wall. "We need to catalogue all that into that." She pointed to the computer. "Technology," she sighed. "But," she smiled, "you're Japanese, so it shouldn't be any problem for you at all."

After about two months, Celia came to my desk one day and asked, "Do you ever get out? Not to be impudent, but what do you do when you leave here at night?" She even winked.

I had to admit that I knew every cheap restaurant, every used bookstore, and every CD shop in the Liberdade, but otherwise I spent most of my time reading, working on the catalogues, consulting them myself, and borrowing all the books that the museum's library never seemed to lend out anyway. I was somewhere on the fifth box of the third row, and I was cross-referencing everything with readings from old newspaper archives of the *Diario Nippaku* and the *Brazil Shimpo*. I had deeply burrowed into the past for reasons only graduate studies can justify. In a few more months, the difference between the computer's and my knowledge of Japanese Brazilian immigration would be only a matter of speed. Anyway, I had to be back at the hotel by 10 or I would be locked out, and besides that, I was also looking for the girl in the Hello Kitty photograph.

After tipping the third bottle of sake, I showed Celia the photograph. She turned the letter around and upside down. At first I felt humiliated, but her laugher was so contagious that I too laughed. We laughed continuously for minutes until tears dribbled down our cheeks. It was a great relief that I cannot describe exactly. Perhaps it was the sight of Celia gasping for air and pressing her stomach in pain; she had felt my great need and release. Finally she wiped her eyes, shiny with sympathy, and said in a slightly slurred voice, "Tamahori-san, we've got to find that girl."

The problem with finding *that girl* was that I had only this letter, no return address, no name except Silvia, and no other information except that she was a dancer and a Nikkei born in Brazil. "Do you know how many nisei girls are named Silvia?" Celia shook her head. "Well," she said, examining the postal markings, "it was sent from São Paulo. At least you got that right." But I knew by now that, although I hadn't ventured outside the Liberdade for lack of money and direction, there were 25 million people in the city alone and maybe 1.5 million Nikkei in the country. "Good luck," sighed Celia. There might be better reasons for coming to Brazil, but after the fourth bottle of sake, neither of us could think of any. That night, locked out of the Nagano-ken Hotel, I slept on Celia's couch.

Celia had needled me. "A dancer? Maybe you should be checking out all the nightclubs." I hadn't thought about that because I associated Silvia with my sister, who happened to be taking modern dance lessons at the same studio. I would meet my sister there early and watch her end her lesson, but after a while I found myself coming earlier and earlier to follow the movements of one girl in particular. When I asked my sister about the girl, she was miffed, probably jealous, and said, "Her Japanese is weird. She's one of those from Brazil."

One day I went to the dance studio knowing my sister wouldn't be there and followed the girl, chasing her as she pranced out with her bags. "Wait," I said. "Have you seen my sister?" I asked lamely. Then, even more lamely, "Would you like to go for coffee? My sister and I usually go for coffee after." Her smile was brilliant, as if a gorgeous blossom had opened her petals before my very eyes, and I took this all in even though every word she spoke was *no*.

Celia, who was recently divorced and always ready to play, arrived at the hotel with her girlfriends and her gayfriends, and we began our search, hopping through the nightclubs of the Liberdade and then taxiing in a wider and wider circle from the original center of my otherwise computerized existence. On these nights, I slept on Celia's couch. On my off-days, I crossed the city by bus and metro to every dance studio advertised: tap, modern, jazz, samba, flamenco, belly, ballet, Japanese folk. I also spent all my money on every dance performance in the city. I was beginning to know Brazil through a maze of twirling and gyrating bodies, the pulsing of one rhythm or another, from techno beats to classical intonations. My dreams were a carnival, a swirl of silken dresses swishing around bodies in fleshy leotards through the bump and grind of jittering buttocks, and the mysterious Silvia nowhere to be seen. "Celia," I begged, "I can't stand it anymore."

Her eyes were red, though not quite blood-shot, from our carousing the previous night. She admitted, "This might not be the way. But," she smiled, "sempre ha un jeito." She was in the middle of a pile of papers and old posters thrown onto the floor from a closet behind her desk. "First," she pointed at the pile, "help me throw this junk out." Sneezing into the dust, she said, "I should have done this years ago."

I marched after her with the scrolls of old posters of cultural events in my arms. At the trashcan I said, "Shouldn't we save some of these as archives?"

"Oh," she said, her sense of the collector returning to her senses. "One of each, then. You do it. But these papers go." She dumped an armful.

Unrolling one discarded scroll, I already knew the layout of a dance poster, the promiscuous flash of the body that forces the head to turn to notice the skill of contorted muscle and healthy flesh, the haughty sense of the dancer's hard-won ease. Amid a posed group of young Nikkei dancers, I recognized her as sure as I knew the fuzzy existence of Hello Kitty.

That weekend, Celia put me on a bus to Esperança, an old Japanese farming colony in the backwoods of the state. "Why didn't I think of it?" she said in exasperation. "Who else dances in the *colônia*? Where you're going is a commune of dancers, you know. They're communist but Christians, so it's okay, I guess. Imagine looking for your Silvia in strip joints. Ahgh!" She groaned. "Don't tell them that. Oh," she guffawed, "but we had such a good time!" Celia chattered on with details. "Don't be shocked. Nothing in Esperança has changed for fifty years, and that's way before you were born. You see the installations in the museum? Like that. Well, not that old, but don't say I didn't warn you."

But when I got there and unrolled my poster, there was not a dancing girl in sight. An old woman with a rag and a short broom made from rice thatching came out of a large kitchen at the back of the long hall. She sat me down at the end of a long rustic table with a copper teapot and a plate of sliced pound cake. "You should have stayed in Japan. That's where they are now. Everyone dancing in Japan. Traveling to seven cities. Another two months maybe. Around here without our girls, it's lonely." The old grandmother shook her head.

In another two months my fellowship was over. Still I pointed at the poster and pressed the woman for information. She named the girls one by one. "This is an old poster. They are more grown up now," she said. "That one there," she pointed at my Silvia, "Haruko," she said.

"Not Silvia?" I asked.

"Oh, you want to meet Silvia? She's visiting here now. Now, where is she? She must be in Mizuoka's museum. Come along."

My heart skipped a beat, and I followed the woman bent before me in her handmade clogs down the flowered paths, around the simple houses, peeking past shutters into dark interiors, fluttering curtains and laundry shifting in the morning breeze. An old man sat sunning himself. A woman looked up from her sweeping. A cat stretched itself in a patch of sunlight. I felt the idyll of a simple place unchanged by time.

But as soon as I saw Silvia, I knew it was not she. I tried to hide my disappointment as we stepped into the small structure that was a single room. Silvia was wiping down the cobwebs from the rafters with a broom, her figure stretching and swiping. She looked at me, spitting away a stray web from her lips, and adjusted the scarf on her head. I looked around at the display of Indian pots and divided boxes of pottery shards, carefully marked.

The old woman went over to a large pot in the corner of the room and ritually placed her hands together, bowing quietly for a moment. "That's Mizuoka-san." Silvia nodded toward the pot with her nose. When I looked surprised, she said, "In the pot. I mean his bones." She smiled.

Silvia gave me the tour. "Mizuoka was an amateur archaeologist. When his wife died, they transferred his museum here. They also transferred the first house built in Esperança. It's over there. Look inside. It's filled with old paintings."

I wandered around the rooms, recognizing some of the artists as those whose work was also displayed at the museum in the Liberdade. "What happened to these?" I asked about a series, all by the same painter, a few of which seemed discolored by soot and partially destroyed by fire.

"They say there was a fire. Lucky they got saved." Silvia shrugged. "This whole place is like a museum. Even the people." She pointed to the granny who, having turned me over to Silvia, was busy again at her chores. "When I was in the United States, I visited the Amish. Like that," she chuckled. "What brings you here?"

I could have lied to her about being a graduate student, but instead I showed her the poster and the girl whose brief acquaintance I had made.

I had finally gotten my sister to give the girl a letter with my address and a wish to meet her, but one day she disappeared, never returning to her dance lessons, and all I received was that cryptic letter mailed probably on a whim from Brazil.

"Ah, Haruko," Silvia nodded. "It's an old game we used to play. She would be me and I her. Silly, huh? She was like my little sister. Now I heard she's going to be a great dancer. Maybe she'll go to New York. That's what they say. It's her dream. When she becomes famous, she's threatened to change her name to Silvia. It's more Brazilian." She laughed.

But who was Silvia, I wanted to know. "I was an exchange student in America. Indiana," she said. "That's really America. Not like New York or Miami. Anyway, when I came home, I felt confused, so I came here, where we kids always used to come in the summer, like camp. My grandfather was an old friend of the original founder, so our ties go way back. And one day, I got married to one of the guys I used to play with as a kid, but it's one thing to be a kid, but not forever." Her eyes danced about, a happy sort of pain and knowing. "So now we're separated, but I come back to play now and then. I'm a city girl, but this place reminds you that innocence can exist."

We walked quietly down a long shaded road. "Mango trees," she pointed. "Come back in the summer," she suggested. "There'll be so many mangoes, they feed them to the pigs."

We sat on a makeshift bench, peeling a cache of tangerines Silvia had brought in her pockets. I wondered about Haruko and to what I had been attracted. Was it her difference? Her body movements that seemed to take on other articulations, that blossoming smile I'd never seen before on any face I'd ever known? I had exchanged hardly a word with her, but when she disappeared I became fascinated with anything having to do with Brazil. I chased the music and the films and the literature, and I chased a plan to study something that would bring me to that place where her movements and smile existed, or so I thought. Everything had become faded and yet clearer. My heart felt suddenly heavy, for I knew at that moment I would never meet Haruko, and that perhaps it was never she who I really wanted to meet.

"Come on." Silvia stood up suddenly, brushing the tangerine peelings into the red dirt and pulling away her head scarf. "Let's go see Terada-san."

"Who?"

"My guru," she said mischievously.

Silvia commandeered a small truck, and we negotiated a series of back roads from one commune to another. After a short hour, we pulled up to a similarly constructed farming community with the same water tower, the same long dining hall, the same scattering of simple houses and barns, the same squawk of chickens in the near distance. It was a mirror image from which I felt a momentary dizziness.

We had to look for Terada, who was milking the cows. We found him in a small barn, struggling with a calf, pulling it away from its mother's teats. "Shoo!" he yelled at the calf, corralling it back into the fold. Then he got to business, stationed himself on a one-pegged stool and started to squirt milk from the cow's teats into a waiting pail. I noticed he'd lost a forefinger on one hand, but still he milked the old cow handily. When he was finished, he came to shake my hands Brazilian style, then removed his hat and bowed to my bow. His old eyes wrinkled with pleasure, and he wiped his freckled brow and pushed his cap over his sparse head of white hair several times. Silvia had said he was more than eighty years old, but he was spry and quick, and we had to hurry to follow him as he did his chores.

As soon as we arrived, he started talking excitedly about everything. He was clearly pleased to see Silvia, asking her about her life these days, exchanging gossip about people of whom I then knew nothing and later would know possibly too much. I could see that his questions were testing me, and I wanted for some reason to pass muster.

Silvia joked, "Eh, Terada-san, this Tamahori here came to Brazil for love."

I looked down in embarrassment, but Terada said, "Love is better than sociology. Some of you come here to study us, you know, but what's there to study? Our lives are an open book. Study if you want." He waved his arms and continued to walk. Then he turned to Silvia and said, "Why are you embarrassing him? Poor guy." He looked back at me. "Don't take it personally. She's a terrible teaser." But by the time we sat down at the long rustic tables, again with a pot of tea and a pile of cake, he sighed, "Love, eh?"

In the many hours of conversation that passed from that moment on, we never talked about love directly, but years later, swinging my own tiny daughter in my arms, I realized that that was really all we talked about. At some late hour, Silvia must have excused herself and disappeared, leaving me there to continue my long mentorship with Terada, a mentorship that lasted the remaining months of my fellowship in Brazil. We talked daily. I learned to milk the cows. I hung about the kitchen and kneaded bread with the women. I gathered eggs in the morning. I took produce to market with the men. And every night, Terada and I exchanged the long stories that made his life long with the long questions that I was too young to know the answers to but smart enough to ask.

On the phone Celia asked, "So what's she like? Hey, watch out. You could get trapped into marriage. You wouldn't be the first."

At first I thought to tell Celia the truth, but she seemed willing to leave me in Esperança in exchange for a good story, and I couldn't see my way to returning to the mahogany desk with the computer. "She's beautiful," I waxed romantically on the phone.

"It's the light in Esperança," she said. "The people there have a reputation for fuzzy heads. Don't say I didn't warn you." She hung up.

So I stayed as long as I could, and one day I told old Terada I would have to leave. He said, "I will miss our conversations. Who would think there would be so much to talk about? Of course at my age, nothing but memories, and you are a good listener. You have been overly generous in your listening, I suspect. My wife says your kind listening polishes my ego. She also says all this memory," he pointed to his old head, "is just a dark museum."

He chuckled softly, then remembered, "I've told you about this American sansei who came here many years ago. We also had such good conversations. I think she came like you, too, for love. She wrote this book, she says, a great fiction about us. Imagine." He paused as if looking around for her ghost. "But it's in English, so she left me a book I cannot read. Here," he said.

And he pressed the book into my open hands.

Glossary

Maru: noun meaning circle, purity, or perfection; in this case (*Brazil-Maru*), a suffix designating the name of a ship or floating vessel.

Meiji: Japanese historic era designated by the lifetime of the Emperor Meiji, 1868–1911.

Edokko: a native of the city of Tokyo, also known as Edo.

Taisho: Japanese historic era designated by the lifetime of the Emperor Taisho, 1912–1925.

sansei: third-generation Japanese descendent.

Tamahori: the surname of the protagonist and narrator of this epilogue, but also Takao Asano's alias and pen name, even alter ego.

***dekasegi*:**   verb meaning to work away from home; Brazilians and other migrant workers of Japanese descent have turned this word into a noun meaning migrant worker in Japan (spelled *dekassegui* in Portuguese).

nisei: second-generation Japanese descendent.

Nikkei: of Japanese ancestry or lineage; belonging to the Japanese tribe; some dictionaries translate this word as Japanese emigrant or even Japanese American.

***Sempre ha un jeito*:**   Brazilian expression meaning, "There is always a way."

Mizuoka-san: character in *Brazil-Maru* who is a scholar and amateur archaeologist.

Terada-san: the first narrator of *Brazil-Maru*, also known as Ichiro or Emiru, who immigrates as a nine-year-old boy in 1925.

Selected Bibliography

Anderson, Benedict. *Imagined Communities: Reflections on the Origin and Spread of Nationalism*. London: Verso, 1991.

Andrea, Bernadette. "Columbus in Istanbul: Ottoman Mappings of the 'New World.'" *Genre: Forms of Discourse and Culture* 30.1 (1997): 135–65.

Azougarth, Abdeslam. "Martí orientalista." *Casa de las Américas* 210 (1998): 12–20.

Barfoot, C. C., and Theo D'haen, eds. *Oriental Prospects: Western Literature and the Lure of the East*. Amsterdam: Rodopi, 1998.

Behdad, Ali. *Belated Travelers: Orientalism in the Age of Colonial Dissolution*. Durham, N.C.: Duke University Press, 1994.

Bhabha, Homi K. *The Location of Culture*. New York: Routledge, 1994.

Bongie, Chris. *Exotic Memories: Literature, Colonialism, and the Fin de Siècle*. Stanford: Stanford University Press, 1991.

Breckenridge, Carol A., and Peter van der Veer, eds. *Orientalism and the Postcolonial Predicament: Perspectives on South Asia*. Philadelphia: University of Pennsylvania Press, 1993.

Camayd-Freixas, Erik, and José Eduardo González, eds. *Primitivism and Identity in Latin America: Essays on Art, Literature, and Culture*. Tucson: University of Arizona Press, 2000.

Cho, Jane. *Asians in Latin America*. San Francisco: Bolerium Books, 1999.

Civantos, Christina. *Between Argentines and Arabs: Argentine Orientalism, Arab Immigrants, and the Writing of Identity*. Albany: State University of New York Press, 2006.

Clifford, James. *The Predicament of Culture*. Cambridge, Mass.: Harvard University Press, 1988.

Dallmayr, Fred R. *Beyond Orientalism: Essays on Cross-Cultural Encounter*. Albany: State University of New York Press, 1996.

D'haen, Theo, and Patricia Krüs, eds. *Colonizer and Colonized*. Amsterdam: Rodopi, 2000.

Dussel, Enrique. "Eurocentrism and Modernity." *Boundary 2* 20 (1993): 65–76.

Ette, Ottmar, and Friederike Pannewick, eds. *Arab Americas: Literary Entanglements of the American Hemisphere and the Arab World.* Frankfurt: Vervuert, 2006.

Fokkema, Douwe. "Orientalism, Occidentalism, and the Notion of Discourse: Arguments for a New Cosmopolitanism." *Comparative Criticism* 18 (1996): 227–41.

Fombona I., Jacinto R. "Writing Europe's 'Orient': Spanish-American Travelers to the 'Orient.'" *Between Languages and Cultures: Translation and Cross-Cultural Texts,* ed. Anuradha Dingwaney and Carol Maier. Pittsburgh, Pa.: University of Pittsburgh Press, 1995. 119–31.

Foucault, Michel. "Of Other Spaces." Trans. Jay Miskowiec. *Diacritics* 16.1 (1986): 22–27.

Goga, Masuda. *O Haicai no Brasil.* São Paulo: Oriento, 1988.

Gómez Carrillo, Enrique. *El alma japonesa.* Paris: Garnier, 1907.

———. *De Marsella á Tokio, sensaciones de Egipto, la India, la China y el Japón.* Prologue by Rubén Darío. Paris: Garnier, 1906.

———. *El Japón heroico y galante.* 1912. Guatemala City: Editorial del Ministerio de Educación Pública, 1959.

———. *Páginas escogidas II: Impresiones de viaje.* Guatemala City: Biblioteca de la Cultura Popular, 1954.

Graf, E. C. "When an Arab Laughs in Toledo: Cervantes's Interpellation of Early Modern Spanish Orientalism." *Diacritics* 29.2 (1999): 68–85.

Graham, Richard, ed. *The Idea of Race in Latin America, 1870–1940.* Austin: University of Texas Press, 1990.

Greenblatt, Stephen. *Marvelous Possessions: The Wonder of the New World.* Oxford: Oxford University Press, 1991.

Helly, Denise, ed. *The Cuba Commission Report: A Hidden History of the Chinese in Cuba.* Baltimore: Johns Hopkins University Press, 1993.

Heredia, José María. *Cuentos orientales y otras narraciones.* 1826–31. Philadelphia: Ediciones La Gota de Agua, 2008.

Herut, Syrene-Chafi. *Viewing Europe from the Outside: Cultural Encounters and Critiques in the Eighteenth-Century Pseudo-Oriental Travelogue and the Nineteenth-Century "Voyage en Orient."* New York: Peter Lang, 1997.

Hu-Dehart, Evelyn and Kathleen López, eds. "Afro-Asia" (Special Issue). *Afro-Hispanic Review* 27.1 (2008).

Hu-Dehart, Evelyn and Lane R. Hirabayashi, eds. "Asians in the Americas: Transculturations and Power" (Special Issue). *Amerasia Journal* 28.2 (2002).

Kabbani, Rana. *Europe's Myths of the Orient.* Bloomington: Indiana University Press, 1986.

Knight, Diana. "Barthes and Orientalism." *New Literary History* 24.3 (1993): 617–33.

Kushigian, Julia A. *Orientalism in the Hispanic Literary Tradition: In Dialogue with Borges, Paz, and Sarduy.* Albuquerque: University of New Mexico Press, 1991.

Lafaye, Jacques. *Quetzalcóatl and Guadalupe: The Formation of Mexican National Consciousness, 1531–1813.* Chicago: University of Chicago Press, 1987.

Lesser, Jeffrey. *Negotiating National Identity: Immigrants, Minorities, and the Struggle for Ethnicity in Brazil.* Durham, N.C.: Duke University Press, 1999.

Loomba, Ania. *Colonialism/Postcolonialism.* New York: Routledge, 2002.

López, Kathleen. *Chinese Cubans: A Transnational History.* Chapel Hill: University of North Carolina Press, 2013.

López-Calvo, Ignacio, ed. *Alternative Orientalisms in Latin America and Beyond.* Newcastle, U.K.: Cambridge Scholars Publishing, 2007.

Lowe, Lisa. *Critical Terrains: French and British Orientalisms.* Ithaca, N.Y.: Cornell University Press, 1991.

———. *Immigrant Acts: On Asian American Cultural Politics.* Durham, N.C.: Duke University Press, 1996.

Mata, Rodolfo, ed. *José Juan Tablada: Letra e imagen (poesía, prosa, obra gráfica y varia documental).* Facsimile editions on CD-Rom. Mexico City: UNAM, 2008.

Molloy, Sylvia. "Of Queens and Castanets: Hispanidad, Orientalism, and Sexual Difference." *Queer Diasporas,* ed. Cindy Patton and Benigno Sanchez-Eppler. Durham, N.C.: Duke University Press, 2000. 105–21.

Nagy-Zekmi, Silvia, ed. *Moros en la costa: Orientalismo en Latinoamérica.* Frankfurt: Vervuert, 2008.

O'Hanlon, Rosalind, and David Washbrook. "After Orientalism: Culture, Criticism, and Politics in the Third World." *Comparative Studies in Society and History* 34.1 (1991): 141–67.

Pan, Lynn. *Sons of the Yellow Emperor: A History of the Chinese Diaspora.* New York: Kodansha International, 1990.

Paz, Octavio. *The Collected Poems of Octavio Paz, 1957–1987.* New York: New Directions, 1991.

———. *Conjunctions and Disjunctions.* New York: Arcade, 1990.

———. *Convergences: Essays on Art and Literature.* San Diego: Harcourt Brace Jovanovich, 1991.

———. "Dos apostillas: El punto de vista nahua; Asia y América." *Puertas al campo.* Barcelona: Seix Barral, 1966. 133–154.

———. *Early Poems, 1935–1955.* Bloomington: Indiana University Press, 1973.

———. *In Light of India.* New York: Harcourt Brace, 1998.

———. *The Labyrinth of Solitude.* New York: Grove Press, 1961.

———. *Renga: A Chain of Poems.* New York: Penguin, 1979.

———. *A Tale of Two Gardens: Poems from India.* New Delhi: Viking, 1997.

Pérez Sarduy, Pedro and Jean Stubbs, eds. *Afrocuba: An Anthology of Cuban Writing on Race, Politics and Culture.* New York: Ocean Press, 1993.

Pratt, Mary Louise. *Imperial Eyes: Travel Writing and Transculturation.* New York: Routledge, 1992.

Rocha, Cristina. *Zen in Brazil: The Quest for Cosmopolitan Modernity.* Honolulu: University of Hawaii Press, 2006.

Román-Lagunas, Jorge. "Influence of Oriental Culture in Latin American Poetry." *Tamkang Review* 22.1–4 (1992): 97–105.

Rustomji-Kerns, Roshni, Rajini Srikanth, and Leny Mendoza Strobel, eds. *Encounters: People of Asian Descent in the Americas.* Lanham, Md.: Rowan and Littlefield, 1999.

Ruy Sáncez, Alberto. *Una introducción a Octavio Paz.* Mexico City: Joaquín Mortiz, 1990.

———. *Los jardines secretos de Mogador.* Mexico City: Alfaguara, 2001.

———. *Mogador: The Names of the Air.* Trans. Mark Schafer. San Francisco: City Lights, 1993.

———. *Los nombres del aire.* Mexico City: Alfaguara, 1987.

——. *The Secret Gardens of Mogador.* Trans. Rhonda Buchanan. Buffalo, N.Y.: White Pine Press, 2008.

Said, Edward. *Culture and Imperialism.* New York: Knopf, 1993.

——. *Orientalism: Western Conceptions of the Orient.* New York: Pantheon, 1978.

Sarmiento, Domingo F. Facundo: *Civilization and Barbarism.* 1845. Trans. Kathleen Ross. Berkeley: University of California Press, 2003.

——. *Recollections of a Provincial Past.* 1850. Trans. Elizabeth Garrels and Asa Zatz. Oxford: Oxford University Press, 2005.

——. *Viajes por Europa, África y América.* 1849. Buenos Aires: Editorial de Belgrano, 1981.

Schaub, Uta Liebmann. "Foucault's Oriental Subtext." *PMLA* 104.3 (1989): 306–16.

Schiavone Camacho, Julia María. *Chinese Mexicans: Transpacific Migration and the Search for a Homeland, 1910–1960.* Chapel Hill: University of North Carolina Press, 2012.

Schurz, William Lytle. *The Manila Galleon.* Manila: Historical Conservation Society, 1985.

Sinor, Denis. *Orientalism and History.* Cambridge, U.K.: W. Heffer, 1954.

Spurr, David. *The Rhetoric of Empire: Colonial Discourse in Journalism, Travel Writing, and Imperial Administration.* Durham, N.C.: Duke University Press, 1993.

Taboada, Hernán G. H. *La sombra del Islam en la conquista de América.* Mexico City: FCE, 2004.

Taylor, Marc C. *Altarity.* Chicago: University of Chicago Press, 1987.

Taylor, Patrick, ed. *Nation Dance: Religion, Identity, and Cultural Difference in the Caribbean.* Bloomington: Indiana University Press, 2001.

Tinajero, Araceli. *Orientalismo en el modernismo hispanoamericano.* West Lafayette, Ind.: Purdue University Press, 2004.

Torres-Pou, Joan, ed. *Orientalismos: Oriente y Occidente en la literatura y las artes de España e Hispanoamérica.* Barcelona: PPU, 2010.

Turner, Bryan S. *Orientalism, Postmodernism, and Globalism.* London: Routledge, 1994.

Valencia, Guillermo. *Catay.* Bogotá: Cromos, 1928.

Vasconcelos, José. *The Cosmic Race: A Bilingual Edition.* Baltimore: Johns Hopkins University Press, 1997.

Vogeley, Nancy. "Turks and Indians: Orientalist Discourse in Postcolonial Mexico." *Diacritics* 25.1 (1995): 3–20.

Weckmann, Luis. *La herencia medieval de México.* Mexico City: FCE, 1994.

Wilson, Andrew R., ed. *The Chinese in the Caribbean.* Princeton, N.J.: Markus Wiener, 2004.

Yegenoglu, Meyda. *Colonial Fantasies: Towards a Feminist Reading of Orientalism.* Cambridge: Cambridge University Press, 1998.

Young, Robert. *White Mythologies: Writing History and the West.* London: Routledge, 1990.

Zavala, Iris M. *Colonialism and Culture: Hispanic Modernism and the Social Imaginary.* Bloomington: Indiana University Press, 1992.

About the Contributors

Erik Camayd-Freixas is a professor of Hispanic studies and the director of Graduate Studies in the Department of Modern Languages at Florida International University. He has written *Realismo mágico y primitivismo* (University Press of America, 1998), *Primitivism and Identity in Latin America* (University of Arizona Press, 2000), *Postville: La criminalización de los migrantes* (F&G Editores, 2009), *La etnografía imaginaria: Historia y parodia en la literatura hispanoamericana* (F&G Editores, 2012), *U.S. Immigration Reform and Its Global Impact: Lessons from the Postville Raid* (Palgrave Macmillan, 2013), and numerous articles in collected volumes and journals throughout the Americas and Europe. Dr. Camayd specializes in cultural studies and anthropological approaches to narrative, poetics, and historiography of the colonial and contemporary periods of Latin America and the Caribbean.

Christina Civantos is an associate professor in the Department of Modern Languages and Literatures at the University of Miami (Florida), where she researches and teaches in the fields of nineteenth- and twentieth-century Latin American and Arabic studies. She is the author of *Between Argentines and Arabs: Argentine Orientalism, Arab Immigrants, and the Writing of Identity* (State University of New York Press, 2006) as well as various articles on the Arab diaspora, Orientalism, and the politics of literacy. She is the recipient of a National Endowment for the Humanities fellowship for her project on the Lebanese author Elias Khoury and his reworking of the Gabriel García Márquez novel *Crónica de una muerte anunciada*.

Zoila Clark is an assistant professor of Spanish at Florida Memorial University. She began her university studies in her native Lima and received her PhD in Spanish and Latin American literature from Florida International University. She is the author of *La sexualidad femenina: Reconceptualización surrealista y posmoderna por Cristina Escofet e Isabel Allende* (University Press of America, 2010) and *Grammar in Context for ESL College Students* (Educational Resources Information Center, 1999). She has published numerous articles on women's studies, literature, and film, including critical studies of Escofet, Allende, Bombal, Chopin, Cambaceres, Galdós, Almodóvar, and Buñuel.

Debra Lee-DiStefano is an associate professor of Spanish at Southeast Missouri State University. She is the author of *Three Asian-Hispanic Writers from Peru: Doris*

Moromisato, José Watanabe, Siu Kam Wen (Mellen Press, 2008) and "When East Meets West: An Examination of the Poetry of the Asian Diaspora in Spanish America" (PhD dissertation, University of Missouri–Columbia, 2001). She has published several articles on the Afro-Chinese Cuban poet Regino Pedroso and the Japanese Peruvian poet José Watanabe, among others. Her current project is a manuscript that focuses on the works of Limeña writers of Asian descent.

Brett Levinson is a professor and the director of Graduate Studies in the Department of Comparative Literature at the State University of New York at Binghamton. He is the author of numerous studies on contemporary literature, philosophy, and politics, including *Secondary Moderns: Mimesis, History, and Revolution in Lezama Lima's "American Expression"* (Bucknell University Press, 1996), *The Ends of Literature: The Latin American "Boom" in the Neoliberal Marketplace* (Stanford University Press, 2002), and *Market and Thought: Meditations on the Political and Biopolitical* (Fordham University Press, 2004).

Blake Seana Locklin is an associate professor of Spanish at Southwest Texas State University. She has written "Orientalism and the Nation: Asian Women in Spanish American Literature" (PhD dissertation, Cornell University, 1998). She has taught at the University of Macau and conducted research in Peru, Mexico, Costa Rica, and Taipei. She was elected co-chair of the Latin America and the Pacific Rim Section of the Latin American Studies Association. She has published articles in venues such as *Revista de Estudios Hispánicos, Chasqui,* and *Delaware Review of Latin American Studies* and presented numerous international conference papers on various aspects of Latin American Orientalism.

Kathleen López is an assistant professor of Latino and Hispanic Caribbean studies and of history at Rutgers University. She holds a master's degree in Asian studies from Cornell University (1995) and a PhD in history from the University of Michigan (2005). López has published various articles on the transnational history of the Chinese in Cuba and has coedited a special issue on Afro-Asia of the journal *Afro-Hispanic Review* (2008). She is the author of *Chinese Cubans: A Transnational History* (University of North Carolina Press, 2013). Her research and teaching interests include the historical intersections between Asia and Latin America and the Caribbean, postemancipation Caribbean societies, race and ethnicity in the Americas, and international migration.

Cristina Rocha is a postdoctoral research fellow at the Center for Cultural Research, University of Western Sydney in Australia. Her writings include *Zen in Brazil: The Quest for Cosmopolitan Modernity* (University of Hawaii Press, 2006); "The Brazilian *Imaginaire* of Zen: Global Influences, Rhizomatic Forms," in *Japanese Religions in and beyond the Japanese Diaspora*, edited by Ronan Pereira and Hideo Matsuoka (University of California Press, 2007); and "Being a Zen Buddhist Brazilian: Juggling Multiple Religious Identities in the Land of Catholicism" in *Buddhist Missionaries in the Era of Globalization*, edited by Linda Learman (University of Hawaii Press, 2004). Her current project is a manuscript titled "Buddhism in Australia: Traditions in Change."

Rogelio Rodríguez Coronel is a professor of Latin American and Cuban literature and was the dean of arts and letters at the University of Havana from 2001 to 2006. He is the editor of the review *Universidad de La Habana* and the advisory committee chair of the Editorial Letras Cubanas publishing house. He is a member of Academia Cubana de la Lengua, Real Academia Española, Academia Panameña de la Lengua, and Unión Nacional de Escritores y Artistas de Cuba. He has lectured at universities in Europe, Latin America, and the United States and has published numerous articles on Latin American and Cuban literature in national and international journals. He has published ten books, among them *La novela de la Revolución Cubana* (Editorial Letras Cubanas, 1985), which received the Premio de la Crítica Award, and *Lecturas sucesivas* (Editorial Unión, 2008).

Julia María Schiavone Camacho is an assistant professor of history at the University of Texas at El Paso. She is the author of *Chinese Mexicans: Transpacific Migration and the Search for a Homeland, 1910–1960* (University of North Carolina Press, 2012). She received the Louis Knott Koontz Memorial Award for her 2009 article in the *Pacific Historical Review*, "Crossing Boundaries, Claiming a Homeland: The Mexican Chinese Transpacific Journey to Becoming Mexican, 1930s-1960s," and she received a grant from the Macau Foundation to conduct research on transpacific Latin American Chinese families. She teaches Mexican-U.S. borderlands, U.S., and Chicana/o history, gender and sexuality studies, and Latin American studies.

Ivan A. Schulman is Professor Emeritus of Spanish American and Comparative Literature, University of Illinois at Urbana. He has received grants from the Guggenheim Foundation, Social Science Research Council, National Endowment for the Humanities, and Florida Humanities Council. He has published more than twelve books and 120 articles on the literature and culture of Spanish America. He has been recognized in Cuba, Venezuela, and Nicaragua for his research on José Martí and has taught at several universities in the United States, in addition to the Federal University of Rio de Janeiro, the University of Buenos Aires, and the National University of Mexico. His research centers on revisionist concepts of Spanish American Modernism (with respect to the writings of Martí, Rubén Darío, Julián del Casal, Manuel Gutiérrez Nájera, and Salvador Díaz Mirón), Cuban literature, and Cuban slavery narratives.

Hernán G. H. Taboada is a professor of history at the Universidad Autónoma de México and the editor of *Cuadernos Americanos*. He has published extensively on Latin American Orientalism, Eurocentrism, and the history and culture of Islam and its relation to Latin America, including articles in *Revista de Occidente* and *Estudios de Asia y África*. He is the author of *La sombra del Islam en la conquista de América* (Fondo de Cultura Económica, 2004).

Margarita Vásquez is a professor and the chair of the Department of Literature at the University of Panama. She has published *Acechanzas a la literatura panameña* (Editorial Universitaria Carlos Manuel Gasteazoro, 2007), which received the Rodrigo Miró Grimaldo Award, *Contrapunto: Doce ensayos sobre la literatura en Panamá*, with Rogelio Rodríguez Coronel (Editorial Universitaria, 2008), and numerous articles of literary criticism in Madrid, Salamanca, Metz (France), Havana, and Panama. She has been a guest speaker at conferences in Warsaw, Mexico City, Santo Domingo, and Miami. She is a member of Academia Panameña de la Lengua and is currently the culture coordinator for the Humanities Department at the University of Panama.

Karen Tei Yamashita is a professor of creative writing and Asian American literature at the University of California at Santa Cruz. She traveled to Brazil in 1975 to study the history and anthropology of Japanese immigration. After interviewing and gathering information from commune members, Yamashita found fiction a more suitable genre for exploring the Japanese diasporic experience, producing a series of novels: *Through the Arc of the Rainforest* (Coffee House Press, 1990), which received the Before Columbus Foundation American Book Award and Janet Heidinger Kafka Prize, imagines the contact between technology and rural culture through the lens of magical realism; *Brazil-Maru* (Coffee House Press, 1992) traces the rise and fall of a Japanese experimental community in the Brazilian interior; *Tropic of Orange* (Coffee House Press, 1997) maps the multilayered grids of meaning in Los Angeles and the borders between Latin America, Mexico, and North America; *Circle K Cycles* (Coffee House Press, 2001) is based on her research on the Brazilian community in Japan. *I Hotel* (Coffee House Press, 2010), a fictional account of the civil rights movement in San Fracisco's Chinatown, received the California Book Award and the Asian/Pacific American Library Association Book Award, and was a National Book Award finalist.

Index